Dawson's
Practical Lawncraft

Dawson's Practical Lawncraft

Revised by R. HAWTHORN

Former Secretary to the Education Committee
Institute of Groundsmanship

Seventh Edition

Crosby Lockwood Staples   London

Granada Publishing Limited

First published in Great Britain 1939 by
Crosby Lockwood & Sons Ltd.
Second edition 1945
Revised and Reprinted 1947
Third edition 1949
Fourth edition 1954
Fifth edition 1959
Sixth edition 1968
Seventh edition published 1977 by
Crosby Lockwood Staples Frogmore St Albans Herts and
3 Upper James Street London W1R 4BP

ISBN 0 258 97029 4

Printed in Great Britain by William Clowes & Sons, Limited,
London, Beccles and Colchester

Preface

SEVENTH EDITION

A number of years ago, a great friend of mine, F. J. Reed, wrote a book on turf culture called *Lawns and Playing Fields*. On the dust jacket, he apologised for 'adding another book to the many already on the subject that were circulating at that time'.

I have no such apology to make for this edition of *Practical Lawncraft*. There is a great scarcity of up to date books on the subject, and while Dawson's book has long been considered the 'Bible' for practical groundsmen, for students and educational establishments, indeed for all those responsible for the maintenance of turf areas, it also has been for a long time out of print.

Sports grounds are provided by local authorities, the services, colleges, universities, industrial and private sports clubs. There are many variations in these grounds in size and facilities provided, but one thing is common to them all—that it costs a vast amount of money in the first place to purchase the land and to construct the sports-ground, and a vast amount of money in labour, materials and equipment to maintain them.

It follows then, that these expensive resources must not be wasted. Indeed they are not. Extended hours of play and even higher standards of playing surfaces are demanded by the users of the facilities provided, and consequently those responsible for the provision of the pitches, who become eventually the groundsmen, have to marshal all their knowledge and skills to provide and to restore the areas after play. It can truly be said that the groundsman puts forth his skill to provide a pitch for the players to destroy, and if this book can add to the store of knowledge possessed by groundsmen, then its aim will be fulfilled.

Basic turf culture has not changed much over the years, but some of the techniques involved have changed out of all recognition. New materials have appeared so that the groundsman can have more success in dealing with the weeds, the pests, and the diseases of turf.

The wise groundsman will treat all these wonderful things as an aid to management, and not as an emergency crutch. Tremendous improvements have come about in recent years in the provision of new varieties of grasses used on sportsfields. The groundsman has to keep abreast of all these new trends, so that he will be able to construct and maintain the ground for which he is responsible within his budgetary limits.

In this present edition, the general format and purpose of the original book has been preserved. New information and new illustrations have been incorporated, but all mention of prices has been eliminated. In these inflationary days, any indication of costs, except those mentioned in the daily newspapers, are made to seem ridiculous within a few short months.

It is my sincere hope that new readers of this edition of *Practical Lawncraft* will find it as useful and helpful as I did, when I read and was helped by one of the earlier editions way back in 1945.

R. HAWTHORN
(1977)

Acknowledgements

I would like to express my thanks for the information and photographs supplied for this new edition to the following:
Mommersteeg International Seed Company Ltd.
Mr J. Bradbury.
Synchemicals Ltd.
Mr D. G. Gooding
Norwich Airport
Mr W. E. Pettifer.
Mr G. Warwick.
Cameron Irrigation Co. Ltd.
Mr G. Barnes.
Ransomes, Sims and Jefferies Ltd.
Mr K. Buckledee.
Mr Van der Ryden.
Mr R. J. Corbin
Sisis Equipment (Macclesfield Ltd.)

R. HAWTHORN

Contents

Part three: Maintenance of established turf

Part four: Turf for sport and other purposes

PART ONE

Introduction

CHAPTER ONE

The lawn as a feature of home and garden

From early times an adequate, well-maintained lawn has been an essential and basic feature of the gardens of this country. Indeed, our lawns and sports grounds are as characteristic of our national life as our homes and firesides. Wherever men of these islands have made their homes, even in the most inhospitable parts of the earth, they have striven to produce and maintain lawns as an unconscious link with their Homeland.

The amenity that a lawn confers upon a home is well recognised by nearly all garden and home lovers. It provides a feeling of restfulness and is a foil to the flower display. Further, it has an æsthetic value in making the garden look better, and the peaceful, soothing effect of green coolness on a good, well-designed lawn, is perhaps the main delight.

To be a success, however, the lawn must be related to the design of the garden and must conform to its general contours. A well-planned lawn should be the result of a definite mental picture, and the aim should be to produce something that is at the same time beautiful and useful, yet avoiding extreme plainness as well as extreme ornamentation. One American writer upon lawns has rather aptly described the lawn as 'the carpet of the outdoor living-room'. The quality of that carpet is dependent in large measure upon colour, texture, density of pile, and uniformity, as well as upon its outlines and its relationship to the other furnishings of the outdoor room.

It is not necessary to have a large piece of land to produce a lawn —even the tiniest area can have its plot of grass, and perhaps one of the most striking features of modern housing estates is the way in which almost every householder endeavours to provide at least a small grass plot, even if some other feature be omitted. Unfortunately many of these grass plots are of poor quality, though there is no reason why they should not be greatly improved with a little extra endeavour and with very small extra expense. For the lack of a little well-directed advice, especially at the start, the result is too often mediocre.

While we, in this country, are blessed with a climate that is favourable to the production of grass, we do not always take advantage of our good fortune: although the high reputation enjoyed by our turf is well deserved in many instances, yet sad to say there exist countless lawns that are a disgrace to any country. Even some of the college lawns of the older universities, with their high reputation for beauty, are more to be commended by their architectural surroundings and their associations than the quality of the turf, which is often much poorer than one finds on a working-man's bowling green or on the putting greens of an average golf course. In spite of their blemishes, however, our lawns are invariably the envy of visitors from abroad.

An area of turf in a garden may well determine the character of that garden, but it may equally be said that the quality of turf on a sports lawn will make or mar the game for which it is prepared. Intensive training and better accessories will no doubt improve one's game, but this advantage is quickly lost unless there are corresponding develop- ments in the quality and suitability of the turf. Of what use are the modern refinements of say the lawn-tennis ball and golf ball, or the present-day golf club and tennis racquet, if the advantage is largely nullified by the poor condition of the turf sward? It is perhaps not too much to say that if we are to retain our national position in sport we must in future pay greater attention to the improvement of our sports turf. In many cases the poorness of the turf can largely be attributed to incorrect balance in club expenditure, too much money being spent on unnecessary apparatus, patent mixtures or an imposing club-room and too little on employment of adequately trained ground staff and the purchase of essential greenkeeping materials.

In recent years the number of sports grounds attached to industrial concerns and run in conjunction with welfare schemes has increased. There has also been an increase in school grounds associated with new secondary schools. Much remains to be done, however, in the provision of recreational facilities for both sexes not only in urban areas but in the countryside where it has been shown by the National Playing

Fields Association that in many rural parishes little or no provision exists for organised games.

The National Playing Fields Association recommends that to ensure adequate communal playing facilities a minimum of 6 acres (2·4 ha) of publicly owned and permanently preserved playing fields per 1,000 of the population is essential. This, it is recommended, must be exclusive of any privately owned sports facilities, commons, pleasure grounds, or ornamental gardens where the playing of games by the general public is neither encouraged nor permitted. Full-length public golf courses are not to be counted in the recommendation of 6 acres (2·4 ha) per 1,000, though putting courses or pitch and putt courses may be included.

The provision of school playing fields is not included in the above recommendations. When schools are being planned, planning authorities will set aside land to be developed for playing fields, which ultimately, because of the lack of general recreational facilities, may be used by the community for sporting activities. Sites for new grounds become increasingly hard to find so that at times some 'left over' areas are chosen, perhaps with awkward shapes, uneven contours and bad soil. Many difficult problems can arise in these circumstances.

The improvement of lawn and sports turf in this country is a matter of national prestige. Fortunately, there is an enlivened consciousness to-day among local authorities and others concerned with turf and a steadily growing interest in turf upkeep especially from the scientific angle. It is to be hoped that the wider interest at present showing will lead to the alteration of many of those inferior turf swards that are so lacking in quality and 'character'.

CHAPTER TWO

The history of the lawn and the scientific study of turf

Lawns, like most garden features, have been the subject of evolution and have suffered changes dictated by fashion, yet they have invariably emerged little changed and defiant to maintain their own unrivalled position in garden architecture. Although it is probable that lawns (possibly made of plants other than grasses) formed a part of classical gardens, real knowledge only becomes available in the literature of mediæval times. All lawn lovers should be grateful to Miss Eleanour Sinclair Rohde, who has searched the literature and brought together the early references to lawns in a fascinating article that deserves to be much better known. Thus it appears from Boccaccio's *Decameron* and a later edition of the thirteenth-century *Romance of the Rose* that the mediæval lawn was not the pure grass sward we strive for to-day but an imitation of a natural meadow 'starred with a thousand flowers'. In the old monastic cloisters, also, the central green plot was planted with flowers and divided into quarters by paths intersecting in the centre—an arrangement, as Miss Rohde points out, suggestive of the rectangular garden plots portrayed in Persian garden-carpets. One constant feature of the mediæval garden was the orchard, carpeted with short grass and flowering plants, whilst another was the turf-topped seat planted with flowers, and built around trees or enclosed in an arbour built at the side of the lawn.

In the sixteenth century the tendency was for the garden to increase in size and to comprise separate 'gardens within a garden' and including an orchard, a knot-garden, a herb-garden, a physic-garden, and a bowling green, and contemporary descriptions of the preparation of the turf are in existence. Turfed paths or walks were also a feature of the gardens of this period, but the lawns and walks were not always made of turf. Thus John Evelyn, born 1620, gave in his diary (*Kalendarium Hortense*) under October, instructions for the maintenance of camomile lawns, and other garden books of this period make a point of referring to this plant. Areas of it still survive in the lawns of some of the royal parks, thus forming an interesting link with the past. It has been suggested that the turf upon which Drake played the historic game of bowls on the eve of the appearance of the Armada was not comprised of grass but of camomile.

It was not, however, until the eighteenth century that the lawn really came into its own and every garden book of the period treated the subject. The ruling fashion then was to provide a large expanse of closely-tended grass unadorned by flower beds or shrubs and falling in sweeps and undulations about the house. Round about this time, too, the garden experts began to comment upon the difficulties of obtaining good seed, and Miss Rohde in her history of the lawn quotes one anonymous author as directing that on no account should hay seeds be used for sowing lawns and that seeds for this purpose should always be obtained from 'the grass of clean upland pastures'. One would like to have honoured the name of this unknown author, for he must surely have been the first to appreciate the value of turf made from the fine-leaved grasses, the bents, fescues, and wavy hairs such as one would expect to find in a pasture so described and where the weed flora would be much reduced.

The antiquity of the bowling green and the fact that bowls was played in the thirteenth century are well established, and while the mediæval lawn was the forerunner of the present-day garden lawn, the original bowling lawn was the precursor of the modern greens, and indeed of all the turf areas that, with their several requirements, we need to-day for our wider range of outdoor sports. A turf area that is required for purely ornamental purposes or for outdoor games, must rightly be classified as a lawn, and will be subject to the same general principles of management.

Turf upkeep is among the oldest of arts, but has depended upon scraps of knowledge handed on from father to son, and perhaps often forgotten through the passage of time or by being buried with the dead. In fact, management was conducted by rule of thumb, and while a certain set of operations produced in some instances tolerably good results, the operator was unable to explain the reasons for carrying them out. The results when positive were only satisfactory through the fortunate coincidence of circumstances—in other words, through good luck.

Perhaps the most epoch-making event in the history of the lawn was the invention of the cylinder mower, the principle of which appears to have first occurred to one Edwin Budding in 1830. The first petrol-motor-driven lawn mower was produced about 1900. The cylinder mower marks the inception of modern turf management, and whilst it made fine lawns generally possible it also introduced a new factor as far as the composition of the turf was concerned. Further discussion of this topic will be introduced later but it is often forgotten that prior to the wide adoption of mechanical mowers, close scything, followed by sweeping up the clippings, was the only method of keeping turf short. To-day it is only seldom that one finds a gardener or green-keeper able, or even willing to attempt, to do this operation.

The more recent developments in the upkeep of lawns are mainly concerned with improved methods of maintenance, better seeds, better tools, and better materials, and with the more intensive study and application of scientific methods to the subject. It may not be without interest to review briefly the progress that has been made in the direction of scientific investigation, though unfortunately this country has in certain respects lagged behind others in the critical study of turf management, or turf culture, as one should perhaps describe the science of managing turf.

The first experiments with turf grasses appear to have been carried out in the Olcott turf gardens, Connecticut, in 1885, and were continued until the death of J. B. Olcott in 1910. His aim was to search for species and types of grasses that approached his ideal of perfection, and to this end he selected about 500 strains from some thousands of plants and multiplied his stock of many of these strains so as to give comparative turf plots. It is significant that he came to the conclusion that the best types of grasses for lawns were to be found in the genera *Agrostis* and *Festuca*, among which groups work is still being done to-day. Olcott invariably referred to the upkeep of turf as 'grass-gardening' and not greenkeeping, which term appears to have come later and doubtless owes its origin to the 'keeping of the green' for the game of golf.

The next stage in the experimental study of turf took place in the United States with the setting up of experiments in 1890 at the Rhode Island State College of Agriculture. The plot trials at this Institute were extended in 1905 and yielded valuable information that has proved the starting-point for many turf gardens and new investigations.

Largely as a result of the enthusiasm of Dr Charles V. Piper and

Dr R. A. Oakley of the US Department of Agriculture interest in turf upkeep steadily increased, many of the State colleges and experiment stations establishing turf gardens. In 1920 the United States Golf Association established a 'Green Section' with Dr John Monteith, Jr, as director, and experimental work, devoted at first to the requirements of golf turf, was started at Arlington, near Washington. Later came a widening of the scope of the work under the Direction of Dr F. Grau at the Plant Industry Station, Beltsville, Md. The work is now largely regionalised and research work has grown considerably at State experiment stations, universities, and other places. Interest has been strengthened by much extension work, including turf conferences held at centres throughout the country.

Since that time, schemes for the scientific study of fine swards, as distinct from agricultural grass land, have steadily increased, and in this country the credit of suggesting that research work should be devoted to the science of greenkeeping must be given to the Green Committee of the Royal & Ancient Golf Club. In 1924 this Committee convened a meeting of club representatives, which was unanimous in its desire that the matter of research should be further investigated. Unfortunately, a subsequent appeal to the clubs for the necessary funds met with insufficient promises of support, and it was not until 1928, when, at the request of the Royal & Ancient Golf Club, the British Golf Unions' Joint Advisory Council, a body representing the National Golf Unions of England, Scotland, Ireland, and Wales, took up the question that any further progress in the matter of a research scheme was made. A further effort was made to enlist the support of the clubs, and in 1929 it was possible to pass a resolution setting up a Board of Greenkeeping Research in the knowledge that all the National Golf Unions had guaranteed their quota of money.

Following this was established a research station and experiment ground on the St Ives estate at Bingley in Yorkshire, which has come to be known as the centre for turf research and advice in this country. The enthusiasm of the late Mr Norman Hackett, who had been closely associated with golf greenkeeping for many years, was a major factor in obtaining the support of the clubs and emphasising the need for experimental work. The main experiments are laid out in old park land at 600 ft (183 m) elevation, with various soils and other altitudes available. Recent years have seen the steady expansion of the work to in-clude the interests of all users of turf while the whole organisation has been reconstituted. As from September 1951 the original Board of Green-keeping Research ceased to exist, being superseded by a new body known as The Sports Turf Research Institute having as members the controlling bodies of other sports besides golf. This scheme is more closely analogous to an industrial research scheme without State support, and from which subscribers expect certain very definite benefits. Since 1929, series of experiments in turf upkeep have been in progress and continue to yield valuable results.

In other countries the development of greenkeeping investigations has followed parallel lines. In 1932 the New Zealand Golf Association set up a research committee, this being reconstituted in 1949 as the New Zealand Institute for Turf Culture. The experiments are following very closely the lines of those in progress at Bingley. Prior to 1939 research into turf problems in Australia was gaining ground. World War II caused a cessation but information to hand indicates strong revival of interest in turf research and advisory schemes. In South Africa the pioneer work is very largely associated with the late Dr C. M. Murray of Capetown. It was in 1904 that Dr Murray first took an interest in the development of greenkeeping, and by the end of 1906 had established a complete series of grass greens at the Royal Cape Golf Course. Previous to this few greens in South Africa were of grass, though some had been put down to grass at Durban as early as 1891 or 1892. In the Transvaal, the first South African Golf Championship was played on grass greens in 1909.

Research in South Africa was established under the direction of Dr T. D. Hall at Frankenwald in association with the University of Witwatersrand. The outcome is The South African Turf Research Station which, with its advisory service, is planned on a scheme similar to that in Britain and New Zealand but on a smaller scale.

Occasional bulletins are issued by the respective research bodies in Great Britain, New Zealand, and USA, while articles on turf establishment and upkeep in Australia, Canada, India, South Africa, and Malaysia have also appeared. Reference will be made later to a selection of the literature. It is probably true to say that in the United States of America nearly as much attention has been paid to lawns as to grass land, and a valuable literature has been built up.

One significant fact emerges from a consideration of the history of investigational work, and that is the part played by the Golf Unions and Associations in setting up their own research departments, and further that very little scientific work directly bearing on greenkeeping has been carried out by agricultural colleges and institutes. In at least five countries the initiative has been left to the golfing organisations or individual golfers.

The conduction of research on fine turf in so many countries indicates a world-wide desire for reliable information on turf matters, and the present interchange of literature and ideas between the various research organisations is found mutually helpful. In the case of fine turf, at any rate, the habitat should be more or less under strict control, and the requisites being so similar the findings of greenkeeping researches should have a wider application than, say, the findings of grass land investigations. Much of the findings in one district or even country can be applied to another district or country where similar climatic conditions obtain. Thus the same general lines of earthworm control, insect and fungal control, the same manurial treatments, the same cutting treatments, the same methods of soil sterilisation, should be almost equally applicable wherever applied, though small local refinements may be necessary. Obviously, for instance, a ribwort plantain in New Zealand and another one in England will react to weed-killing in like measure, and the same may be said of many other operations, though of course extreme climatic conditions will have their effects in determining the degree of, say, fungal infection and thus of the amount of fungicide required. The amount of money available for purchase of materials and employment of an adequate labour force for general maintenance will often determine differences in the quality of turf to a greater extent than will any inherent differences in the soil or the climate.

CHAPTER THREE

Good and bad lawns

The causes of bad lawns

A brief consideration of the causes of imperfect lawns is a necessary prelude to the subject of establishing a new lawn and maintaining or renovating an area that has been in existence for some time. Experience shows that very often the lawn owner, especially if he be an amateur, expends countless hours of toil upon his garden lawn attempting to produce a satisfactory sward. If, in spite of these efforts, the results are bad then the conclusion is often reached that the failure is due to infertile soil or some peculiarity that makes it unsuitable for lawn purposes. It may also be argued that the local climate is such that it is unsuited for growing turf; yet, the desirable turf grasses are found growing naturally in soil of low fertility and also at high altitudes or in exposed positions where conditions are anything but ideal or favourable to good growth. Failure to produce the desired result may therefore be attributed more probably to some other cause or group of causes counteracting the work and so operating to produce the poor result.

With new lawns, failure to attain success is generally due to early mistakes that may be enumerated as follows: (1) cheap or hasty construction of the site; (2) insufficient or incorrect preparation of the top-soil for the reception of the grass; (3) the sowing of impure seed, or seed of low germinating capacity, or even seed of species more suitable for the production of a pasture or meadow than a fine sward; (4) uneven sowing; (5) when the lawn is sodded and not sown, the selection of turf containing the wrong grasses; and (6) in a

Fig. 1. Good and bad turf. Experiments on the use of fertilisers. *Foreground*: Untreated plot invaded by moss.

Fig. 2. Neglected lawn infested by earthworms.

sodded lawn, failure to lay the turves uniformly. Of the above perhaps the commonest mistake is undue haste, which is wasteful and more expensive in the long run. The lawn owner who has failed to observe the rules in establishing his turf thus spends his time in trying to put things right rather than in well-directed work in improving the sward or maintaining it in good condition.

When lawns have been longer established the causes of failure lie in neglect and mismanagement, the latter including (1) insufficient or wrong manuring; (2) abuse of the roller; (3) the use of a lawn mower that is old or ill-set, or even too heavy; (4) failure to use the mower sufficiently often to obtain the desired uniformity. Established lawns are often unsatisfactory owing to excessive wear and tear, and if the area is small this is apt to be a serious drawback to improvement, but general neglect of the turf is usually found to be the cause of failure. The effects of wrong treatment and neglect show themselves in a turf that is sparse, containing other than dwarf-growing grasses, a raggy surface, sharp undulations that skin with the mower, an extensive weed population, moss invasion, water-logging, and very often a slimy sticky surface that is unsuitable for the production of any growth except green algæ or even liverworts.

Perhaps one of the chief reasons for poor lawns is the failure of lawn owners to realise that turf production and maintenance are exacting and require just as much work, if not more, than any other branch of gardening practice. Very often one finds that a glorious display of bloom in a garden is accompanied by an execrable area of turf. This is a pity—yet such a lawn may have been regularly mown and occasionally rolled, though such treatment alone is not sufficient to produce a pleasing sward.

While there is to-day an undoubted increase in lawn-mindedness and a higher standard of turf requirement, very few people realise that the time factor is so important and that 70 to 80 per cent of the cost of producing a first-class lawn can be put down to labour. The amateur often wonders why a monthly roll and a fortnightly mow fail to give as good a result as obtained at his local bowling green or on the greens of the golf course of which he is a member. It should be remembered that the results on these two classes of turf have not been produced by haphazard attention, but are due to unremitting care and to a higher expenditure upon the sward than the amateur will give. Further, the results follow very careful study and attention to details. This difference may readily be made clear by quoting some figures from golf-course upkeep. Thus, a club of first-class standard holding about 120 acres (48·0 ha) of land maintained to a high standard, will find that most of the work is accorded to some $2\frac{1}{2}$ to $3\frac{1}{2}$ acres (1·0 to 1·4 ha) of putting green surface, and actually about one-third of the total annual cost of upkeep on the course may be allotted to the production of the turf on the greens. Perhaps this will serve to bring home the point about expenditure.

The ideal lawn

In some instances the owners of neglected lawns are fortunate in having associated with weeds a desirable grass species that will respond readily to treatment. On the other hand, the lawn may have been established with unsuitable grasses and then become invaded by weeds, or it may be afflicted by other complaints. A decision must therefore be reached as to whether it is worth while endeavouring to renovate the lawn or whether it will be easier in the long run to make a fresh start and to establish an entirely new turf from seed or sods. Perhaps a consideration of what constitutes an ideal lawn will assist in coming to a decision on this matter.

Looking at the ideal ornamental lawn from the turf aspect, and not from its general lay-out in conjunction with other garden features, it should first of all be free from weeds. It should also be uniform in colour and provide a true surface. Though the lawn may only be required for ornament and not for putting, trueness of surface is still required because without it close regular mowing is not possible, so that uniform density, texture and colour cannot be attained. If the herbage consists of several species of grass they should be intimately mixed and should not be in patches. Further, the soil should be free from earthworms because the casts thrown on to the surface upset the trueness, lead to caking of the surface, and are favourable to weed invasion. The ideal lawn should not only look well when closely examined, and provide a firm yet soft resilient sward to the foot, but it should provide a satisfactory appearance when viewed from a distance. The lawn should also be reasonably drought-resistant though during severe drought it may become necessary to apply water artificially. In addition, the turf should retain its colour, density, and uniformity to a marked degree throughout the winter months, and should be free from disease at all times.

The aim in lawn upkeep should be to produce a turf that gives satisfaction and pleasure throughout twelve months of the year, and the attainment of this ideal is not easy. A near approach to the ideal can, however, be attained by patience and by attention to detailed treatment, as has been found on many golf greens where the putting surfaces are expected to be playable for 365 days in the year and yet retain their surface and much of their general excellence during the winter. The exacting conditions required on a putting green are, of course, much greater than those on the ornamental lawn; for one thing the cutting required is keener and any small irregularities of the surface must be eliminated, or putting cannot be accurate. As the conditions to be satisfied on ornamental lawns are less exacting than on a putting green, all-the-year-round excellence should be more easy of attainment, but will involve regular and systematic attention, which should be related to weather and seasonal conditions. As the greenkeeper on a golf course or bowling green finds early in his career, all treatments must be carried out with as little inconvenience and spoiling of the appearance and surface as possible.

The lawn owner, unlike the farmer, is not concerned with the production of a big bulk of leafage, or with the palatability of the grass he produces; in fact, the grasses (bents, fescues, and meadow-grasses) normally found on good lawns are those that are of least value to the stock farmer and those which he generally endeavours to eradicate from his pastures. Similarly, the presence of wild white clover and perennial rye-grass on a lawn is undesirable, although these two species are the stand-by of the grazier. Even the earthworm, the friend and cultivator for the farmer, cannot be tolerated for long on a lawn. Constant mowing is also necessary so that any period of rest or laying up that the farmer's pasture enjoys through the removal of the stock, is not easy under turf conditions. Strains or species of grass that are markedly perennial and strongly aggressive, must be present if the lawn is to withstand constant mowing, and coarser-leaved grasses like Yorkshire fog and creeping soft-grass should be absent.

The conditions required for an ideal lawn are thus very exacting, and one result of this is that the botanical composition of lawns is restricted as regards both the weed and grass species found in them. In this connexion it is seldom realised that the cylinder mower is one of the most potent factors in turf upkeep because it shows no selectivity, like the grazing of the farmer's stock, but defoliates all species of grass or weed that are not adapted to growing very closely adpressed to the ground. The number of grasses able to withstand keen mowing and yet remain persistent is strictly limited, and while further reference will be made to this point in another chapter, the amateur must realise at this point that the mowing machine must be carefully managed, and that it is a factor leading to certain results and so necessitates other auxiliary treatments to help maintain the turf.

While most of the above remarks apply in particular to the ornamental or private lawn, it may be taken that they apply in general to turf for sport, though each class of sports turf must be considered in relation to the game for which it is intended. Hard-and-fast rules are impossible. This may be illustrated by the following example. On golf greens weedlessness is the ideal, but on fairways, complete freedom from weeds is not so essential though it is nevertheless desirable. There are, however, on golf fairways, certain weeds that are harmless and that it is not necessary to take special steps to control. Thus, if thyme is extensively present among the grass of a golf fairway, not only does it form an essential part of the turf, but, when flowering, it provides a wonderful carpet of colour, so that for both reasons attempts at eradication would be unwarranted. The same consideration applies to heather which on moorland golf courses provides a valued feature. So long as they do not become excessive, wood-rush, heath bedstraw and ladies' bedstraw form useful constituents of acid turf on golf fairways. Even the persistent yarrow has a use on light land as a binding constituent of the sward. The provision of suitable turf for each sport will be dealt with under the appropriate section, but the above general points about the ideal sward and the causes of bad lawns must be borne in mind throughout.

CHAPTER FOUR

Lawn grasses

The number of grass species structurally adapted to making good turf is strictly limited, but there is no question that the best lawn grasses for temperate climates are found in the bent (*Agrostis*) and fescue (*Festuca*) genera. The species found in these two groups are dwarf growing and generally described as 'bottom' grasses. Being low growing they are able to survive where competition from tall vigorous growing species does not exist or has been removed. They are fine in leaf and markedly persistent even when not allowed to grow above the height of cut of the mowing machine. Altogether the bent grasses and fescues satisfy the conditions imposed to a marked degree, though the bent grasses are more aggressive and persistent than the fescues.

The bents, and to a lesser extent fescues, are capable of with-standing defoliation, and they show powers of aggression in spite of the mowing. They owe this to their propensity for forming tussocks, surface runners, and underground stems or rhizomes. The degree of aggressiveness is partly a reflection of species but is very largely decided by the strain of grass and its capacity for forming new shoots and leafage from buds at the base of the stems. Like other grasses the leaves are capable of growing up again from the base when clipped. Thus it is possible to make turf vegetatively from each of two plants of *Agrostis tenuis* that look outwardly identical, and to find the turf slow to form, less persistent and less vigorous in the one, whilst in the other a dense thick pile of permanent turf rapidly develops.

The species going to compose a good lawn are comparatively few as compared with the numbers found in a pasture or meadow. Indeed, good turf can be made of a single species or a single strain. Although the species are few, the number of strains of finer grasses is very great, and the strain present may well be the determining factor of condition. The degree of improvement that can be effected in a lawn is often limited by the strain of grass present. The realisation of the significance of strain in the grasses used for turf is important, and this aspect of turf management has assumed great importance in recent years.

There are only four species of bent, or *Agrostis*, of any real significance in turf culture, but each is represented by an almost endless chain of types or strains. Of these four species Browntop (*Agrostis tenuis* Sibth.) is the commonest, and it is safe to say that no lawn or turf area is entirely without it. The finest lawns are almost entirely composed of browntop, which spreads by short overground runners or by the development of underground rhizomes. Good strains provide a dense thick carpet of grass. Velvet Bent (*A. canina* subsp. *canina*) and Creeping Bent (*A. stolonifera* var. *compacta* Hartm.) are also found in lawns, but not to the same extent as browntop. These species spread by a series of overground runners, so that a small patch of either will tend to increase, provided the conditions are suitable. They are very variable in vegetative characteristics. The fourth species, Redtop (*A. gigantea* Roth.), is seldom found in good lawns but occurs at times in coarser and longer swards. It spreads by rhizomes but fails to tolerate keen mowing. The commercial seed of these species will be described later.

Among the fescues there are a number of species found in turf, some of which have commercial counterparts. Red Fescue is perhaps the commonest, some types being extensively creeping (*F. rubra* subsp. *rubra*), while others have only short creepers or no creepers at all. Fine-leaved Fescue (*F. tenuifolia* Sibth. or *capillata* Lam.) and Sheep's Fescue (*F. ovina* L.) are tufted species of fescue found in turf, though they do not blend very well in closely-cut swards.

The variability in these species is very great indeed, some of them being more leafy while others are less leafy and more disposed to panicle production than leaf production. These species of bent and fescue are found growing naturally in poor soils; they are in fact poverty grasses, having fine leaves, which in the fescues are markedly xerophytic or drought-resistant. Though bent is coarser-leaved than fescue it fines down under the influence of the mower, so that the leaves are often difficult to distinguish by the naked eye from those of fescues.

We are not concerned at the moment with the species or varieties of fine grasses obtainable through seedsmen, but with the grasses found on turf areas that have never been sown down with commercial seeds but that are inhabited by species native to the district. Such indigenous strains are those that have adapted themselves to local conditions of soil and climate, and one advantage of making turf with sods is that, if local turf is used, strains of grass indigenous to the district are obtained.

Other grasses found in lawns may briefly be described. Thus, Annual Meadow-grass (*Poa annua* L.), or Annual Blue-grass as it is called in the USA, is a common constituent of turf, being a vagabond or volunteer species. Though some forms produce short stolons persistence is due primarily to its habit of forming large numbers of panicles below the level of the mowing-machine blade. Even though keenly mown, annual meadow-grass is capable of flowering and setting seed, and so maintaining or even increasing the number of plants in the sward. Other grasses do not adapt themselves to seeding in this way.

Other meadow-grasses found in small quantity in turf are: Rough-stalked Meadow-grass (*P. trivialis* L.), which, though useless for fine turf because of its tendency to form on the surface runners that do not root down, is nevertheless a valuable constituent of sports turf; Smooth-stalked Meadow-grass (*P. pratensis* L.), which is more valued in the United States than in this country, being known there as Kentucky Blue-grass; Wood Meadow-grass (*P. nemoralis* L.), which is not common and is confined to shady places; Bulbous Meadow-grass (*P. bulbosa* L.), which is occasionally found in turf in southern parts of this country, but never on keenly-mown or intensively-managed turf. For instance, it may be found on fairways of certain seaside golf links in Kent. It is mainly useful in winter since in the drier months of summer the plant browns off leaving the drought-resistant bulbules.

On richer soils and on second-class lawns and sports grounds, Perennial Rye-grass is a common constituent, and there are many leafy forms that are markedly persistent in spite of mowing, but in competition with bent and under keen mowing perennial rye-grass is less aggressive and may gradually die out. Crested Dog's-tail (*Cynosurus cristatus* L.), though not a suitable grass in the finest swards, is often found on poorer soils on heaths and seaside places, where it forms a valuable constituent of the natural herbage. In turf on soils that are markedly acid or approximating to moorland conditions, Wavy Hair-grass (*Deschampsia flexuosa* (L.) Trin.) is found, and even the Early Hair-grass (*A. præcox* L.), which is capable of seeding, though mown, like annual meadow-grass. Under very acid conditions, even though the turf is being systematically cut, Moor Mat-grass (*Nardus stricta* L.) may be found. Care must be taken not to confuse these wiry-leaved grasses with any of the fescues.

Sometimes Heath-grass (*Sieglingia decumbens* (L.) Bernh.) contributes to swards on heathlands. Occasionally leafy strains of yellow or Golden Oat-grass (*Trisetum flavescens* L.) Beauv.) are to be found in closely-mown swards.

This chapter would not be complete without making some reference to a weed grass found in fine lawns and greens and known loosely as Yorkshire Fog. Sometimes the patches called Yorkshire Fog (*Holcus lanatus* L.) are in reality another species—Creeping Soft-grass (*H. mollis* L.) and both species are markedly persistent in spite of keen mowing. While no doubt useful in coarser classes of turf these species are weeds as far as fine turf is concerned and therefore constitute a serious difficulty in mown herbage.

It will be seen from the above that the number of grass species found in natural turf swards is very limited. In a later chapter the commercial equivalents will receive attention.

PART TWO

New Lawns

CHAPTER FIVE

The construction and drainage of lawns

The construction of a new lawn is usually associated with the building of a house or with a scheme of general re-design of the garden, but on occasion the owner is fortunate enough to take over an area of un-disturbed pasture, and, with little or no constructional work, achieves a tolerably good result. Such instances are rare and usually there is involved a constructional scheme depending in size upon the aspirations of the would-be lawn owner or upon the nature or condition of the terrain.

In making a new lawn the usual methods are either sowing or turfing, though, as will be shown later, there is the third method—vegetative propagation. The general preparation of the site, its lay-out and cultivation, are virtually the same for each method, but it is necessary to come to a decision on the matter in the course of the preparatory work, as the final details vary to some extent.

Assuming that the site is a natural one and that little or no alteration in contours is necessary, it is still important to decide, for example, as to whether the turf on the site is worthy of attempts at improvement, or whether it must be removed. If the existing sward is to be retained and if the land is wet it may be necessary to put in a system of drains. Should the condition of the turf be such that removal is advisable, then the general lines of preparation for re-turfing or re-sowing must be followed in accordance with the description below. Assuming, on the other hand, that either general re-design is called for or a construction scheme is decided upon, then the first step is to plan the outlines of the lawn and any banks or undulations desired. This is where the ability to picture the finished effect is important, and assistance may be given to the mind by means of stakes and lines. It may be the intention to use the lawn for clock golf, or as a miniature golf putting green, or as a combined croquet and putting lawn, or even to lay it out as a single rink for bowls. The future use of the lawn has a bearing upon the garden lay-out.

Grading the site

Grading of the site for the future lawn is an important matter, and one in which many errors are commonly made. Every lawn has certain fixed levels, such as the paths, the house foundation, or perhaps the base of a tree or the bank of a stream. With these in view a correct yet pleasing and practical grading should readily be achieved. In arranging the contours, the question of surface drainage should be kept in mind, and also the fact that grading of any type is a costly process. Often the scheme involves obtaining a level surface from a slope or series of undulations, and in such instances a datum point or line should be selected and a peg driven in, leaving the peg 4 to 6 in (10 to 15 cm) above the soil. From here should be set a series of pegs arranged in lines and cross lines at measured distances. Then by the aid of a straight edge and spirit level these stakes can be set level. To level up, soil is then applied to the surface in shallow layers and gradually levelled up with the tops of the pegs, using another straight edge. In other instances the question is one of providing a gradual slope or a series of gentle undulations to provide variety, or to cover obstacles like outcropping rock. Here stakes and lines will be found most satisfactory in guiding the moulding of the surface. By adjustments to the lines and stakes the work may be reviewed and modifications effected.

Where construction or re-construction involves only small changes in the grading, the changes can be made by the addition of extra top-soil, but if major alterations are in view it is important that they should be made with the sub-soil, the top-soil being removed, placed at one side and carefully saved until the grading is finished, when it can be returned. On large schemes involving the use of heavy earth-moving equipment there is a tendency for top-soil removed to become compacted in the process with consequent loss of physical structure. Furthermore, such machinery tends to compact the sub-soil especially if heavy and when handled in poor weather conditions. It must therefore be well broken up before replacing the top-soil and this in turn must receive thorough cultivation. A similar depth of soil throughout is important because it will determine, to a large extent, uniformity of texture and colour in the subsequent sward. Whatever the size of scheme, however, mixing of top-soil and sub-soil must at all costs be avoided. It should be realised that a medium loam soil will settle 20 per cent or one-fifth, and allowance should be made for this. Neglected grading is a frequent cause of failure to produce a good turf. Occasionally it is necessary to construct a lawn on a hillside, and here the draw and fill method is adopted, an excavation being made, and the material thrown forward to produce the site, which may or may not be quite level. Here again the top-spit should be removed and the work carried out with a sub-grade. The common fault in this type of construction is to provide too shallow a depth of top-soil at the back—the deep part of the excavation—and an excess of soil on the filled portion; with care this can easily be avoided.

Pre-treating and cultivating the soil

Discussions frequently take place as to the best and most suitable depth of soil for the production of a lawn. In general a layer of 9 in (23 cm) of firm top-soil is required but in large schemes involving big volumes of soil it is seldom practicable to provide more than 6 in (15 cm). This often gives quite satisfactory results. Where the top-soil from a lawn has been removed for constructional work to take place, an excellent opportunity is provided for digging over the sub-soil and incorporating vegetable matter that will decompose and open up the soil. While it is true that the bulk of grass roots are concentrated in the top 6 in (15 cm), nevertheless the longer ones will penetrate to a lower depth if encouraged to do so, and roots of the finer lawn grasses have been traced to 16 to 18 in (40 to 45 cm). If there is no question of removing the top-spit, the bulk of the cultivation should be given to that layer, but it is an advantage to double dig the soil, so giving an opportunity for improving the sub-layer but this should not be left too soft or subsequent sinkages may occur.

For small lawns and lawns in restricted areas, hand cultivation is, of course, the only possibility, but on larger areas like sports grounds and playing fields, or on golf courses, large-scale operations become necessary and the cultivation is then carried out by plough and other agricultural implements. For areas that are intermediate between small private lawns and large areas, there are various small mechanical cultivators on the market to-day. Some of these cultivate by rotary action of the tines, while others consist of small power units capable of drawing a plough, cultivators or even disc harrows. On large reconstruction schemes such as are necessary where sports grounds are to be levelled or greens built up on a golf course, from sloping or uneven land heavy earth-moving equipment (scrapers and bulldozers), excavators, and tractors are now widely used while surface cultivations are of course carried out rapidly by tractor power.

In constructional work and preparation for turfing or sowing, thorough cultivation of the top-spit is essential, and it should be realised that any material alteration of this layer during the subsequent history of the turf will be very difficult, and therefore while the soil is bare every opportunity should be taken to improve it. Thus on very heavy soils the aim should be to incorporate gritty material such as coarse sand or fine coke breeze, and to work in well-rotted stable manure at the rate of 2 to 3 tons per 500 sq yd (per 400 m²). In doing so care should be taken that the organic matter* is well broken up, since if it is buried in large lumps, subsequent decomposition leads to settlement in irregular patches. This has sometimes been found the cause of trouble on artificially-made golf greens. Other organic materials that may be used for the amelioration of heavy soil are granulated peat, spent mushroom manure, hop manure, and dried sewage. With sandy soils it is advisable to work in well-decomposed manure at the rate of about 3 tons per 500 sq yd (per 400 m²) and well-rotted cow and pig manure are useful on this type of soil. Dried sewage may also be used at, say, 10 cwt per 500 sq yd (500 kg per 400 m²). Further, if a supply of more loamy material or leaf mould can be obtained it may be added and worked into the top spit. The amount of amelioration that is possible is, of course, dependent upon the funds available, the size of the scheme, and the availability of organic matter. The addition of organic matter on sandy soils improves the water-holding capacity and encourages a deeper root system, while on heavy soils the introduction of grit and organic matter improves the soil texture and the porosity of the soil.

Before a newly-constructed lawn or a sports ground can be sown or sodded, consolidation must be carried out. On small areas like lawns or putting greens this is best done by means of the feet; thorough trampling is the most efficient way of finding the hollows. On larger areas the usual methods adopted are rolling followed by cultivation and further rolling.

---

* The term 'organic matter' and not 'humus' has been adhered to throughout. 'Humus' is a constituent of the colloidal complex of the soil which acts as a reservoir of bases like lime, potash, and magnesia. The 'humus' content influences the fertility, water-holding capacity, and physical condition of the soil, and the supply is increased by the incorporation of organic matter like dung.

Fallowing

The next question to consider in connexion with a new lawn is that of fallowing, which involves the destruction of the weeds that develop from the dormant weed seeds present in the soil. This operation also assists in producing a tilth and is most important where the land is going to be sown, but is less so when sodding is to be done. While it is true that the usual weeds that germinate along with the seeds are annuals, they nevertheless may cause a great deal of difficulty. In the seedling stage the finer grasses do not compete favourably with weeds. The following are the species of annual weeds that may cause most difficulty: groundsel, mayweed, various speedwells, common chickweed, annual meadow-grass. Of these, annual meadow-grass is probably the worst. Very often, imported soil is a source of weed invasion, because many soils purchased for the purpose of making up levels have been removed from arable fields or from building sites that may have lain idle for some time and thus become heavily charged with weed seeds. The importance of fallowing the soil cannot be too strongly stressed, because it is an aspect of lawn production that is almost invariably neglected. There is no sound alternative to it. Numerous instances are known where a crop of weeds has appeared amongst the finest grasses, and the seedsman has been wrongly blamed for the condition. Actually many of the weeds that appear in newly-sown turf are of a type that never appear in properly-cleaned purchased grass seeds. A weed-free sward cannot be made on a soil bed containing dormant weed seeds.

The period from May to August is the best in which to carry out fallowing, which is done by alternate hoeings and rakings to destroy the weed seeds as they germinate and encourage another crop to sprout for similar treatment. The rhizomes or underground stems of creeping soft-grass, couch, convolvulus and thistle, are occasionally found in soil to be used for lawns, and while three of the species do not cause much difficulty it is important to remove all the rhizomes or portions of creeping soft-grass, because this is a species that will establish itself from portions of rhizomes among sown grasses, and will remain persistent in spite of regular mowing.

On some occasions, the time factor may not allow adequate fallowing, and spraying with the herbicides Paraquat or Diquat is an accepted practice. A crop of weeds and unwanted vegetation can be killed off without adverse affect on the soil.

Although it is not often practised in this country, green manuring of an area to be sown for a lawn is a practical proposition. It may be best carried out by sowing white mustard at the rate of 14 to 20 lb per acre (15 to 22 kg per ha). The crop helps to choke weed plants and when 6 to 8 in (15 to 20 cm) high is rolled and dug into the top soil, thus increasing the organic matter and conserving soil nitrogen. Another way is to grow a crop of early potatoes on the site, getting these off by early or mid-August in time to enable autumn sowing to be carried out. This method, however, is apt to leave the land too spongy.

Final preparation of the soil bed

Finally, the preparation involves the production of a soil bed that should have a fine tilth, and if grass seeds are to be sown no particle of soil should be greater than a grain of wheat. Alternate cross-raking and cross-rolling should be carried out, choosing weather conditions that will enable the soil particles to be crushed and worked down. The rake should also ensure the removal of rubbish like roots, surface stones, and twigs, and should be so manipulated that the surface is not left in humps and hollows that will cause subsequent difficulty. While a very fine tilth is necessary for sowing the seeds of the finer grasses, it is not so essential that the surface should be so fine for turfing, nor is it necessary to be quite so particular in the fallowing operations, although it is stressed that the removal of the rhizomes of creeping soft-grass is very important. Both for sowing and sodding, however, the soil bed must be firm so that no settlement is likely to take place subsequently.

Drainage Systems

Some reference must now be made to the drainage of the lawn or sports field. Whether the site is to be sown or sodded attention must be paid to this matter, except where the soil is very light and porous, or in a very dry district, or on land with a good natural slope. Good turf cannot be grown in a water-logged soil, and the indications of the need for draining are soft, spongy areas, prolonged ponding on the surface after rain, and on existing swards the presence of weeds such as selfheal, blinks (*Montia fontana* L.), certain mosses, sedges like carnation grass (*Carex panicea* L.), or dwarf rushes like toad-rush. Proper drainage ensures good aeration, a better distribution of plant foods, an improvement in soil texture, and a circulation of sufficient moisture, so that the plant roots are encouraged to grow deeper; when well drained the soil is also warmer.

Seldom on the garden lawn is anything more than a simple system needed, e.g. a single diagonal drain running in the direction of the fall.

On a sports ground, however, the improvement of drainage is a matter of importance if the maximum number of days of use are to be obtained and a wet puddled surface avoided. In conditions of inadequate draining a bad physical texture of the soil develops through the churning up of the surface and the sealing of the surface layer. Under wet conditions growth is slower in starting in spring and finishes earlier in the autumn. Further, on a badly-drained soil snow lies longer, and this is a point of some importance on turf used for winter games like golf or football. In summer the turf on badly-drained clay soils bakes and cracks, the surface having been 'poached' by the feet of players, just as the farmer finds will happen with the feet of his stock. The rate of loss of surplus water depends on three main conditions:

1. *The gradient of the site*—a gentle slope aids run off.
2. *The structure and texture of the top-soil.* The permeability depends upon the composition and structure of the soil.
3. *The natural water-table of the site.*

Having decided a drainage system is needed, the first step is to locate a disposal point which may be a ditch, stream, or storm water main (subject to permission). On small schemes (e.g. lawns) a soak pit may be the answer.

There are three types of drain from which to choose, viz.

(*a*) *Open* drains or ditches are rarely suitable on playing fields but sometimes of value off the line of play on golf courses.
(*b*) *Closed* or covered drains are suitable. Expensive to install, their life is long and maintenance costs are low. They are the type mostly needed on sports fields.
(*c*) *Mole* drains consist of cylindrical channels drawn in the sub-soil with a mole plough. On consistent clay land with a uniform gradient they will stay open many years. A piped receiving main is desirable.

Pipe draining
Brushwood and stones have been used in wooden and 'stone' country respectively to produce covered-in drainage systems. To-day porous pipes are normally used. They may be clayware pipes or 'tiles' (first introduced in 1843), plastic pipes or porous concrete. Whatever their theoretical advantages, it is difficult to justify their added cost. Plain cylindrical pipes to B.S.1196 (1971) are suitable. Where pipe drains are found to be necessary a scheme should be drawn up on the basis

of one or more of the following systems, according to the contours and
outlet from the site:

1. *Herringbone*. Consists of a series of mains into which discharge,
   usually from both sides, numerous roughly parallel branches (not
   longer than 100 ft (30 m)) at an angle to the main. The system is
   most suitable on nearly level sites.
2. *Grid*. Branches discharge into one side of a main near the
   boundary. Commonly used in lawn tennis court construction.
3. *Fan shaped*. Here the drains converge to a single outlet at one
   point on the boundary. Useful on small sites.
4. *Moat or cut-off system*. The single drain is laid parallel with a
   building or bank to intercept the flow of surface or sub-soil water.
5. *Natural*. Here the drains follow the natural depressions or valleys
   of the site. The system is likely to be of use in large gardens.

Main drains should be laid from 2 ft to 2 ft 6 in (60 to 75 cm) deep and
minors or laterals 1 ft 6 in to 2 ft (45 to 60 cm) deep, the depth being
measured from the lowest point. In clay land laterals should be from
12 ft to 15 ft (3·6 to 4·5 m) apart, in clay loams from 20 ft to 30 ft
(6 to 9 m) and in light loams 40 ft to 60 ft (12 to 18 m). Branches
should enter the main at an angle to the direction of the flow (usually
about 60°) and the main should enter the ditch or stream in the same
way. The falls of the drains should be uniform and lie between the
limits 1:80 and 1:300, though there may possibly be exceptions on
steeply sloping sites. A uniform fall is essential—an uneven fall means an
uneven flow with possibility of deposition of solids followed by
chokage. Sharp bends should also be avoided.

Branch drains should be laid with 3 in (7·6 cm) tiles and should not
exceed 100 yd (90 m) in length. Extra mains should be provided where
longer runs would otherwise be necessary. Mains should be partly
in 4 in (10 cm) pipe but mainly in 6 in (15 cm), stepping up on big
sites to 9 in (23 cm) at the lower ends.

Trenches should be just wide enough at the bottom to permit the
laying of pipes to even falls and proper lines. When digging the trenches
it is important to keep top-soil and sub-soil separate. All pipes should
be butted up all round with open joints, care being taken with the
alignment to avoid both excessive intake of silt and uneven flow.

On heavy land the pipes should be covered with $1\frac{1}{2}$ to 2 in (3·8 to
5·0 cm) washed stone to within 6 in (15 cm) of the surface, after
which only top-soil should be replaced and firmed up without dis-
turbing the pipes. On land carrying grass, a neat job can be made if a

turf rather wider than the future trench is first lifted and laid to one side as in the diagram.

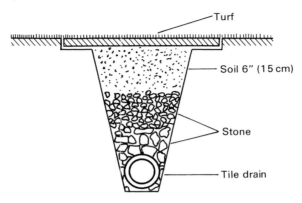

Section of tile drain

Where pipes discharge into an open waterway proper brick or concrete headwalls and aprons should be built and a guard provided to prevent the entry of vermin.

Much of the work of excavation in pipe drainage of lawns and sports grounds must be done by hand, though there are mechanical trenching tools for large-scale work.

Mole draining

Tile draining of large areas of turf is often precluded owing to considerations of cost, and in many instances the adoption of a system of mole draining is possible. Although it may be carried out on open soil it is usually done on turf that has been established. Mole draining is carried out by drawing through the soil a steel cartridge-shaped rod fixed to the end of a knife-shaped coulter, the apparatus being called a mole plough. The rod compresses the soil, so leaving a tubular channel at the required depth. While not so durable as tile drains these channels may last up to 10 or 12 years, although 6 to 7 years is probably nearer the usual period. Deep mole drains, however, have been known to exist for periods of 20 to 30 years. The method is restricted to land having a clay sub-soil and free from stones or pockets of light soil. The land must also have a natural regular slope with a minimum fall of 1 in 200, the ideal fall being 1:100. The fall must be even, and hence on ridge and furrow land the drains must be run parallel with the furrows or they will not be even in depth.

Mole draining of turf is best carried out in the late autumn and winter months when the soil is sufficiently moist to permit the mole plough to move relatively easily. Several types of mole plough are available, and one that is commonly used in draining sports turf is provided with a disc knife fitted in a frame; this cuts the turf and thus minimises the temporary damage. The plough may be drawn either by direct haulage, when it is necessary carefully to choose weather when the surface is dry enough to take the tractor without much damage, or by cable haulage, which has considerable advantages over direct haulage when dealing with turf. When mole draining is contemplated a very careful survey of the land is necessary, especially in regard to slope and contours.

The object of the mole draining is to remove the surface water quickly, and drains at depths between 12 and 18 in (30 and 45 cm) are usual. The drains should, of course, be adequate in size and number to cope with the volume of water reaching the land, and shallow drains of a small diameter close together are more effective than those that are deeper, larger, and less frequent. It is often possible to arrange for a mole drain to lie 3 to 4 in (7·6 to 10 cm) deep in the sub-soil and a total depth of about 18 in (45 cm) is usual. The distances apart will vary with the type of soil and the nature of the land, but from 3 to 10 yd (2·7 to 9·1 m) is the usual distance, although instances are known where, on ridge and furrow land, 2 or 3 drains have been put in in the furrows with only a few feet between them. Drains of $2\frac{1}{2}$ in, 3 in or $3\frac{1}{2}$ in (6·3, 7·6 or 8·8 cm) bore are most common and it is usual to regard 220 yd (200 m) as the maximum length of a drain with $3\frac{1}{2}$ in (8·8 cm) bore. The plough is inserted at the low end of the slope and is drawn uphill and returned to the bottom for the next pull.

The question of outlets in a system of mole draining is of great importance, and deserves more care than is usually given; proper unimpeded emptying of the drains determines their efficiency and permanency. It is sometimes possible to run the moles into an open ditch or into the bank of a stream, but the outlets must be protected from caving in by inserting a few lengths of tile or a length of iron pipe.

This method is not considered to be sound practice. The success or failure of a system of mole drains depends on the provision of good mains and outfalls and it is better practice, therefore, to provide a tiled main cutting across the mole runs at their lower end, the top of the tiles being 2 to 3 in (5 to 7·6 cm) below the floor of the mole channels and covered with gravel, clinker, or similar material.

As regards the cost of mole draining, the size of drains, the distance apart, the depth, and the shape of the area (which determines the length of the tiled main) all have a relationship to this problem.

Mole draining, while very satisfactory on the right soil and sufficient slope, is of course unsuitable for small areas like private lawns where a system of tiles is of necessity usually adopted.

Other ways of draining
Open or surface drainage has a very limited use on sports grounds, but a combination of open drains and tile drains is frequent. Open drains are useful on golf courses and sports grounds for trapping surface water on slopes, for example before it reaches the playing area, but their use is restricted owing to their interference with upkeep operations and the game. They are often useful when a large volume of water is to be removed, or where the water-table is very near the surface, or where the fall is so slight that it is impossible to sink a pipe. Open drains also prove useful for receiving the discharge of tile or mole drains, but they are more expensive to maintain than covered drains and are subject to erosion and chokage by vegetation.

With lawns that have been excavated from a slope on the draw and fill principle, an area at the back is apt to become waterlogged through moisture seeping out of the bank and running over the surface. In such an event, if it is impossible to put in an open drain, a tile drain should be inserted in which washed stone has been filled almost to the top. Such a drain may be helped by placing it in a slight hollow as a further trap for the water.

Vertical drainage is practicable in conditions where a layer of clay overlies a porous stratum of sand or gravel. Small wells are dug through the clay, to contain a column of drain tiles surrounded by washed stone. The end of the column is covered with a slate or flat tile and then with surface soil. Good results have also been obtained by taking out a column of soil with a golf hole cutter or post hole auger and filling to within 4 in (10 cm) of the surface with washed stone.

When constructing a lawn or green on moist heavy soils, it is sometimes the practice to cover the sub-soil with a layer of porous fill, which then comes into direct contact with the washed stone placed in the drains laid in the sub-soil. This method has proved very successful provided a 4 to 6 in (10 to 15 cm) layer of top-spit is replaced to form the surface, and spiking is done to encourage surface water to go through to the porous layer.

Drainage difficulties
In concluding this chapter some brief reference must be made to the troubles attending a system of drains. The most serious is the displacement of tiles, which steadily leads to blockage and the welling up of water on to the surface. The only way in which this can be cured is to

lift the affected part and relieve the blockage. Another cause of trouble is the growth of roots of trees like willow and birch into the pipes. The slowing down of the current of water then leads to silting up and blockage. Collared pipes adjacent to trees are therefore to be recommended. Often, pipes will become choked with sediment through the fall not having been uniform, a dip in the fall causing suspended matter to settle and cause sealing up. Very often, too, silting up is due to a bad outfall of the system. In the event of repairs being required, work is greatly facilitated if there has been kept a proper plan showing, with measurements, the lines of the drains and position of the outlets. On large schemes this is most important.

In many instances surface wetness of the turf is not due so much to bad drainage as to a sticky gluey surface caused by puddling through use under bad conditions. Here, spiking and pricking and the applications of gritty material like sand, charcoal, or coke breeze will greatly relieve the condition.

Sand slitting
This is an efficient and economical way to drain pitches that are prone to surface wetness, by linking the surface through deep sand slits directly to the stone fill above an existing pipe drainage system. In the normal course of surface run-off, some time may elapse before the excess water can move through the often saturated (and sometimes hard-panned) soil to the drainage system. Slits are cut about 2 in (5 cm) wide at about 2 ft (60 cm) apart to a depth of some 8 to 16 in (20 to 40 cm) at right angles to the main drainage, and then filled with sand. This system affords an easy and quick way for the surface moisture to pass into the slits, and so to the drain pipes.

Trenchless drainage
In any pipe drainage system that is installed conventionally, a good deal of disturbance is inevitably due to the digging of trenches, carting about the backfill and the time taken in the operation. Trenchless drainage is a method of laying pipes which overcomes nearly all the problems encountered with the traditional methods.

A very strong blade is winched through the ground bursting open a slot as it traverses the ground. The pipes are led through a hollow section which follows behind the blade and rests on the bottom of the slot. Backfill can be metered above the drain, and the ground closes over the slot like a zip-fastener as the machine moves forward. A high rate of output can be achieved. A slight mound raised by the movement of the blade through the ground settles down within a day or so, and the bursting action of the blade moving through the soil, fissures it and allows the water to flow freely into the drain.

Contractors are available with machines for this operation and for sand slitting.

The question of drainage has been dealt with at some length because it is often neglected when new lawns or grounds are constructed, and it is just as important for small lawns to be well drained as for large areas like golf courses and playing fields.

CHAPTER SIX

How to choose and lay sods

The advantages of lawn making by sowing seed are so frequently stressed in seedsmen's catalogues that the amateur often forgets that lawn production by sodding has in some respects decided advantages over seeding. Perhaps the chief of them is in point of time, because an area of land can be more rapidly clothed in turf, even though it may be overtaken in the long run by a seeded sward. Sodding has the added advantage that it may be carried out in the 'off season', at a time of year when labour in the garden may be more easily allocated to the work, while on the other hand sowing must be done in late summer or spring at times when labour is fully occupied in other directions. Sodding is, however, more expensive in original cost than seeding, for not only does the turf cost more on a yardage basis, but there is the additional cost of carriage, which may be considerable if the turf has to be brought any distance. In many ways it is easier for the amateur to make his lawn from sods rather than seeds because the soil needs less careful preparation and sodding is less tricky than seeding. It is also true to say that some very bad results are achieved with sods by using those containing undesirable grasses. On large constructional schemes sodding is generally precluded because of cost, and here seeding has to be carried out.

The main difficulty in making turf from sods is to locate a source of really good turf—and good turf is exceedingly rare. For one thing it is seldom entirely free from weeds, but in choosing turf it is actually more important to pay attention to the species of grass present than to the weeds. The identification of grass species in a turf sward is not easy, so if the amateur is choosing turf it is desirable either to take advice on the suitability of the species present, or only to deal with a supplier whose stock of turf has already been approved as regards species and suitability. For general purposes old parkland turf is suitable because it lifts readily, is strong enough to withstand transport, and usually contains only finer grasses, mainly species of bent and fescue, which will work up to a turf. Such turf is also reasonably free from weeds, and such species as are present will either die out as a result of cultivation, or may be removed by special operations.

Marsh turf, such as is obtainable from the salt marshes of Lancashire (Morecambe Bay) and Cumberland (Solway estuary near Silloth) as well as other districts, has a high reputation for laying bowling greens. The Cumberland, or Silloth turf, has earned a high reputation, but to-day supplies of good turf are becoming more limited. The species present in sea marsh turf are strains of *Agrostis stolonifera* var. *compacta*, Hartm., and strains or even varieties of *Festuca rubra* subsp. *rubra*. Some inferior classes of this turf contain sea poa (*Glyceria maritima*, Wahlb.), which does not make a turf. The main variety of red fescue found on sea marshes is *F. rubra* var. *glaucescens*. Analyses show that the relative proportions of the red fescue and bent vary from place to place, so that definite analytical figures cannot be given. This turf is lifted in 1 ft sq (30 cm sq) sods for ease of transporting. It is a heavy material and 1 sq yd (0·94 m²) of the turf, cut $1\frac{1}{4}$ in (3·17 cm) thick, will weigh about 112 lb (50 kg) so that the cost of transport for an area like a bowling green is considerable.

Downland turf overlying chalk, mainly in the south and east of England, provides a useful source of turf. The soils underlying this type of turf are thin, and a herbage of sheep's fescue, bent grass, and crested dog's-tail, with some golden oat-grass, is typical. Unless the turf is of the old matted fibrous type leguminous plants may be numerous, as well as miscellaneous weeds, among which burnet is common.

On stiff soils derived from Boulder Clay or other clay formations, much of the land has been worked out and allowed to 'tumble-down' to grass. Semi-natural vegetation has developed and where acid conditions prevail, bent grasses, fescues, dog's-tail and Yorkshire fog occur. The weed flora is more extensive, but good turf may be evolved from this type of sward.

Turf suitable for lifting as sods for lawn work may also be found in extensive areas on the millstone grit or other non-calcareous grits and sandstones. Such turf is characteristic of many parts of the north of England where rainfall is high and smoke pollution aids the depletion of bases from the soil. The semi-natural vegetation found on these types of soil contains grasses suitable for turf production, and good results are obtained by reducing the acidity, applying phosphate, and by reducing the amount of acid mat by boxing the turf. Creeping soft-grass is a frequent constituent of this type of sward so that in choosing sods care should be taken to avoid the patches of it.

Good turf is also found on heaths where the soil is poor and semi-natural associations of plants have gradually become established. On poor uplands in many parts of the country occur large tracts of grass in which the finer-leaved grasses, the bents and fescues, predominate. Unfortunately such areas are usually badly placed or inaccessible from the point of view of disposing of the turf, but such material would provide unlimited supplies of sods. Much heath and moorland turf contains moor mat-grass (*Nardus*) or heath-grass (*Sieglingia decumbens* (L.) Bernh.), but if a good heath or moorland turf containing dominantly bent grass and some fescue can be obtained it works down very satisfactorily for a turf sward. This class of turf is usually very matted, and is therefore not so suitable for lawn tennis or cricket wickets, but makes excellent turf for golf or ornamental swards. Practical experience and experiments suggest that the grasses in heath and moorland associations are to be preferred to those in sea marsh turf, especially as sods of the latter contain a layer of fine sandy clay. Heath and moorland turf is usually very free from weeds, the principal species found being cat's-ear, which is easily removed, heath bedstraw, which dies out under mechanical operations and manuring, and wood-rush, which also gradually disappears with the mowing.

It will be apparent from the above that the best types of turf for obtaining sods are found as semi-natural vegetation on the poor soils, and, indeed, the finer-leaved grasses useful for turf are 'poverty' grasses, a fact that is often forgotten in their subsequent maintenance.

In all instances in which turf from an outside source is purchased, it is worth inquiring whether any preliminary cultivation has been given to it in its natural situation. On golf courses preliminary cultivation can readily be carried out before lifting the turf, but purchased turf has commonly received no such treatment and the subsequent laying and management are thus made considerably more difficult.

The first stage of lifting is to cut the turf into parallel strips, guided by a line and using a turf race or 'half moon' turf cutter; cross cuts are then made to give pieces of the required size, and the sods are lifted by means of a turfing iron. As very few people can lift turf to a uniform thickness it is better in practice to lift the sods say to 2 to 3 in (5 to

Fig. 3(a). Lawn:
turf cutting.

Fig. 3(b). Lawn:
turf lifting.

Fig. 3(c). Lawn:
turf boxing.

7·6 cm) thick and to box them down in a turf gauge-box. These boxes consist of a shallow tray with three sides, the sides being of the same height as required to make the finished sod. The turf is placed, grass down, in the gauge-box and the loose fibre and soil on the underside are removed by planing them off with a scythe blade or a two handled knife. The actual thickness and size of sod must be decided by the strength of the fibre; if the turf is weak, sods of 1 ft × 1 ft (30 cm × 30 cm) should be cut, but turves 1 ft × 3 ft (30 cm × 90 cm) and 1 ft × 2 ft (30 cm × 60 cm) are often used. Parkland and moorland turf when bought is usually delivered in 1 ft × 3 ft (30 cm × 90 cm) sods rolled for convenience of transport.

As regards the most suitable thickness, most practical men agree that the best results are obtained by cutting the turf as thinly as possible, but the usual thickness is from 1 to $1\frac{1}{2}$ in (2·5 to 3·8 cm), though excellent results have been seen where the turf was cut as thinly as $\frac{1}{2}$ in (1·2 cm). Experiments have shown that the practical man's views on the thickness of sods are substantiated by scientific fact. Tests carried out showed that the general trend is for thin sods to grow a better root system than thick ones; thus sods $\frac{3}{4}$ in (1·9 cm) thick had a better root development than sods cut 3 in (7·6 cm) thick. The experiments were carried out with very matted parkland turf.

Before laying the sods on the prepared site it is advisable to pass each sod across a bench for inspection when any rosette weeds present can be pulled out or pushed through from the back. Similarly each should be scrutinised for plants of Yorkshire fog, or creeping soft-grass, and turves heavily contaminated with these grasses should be rejected or placed on one side for turfing unimportant parts of the work. Turves containing small pieces should be rigorously hand picked. In constructional work, especially on big schemes, the use of a turf-cutting machine is convenient for lifting large areas of flat turf rapidly. Such machines are available in a variety of cutting widths from 12 in (30 cm) to 24 in (60 cm) and are capable of cutting turves uniformly to predetermined thickness and length thus eliminating the need for boxing. Also, in the construction of banks and mounds, turf may be cut up into long bands, rolled back spirally for several yards and left standing in situ; after the constructional work is finished the turf is then rolled out again.

Some practical greenkeepers cut the edges of their turves at an angle instead of vertical—there are special turf races for doing this—and while this method gives excellent results in capable hands, it is apt to result in drying out and curling up of the edges where the work has not been carried out so skilfully or where drought has intervened.

Having obtained a supply of turf that has been cut accurately into pieces of equal area and boxed to uniform thickness, laying can commence. If the sods are delivered and it is not possible to commence work at once, they should be laid out flat and any rolled turf should be opened out. If turves are left standing rolled or stacked, they soon discolour and the lawn suffers a preliminary set-back. Even if frost intervenes and delays the work of laying, the sods will not be adversely affected when laid out. Before laying the turf it is a good plan to dress the prepared bed with fine raw bone meal or superphosphate at 2 oz per sq yd (64 g per m²), especially on poor land. The soil may be dressed with lead arsenate at 2 oz per sq yd (64 g per m²), lightly raked in, since it has been shown experimentally that this material when placed under the turf gives a high degree of earthworm control. The material also controls other soil pests. For small lawns or areas near a supply of water this additional initial expense is, however, hardly warranted since deworming the turf can follow soon after establishment.

Before laying the turf it is important to see that the formation level has been accurately finished and that the area has been pegged out at 10-foot (3-m) centres. Turfing should commence at one side or corner and work across the area. Laying should be carried out in a forward direction, i.e. the man laying the turf should face the unturfed soil and he should stand upon a board so that foot indentations are not made in the newly-laid turf. The sods should be laid with the joints alternating, as on a flagged pavement or as the bricks in a wall, and they should be packed closely together. Beating of the turf is sometimes recommended, but should not be necessary if the soil bed has been well prepared and the sods are cut to uniform thickness. If there is a lump in the turf then it should be regulated from below by the removal of soil. Beating down of the turf on such lumps rarely succeeds and often leads to unequal compression of the soil. In the laying of a flat bowling green it is usual to commence at the corner of the green and work at an angle of 45 degrees to the line of play, and 12-in sq (30-cm sq) sods are necessary to ensure accuracy in laying.

Once the laying is completed, top-dressing with sand, or soil containing a high proportion of sand, should be carried out, and the material worked into the joints between the turves because this facilitates knitting in the lateral direction. After this material has been well worked in, rolling can be carried out once over with a roller weighing about 2 cwt (100 kg). An application of fine compost may then be given. If frost lifts the turf or the latter is of a spongy nature, repetition of the rolling may be necessary. At this stage the turf should be left until growing weather commences, when a spring

Fig. 4(a–c).
Lawn: turf
laying.

(c)

Fig. 4(d). Lawn:
turf beating.

(d)

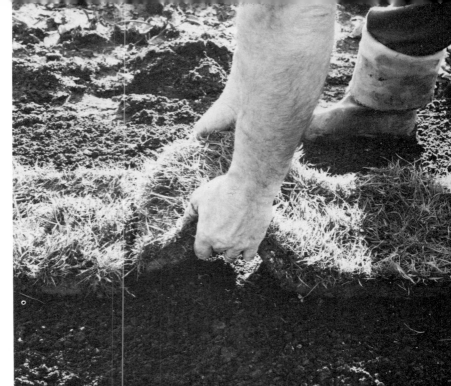

application of fertiliser may be considered necessary. On the other hand, if the soil has been well prepared and pre-treated with bone meal or superphosphate it is probable that it will not require much treatment other than mowing for the first part of the season but a light nitrogenous dressing may be given in spring. Composting of newly-laid turf is valuable because it helps to find the small depressions in the turf, and may be done at intervals during the establishment period. It also acts as a mild fertiliser and mulch.

Sodding of lawns and greens is usually a winter operation, but it may be carried out at almost any time of the year provided there is an adequate supply of water for application in dry periods. In practice, however, most re-turfing is done between September and early February, although good results have sometimes been seen from turf laid as late as April. Late work invites damage in dry weather. On light sandy soils the earlier the re-turfing is completed in the winter the better—in fact, the aim should be to finish before the old year is out. On other soils it is usual to try to complete the work by the end of the first month of the new year.

During summer weather newly-laid turf, especially on clay soils, is inclined to crack and, should this happen, watering will be necessary and top-dressing for the purpose of filling in the cracks; mulching the sods is also desirable. During the spring it is wise to carry out a further inspection for weeds. If they are few, and rosette types, hand weeding should follow, but if numerous or mainly creeping they should be left for mechanical operations and applications of selective weed-killers as soon as the turf is well enough knit and established. This is particularly important with sea washed or sea marsh turf, which may contain plants of sea plantain, starweed, sea milkwort, and thrift.

CHAPTER SEVEN

Grasses procurable in commerce

The number of species and varieties of grass seed suitable for the formation of the finest lawns, obtainable in commercial quantities, is strictly limited, but if the range is widened to include varieties employed in the production of turf for other purposes also, their number is proportionately increased. It must be realised that many of the species obtainable through the seedsman, while often botanically the same as those found in natural turf, may differ considerably in turf-forming capacity, and that many of the strains of grasses grown for seed generation after generation are more adapted to production of seed-stalk than leaf—and it is leafage that is required for turf formation. There is, therefore, room for the production of seed crops from selected strains of grasses, such as those found in the finest indigenous turf, and capable of producing leafy, persistent swards. It may be well to describe the various species and strains obtainable in commerce with their turf-forming propensities, giving details of the usual purity and germination of the seed, as a preliminary to discussing seeds mixtures and the purchase of seeds.

The fescues

Among the fescues used in turf production there are two main groups, the red fescues and the sheep's fescues, which are distinguishable by the nature of the leaf sheath* on the non-flowering stalks. In the

---

* The leaves of grasses are attached to the stem at the nodes and each consists of two parts—a lower portion surrounding the shoot and called the 'sheath' and an upper portion called the 'blade'.

sheep's fescue this sheath is split, while in the red fescue the sheath is entire. The dwarfest of the sheep's fescues is Fine-leaved Fescue (*F. tenuifolia* Sibth.), which forms dense compact tufts and is adapted to peaty and dry soils. The wiry or bristly leaf is permanently folded and the plant forms only intra-vaginal shoots.* It is a perennial and under natural conditions flowers in June and July, producing a seed 2 to 4 mm long with no awn.† The standard of purity and germination is lower than in other fescues, the purity being usually between 80 and 90 per cent and the germination at least 70 to 80 per cent in 21 days. Harmful weed seed impurities liable to be present include sheep's sorrel and Yorkshire fog. As a turf-forming species it has points in its favour for acid land, but it does not blend so well as other species of fescue and should not be used alone. Turf sown from this species alone is dense, dark green in colour with a 'dappled' surface and a tendency to form a grain.

Another fescue belonging to the same group is Sheep's Fescue (*F. ovina* L.) but seed true to name is very scarce and tests with seed purporting to be sheep's fescue have shown that in many cases Hard Fescue or Fine-leaved Sheep's Fescue was being sold. The seed is 3 to 4 mm long, has a short awn point and the plant is tufted and of similar habit to fine-leaved sheep's fescue. Perhaps the commonest of the sheep's fescue group is Hard Fescue, which is the term for varieties grouped together as *F. duriuscula*, a botanical term that has also been applied to some of the red fescue group. It appears however, to consist of a number of varieties and even sub-species, and in fact much of the hard fescue of commerce can be classified as *F. longifolia* Thuill. Commercially the term 'Hard' fescue is almost interchangeable with sheep's fescue and this species, like those mentioned above, is obtained almost entirely from Europe where the suppliers class them as natural grasses.

While sheep's fescue has a habit of forming tussocks and does not blend well with other turf-forming species, cultivars of hard fescue (*F. longifolia*) do blend well.

The name Creeping Red Fescue (*F. rubra* subsp. *rubra*) covers a number of varieties of red fescue able to grow in all kinds of situations and which are markedly drought and cold resistant. The plant produced is wiry leaved and spreads by underground runners, since it produces extra-vaginal creeping stems as well as some intra-vaginal shoots.

* Every new stem arises within the angle (axil) of the old stem and the leaf sheath. If the stems grow up within the sheaths this is the intra-vaginal mode producing tufts of foliage. If the shoots pierce through the sheath close to where they arise and grow out horizontally this gives the extra-vaginal mode and a loose open habit results.

† A bristle-like appendage generally associated with grass seeds. It may be terminal, basal or affixed midway to the glume.

The seed is 4 to 5 mm long with an awn and is employed to some extent in agricultural practice, though mostly in lawn mixtures.

The original stock of seed came entirely from Germany, but in recent years it has been imported from Denmark, Canada, and Holland.

Selection work with red fescue has been carried out in this country at the Welsh Plant Breeding Station, with the result that a variety known as S59 was produced. Supplies of certified seed are available in good quantities. It provides a sward of good colour, resistant to drought and cold, and is markedly uniform, being finer in leaf than other creeping red fescues except that derived from sea marshes. All the varieties tested are susceptible to Corticium disease. A certain amount of red fescue is harvested by hand from the sea marshes of the Solway and on the borders of Morecambe Bay. This is the botanical species *F. rubra* subsp. *rubra* var. *glaucescens*, and the seed harvested has been successfully used in lawn mixtures. The plant is slightly glaucous in colour and forms a turf finer in leaf than the German species, and as the seed is mostly hand gathered it rarely contains any weed seeds. All the above forms of creeping red fescue blend well with other grasses, especially with browntop and Chewing's Fescue.

The remaining fescue obtainable is Chewing's fescue (*F. rubra* L. subsp. *commutata* Gaud) which is a non-rhizomatous perennial species of red fescue. This species is found as a wild plant in different parts of the country. The plant forms a tussock, but it is of a looser type than that of sheep's fescue. It produces both intra-vaginal and extra-vaginal shoots but all the branches ascend in the vertical direction. The species is well adapted to turf formation and blends well with species of bent and other grasses, the only disadvantage in the turf being the tendency for the leaf tips to 'bleed' or discolour after cutting, and for it to lose colour somewhat during the winter months. It is however, markedly drought resistant. When included in seed mixtures containing *Agrostis* there is a tendency for it to be ousted by the more aggressive bent.

Chewing's fescue is mainly grown for seed production in Oregon (USA), Holland, Germany and Denmark.

The story of Chewing's fescue forms a romance of the seed trade. It appears that the original seed was supplied by an English firm of seed merchants about the year 1833. It was sown near Invercargill and two years later the pasture was cut for seed. This crop was taken and sown at Mossburn, a property which was later purchased by a Mr Chewing, who harvested the fescue field and presumably marked the bags of fescue seed as 'Chewing's Fescue'.

Loss of germination has been a problem with this seed, the matter being so serious that the seed unfortunately earned an ill repute

Fig. 5. Sowing seeds. *Left*: sown with 90 per cent Chewing's fescue and 10 per cent perennial rye-grass. *Right*: pure sowing of Chewing's fescue.

amongst seed merchants who often lost more money through unexpected depreciation of germination than in any other grass seed. The causes of bad germination were investigated by Foy and Hide around 1935 when the fescue trade was at its height and when there was no competition from the American grown seed. The fall did not appear to be inevitable, because in some years the seed retained its viability remarkably well. It has been shown, however, that the falling off was associated with unfavourable conditions during shipment, such as high humidity and temperature. Further, immature seed tended to sweat, but seed that was well matured before exportation, and with a low moisture content, retained its viability for some years. Foy's experiments indicated that by artificial seed drying it was possible to overcome the rapid loss in germination, and much of the seed exported later was artificially dried before shipment.

Before concluding references to the fescues, mention may be made of Rat's-tail Fescue (*Vulpia myuros* (L.) C.C), a species of little significance in lawn work as it is an annual, but it is occasionally found as a coloniser in long turf and small supplies of seed are at times offered.

The bent grasses

Amongst the bent grasses Browntop (*Agrostis tenuis* Sibth. = *A. vulgaris* With.) is undoubtedly the most important. It is a slightly stoloniferous tufted perennial found on poor, dry, acid soils in meadows, heaths and moorlands. Some forms have short rhizomes.

Seed used to be exclusively imported from New Zealand, but since 1956 an increasing amount of American seed has reached this country, as also has seed from Europe.

In New Zealand, the main seed production area was confined to the Otago and Southland districts of South Island, where the grass is said to have been accidentally transported as stuffing from palliases by early immigrants from Cape Breton and Prince Edward Island (Canada) in the period 1851 to 1856.

The seed was rarely sown intentionally in New Zealand, but the grass established as a volunteer on poor land. 'Run out' pastures were widely used for seed production, costs thus being low. The seeds are small, being only 1·2 to 1·8 mm long.

Pasture improvement in New Zealand meant that the browntop country declined in area as did production of seed. Some 340 tons left the country in 1947, of which about 50 tons would reach Great Britain. Since 1956, American or Highland Bent has been imported. Licences to import were issued for some 650 tons in 1958 against 14 tons from New Zealand.

Another source of *A. tenuis* was central and south-west Germany, from which a seed known as South German mixed bent or simply German bent was exported. As the name implies it was in reality a mixture, small amounts of *A. canina* and *A. stolonifera* var. *compacta* seed also being present. The mixture is still procurable from reputable seed houses.

A small amount of *Agrostis* was harvested annually in this country and sold under the name of English or Kentish agrostis.

Though found at times in lawns and proved experimentally to provide an excellent sward, little commercial seed of Velvet or Brown Bent (*A. canina* L.) is available. Small amounts are produced in Holland and the USA, but the turf is not so good as an indigenous selected type since there is a tendency for surface creepers to form. The winter colour is poor.

Supplies of another species of *Agrostis* known as Redtop (*A. gigantea* Roth.) reached this country prior to World War II. Actually the commercial material, sometimes called Fiorin, is a collection of types, the plant being vigorous and forming extensive underground rhizomes. When sown alone this grass fails to make a fine sward, though the seed can be included in mixtures for sports grounds, but at present no seed is being imported to this country. The seed was harvested in Southern Illinois, where for some forty years it had been a commercial crop. Unfortunately the seed has often been substituted in mixtures for the seed of other more expensive bents suitable for fine turf.

Wavy hair-grass

In addition to the bent and fescues seeds obtainable in commerce, and forming the basis of fine seeds mixtures, there are a number of other grasses used for purposes other than fine lawns. Very like a sheep's fescue in vegetative character is Wavy Hair-Grass (*Deschampsia flexuosa* (L.) Trin.), a species of limited use in turf establishment but able to establish well on very acid soils. The species can be used in seeds mixtures for heaths and peaty soils, for example on some golf courses. The leaves are dark green in colour, narrow and rolled. The seed is characterised by a twisted kneed basal awn, and tufts of white hairs. The seed is usually of European origin.

The meadow-grasses

Another important group of grasses used in connexion with turf formation are the meadow-grasses or *Poas*, and the commonest and most widely distributed species amongst this group is Annual Meadow-Grass (*Poa annua* L.). Its commonness, is, however, due to its habit of seeding and propagating itself all the year round, but more profusely in the months of May and June. Being dwarf-growing it is adapted to close mowing, but seed when procurable is in the form of gleanings, rarely contains more than 65 to 70 per cent of pure seed, and has only a limited use on account of the impurities. One sample that was examined contained 14·4 per cent of impurities, including rough-stalked meadow-grass (4·4 per cent), perennial rye-grass (3·8 per cent), crested dog's-tail (3·2 per cent), Yorkshire fog (0·8 per cent), as well as seeds of cocksfoot, hawk's beard and slender foxtail.

Smooth-stalked Meadow-Grass (*P. pratensis* L.) is another *Poa* abundant in Britain, but only small amounts are found in fine lawns. It is very much valued in North America for pastures and for lawns under the name of Kentucky Blue-Grass. It is suited to the lighter soils, spreading by rhizomes, but does not reach its full development until the second year. Smooth-stalked meadow-grass withstands a considerable degree of treading and drought, and is a useful plant for

Fig. 6. Fescue turf invaded by annual meadow-grass.

binding slopes and banks. Seed is now imported from the USA, Denmark and Holland.

Rough-stalked Meadow-Grass (*P. trivialis* L.), the third species of *Poa* obtainable commercially, is also abundant in this country, but is best suited to moist soils and districts. In dry places on dry lawns the foliage turns a reddish brown, but in moist fertile conditions it produces a steady yield and is quicker in development than smooth-stalked meadow grass. It is a bottom grass and spreads by thin stolons, which unfortunately preclude its use on the finest turf, but it has its uses for sports turf purposes.

Wood Meadow-Grass (*P. nemoralis* L.), which is indigenous to Europe, is found in woods and moist shady places, and has therefore been advocated for sowing lawns in shade. The foliage is a rich green colour, but supplies of seed are limited. The seed is produced in Germany and Holland, and owing to its scarcity is subject to adulteration.

Another meadow-grass is Flat-stemmed Meadow-Grass (*P. compressa* L.), which although indigenous to Great Britain, is seldom found in turf. In turf it forms a tough coarse sward, but its possibilities in this country have not been fully investigated. It spreads by rhizomes.

As a curiosity Bulbous Meadow-Grass (*P. bulbosa* L.), which is found on some seaside golf courses in this country, particularly in

Kent, is worth mentioning. Commercial 'seed' from America is actually in the form of small bulbils, produced on the flowering stems in place of seed. The species has little value for turf formation, though it is used in the hotter parts of the South of France with fairly satisfactory results.

Perennial rye-grass

It remains to describe in this chapter three groups of grasses of more particular use for play lawns and the sowing down of large areas like sports fields. The first of these is Perennial Rye-Grass (*Lolium perenne* L.), which is a tufted perennial abundant on most soils, and grows best on moist fertile land. Its value is reduced on dry soils. It has an extensive use in agriculture and is reasonably permanent on the richer soils. There are many varieties or strains, and some of the old varieties, described as Pacey's or Devon Evergreen have now lost much of their identity and these terms are now applied to the genuine perennial rye-grass. The Welsh Plant Breeding Station has bred leafy varieties now widely known, described as S23 (pasture type), S24 (hay type), S101 and S321 (dual purpose). Of these the relatively prostrate variety, S23, has a distinct place in turf establishment where leafiness and persistence are required.

The ordinary commercial perennial rye-grass is shorter lived than the indigenous type and is produced mainly in Northern Ireland and to a lesser extent in Ayrshire. Some acres are grown annually in Northern Ireland, yielding 5 to 6 cwt of seed per acre (625 to 750 kg per ha). The small seeds are often graded out and sold as 'small' or 'short seeded' perennial rye-grass.

Other varieties of rye-grass are produced in Denmark, Holland, Sweden and Belgium from selections made by plant breeders, and there is a form that is certified and exported from New Zealand known as Grasslands Ruanui. This type is persistent, but the ordinary New Zealand and Danish rye-grasses are less persistent in this country than the British and the Dutch.

Timothy

(*Phleum pratense* L., and *P. nodosum* L.). These two species are occasionally used in sports turf but cannot be advised for any form of fine turf. They are too coarse and do not persist under very close mowing. The Aberystwyth varieties S48 (*P. pratense*) and S50 (*P. nodusum*) are likely to have uses in some types of turf. Seed of S50 is relatively scarce and expensive, but this creeping grass is likely to gain in popularity for establishing the less keenly-mown types of turf.

Crested dog's-tail

The remaining species requiring reference is Crested Dog's-tail (*Cynosurus cristatus* L.) found naturally on dry hill pastures and even on heavy clays. It withstands drought and cold, but is slow in developing, only reaching its maximum in the second year. The plant grows in tufts with the leaves at the base, and is essentially a bottom grass. Being tough in nature, it is used in mixtures requiring hard wear. Seed is produced in Europe. It is advisable to avoid seed of a canary yellow colour because it is immature and of poor quality. It has been shown that high germination is coincident with maturity of the seed, and this condition is linked with seed colour, which is a dull brown in mature seed. It has also been shown that loss of germination during shipment can be related to the immaturity of the seed.

Seed prices

The prices of seeds have always been subject to market fluctuations. Prices are especially influenced by the season, since poor harvesting conditions lead to lower yields and poorer quality. Advances in the costs of seed can often be offset however, by greater care in seed bed preparation (e.g. good cultivations and pre-treatment with fertilisers) followed by lighter rates of seeding. Up to date quotations should always be obtained for seed requirements from reputable sources.

Breeding of cultivars

For a number of years research and development has been carried out into the management and improvement of grassland for herbage. New strains of grasses have been bred at the Welsh Plant Breeding Station, Aberystwyth, in particular the 'S' numbers, now widely known throughout the British Isles. Some of these have proved very suitable for sports turf use, for instance S23 Rye-grass and S59 Red Fescue.

The breeding of grasses specifically for sports turf has assumed new proportions in recent years, particularly in Holland, breeding being done by about eight private companies, and being supported by the Agricultural University at Wagenigen with fundamental research work.

The main aim of plant breeding is to produce better varieties (or cultivars) in order to replace the so called 'commercial seed' of grasses,

Fig. 7(a). A view of a typical seed-production establishment in the Netherlands. Note the extensive seed testing grounds at the top of the picture.

Fig. 7(b). Testing wear resistance of new cultivars using a 'wear machine'.

many of which had bad characteristics. The new cultivar would be better than the older variety, with the breeder seeking to make improvement in one or more of the following characteristics (among others); establishment, density of sward, persistence, resistance to disease, drought resistance, wear resistance, and colour. Because the breeder will want to produce and market the seed, consideration will also have to be given to seed production of the cultivar, threshing and cleaning behaviour, whether or not, in fact, the production and sale of seed will be a viable proposition.

It would appear obvious that a breeder can only combine a limited number of improved characteristics in one cultivar, and he will aim for a certain target in one breeding cycle, attempting to reach this by combining the improved properties in one variety. This takes years of work in the laboratory, in the warehouse, but mainly in the field.

When the breeder is seeking to create a new variety, he will need new material with as much genetical variation as possible, and can obtain this mainly by collecting plants or seeds in the field, where natural selection may have done some work for him, and by crossing certain varieties he can combine their good qualities.

The new material will then be planted in the field for observation for a period of about two years, during which time attention will be paid to such properties as colour, leafiness, type of growth, disease resistance, winterhardiness and so on. In the summer of the second year, selection of the plants to be retained will be made, and groups of these plants with more or less the same characteristics will be planted together. These groups will be looked at the next spring with a view to further selection, and those plants that fall short of some of the properties needed will be eliminated before flowering. Seed from the remaining plants will provide the first seed of the potentially new variety. This seed, and seed obtained after multiplication of it, is used during the next three to four years for trials of the potential cultivar.

Normally three types of trials will be carried out during this period:

(i) variety trials, to compare the new cultivars with the existing ones,

(ii) turf trials, taken in conjunction with existing varieties as a control. Those characteristics important for lawns and sports turf will be carefully looked at, attention being paid to such things as persistence, resistance to disease, resistance to wear, establishment, density and drought resistance, and

(iii) seed production trials, in order to form some opinion of the seed yield compared with the existing ones.

After these trials, the most promising new varieties will be submitted to the Institute of Variety Research, Wageningen for further research. After three or four years, the cultivar may either be discarded because of deficiencies, or else it may be accepted and added to the list of varieties, after which the seed of the new variety can be marketed. From the first collection of new materials to the acceptance of a new cultivar can take from between seven to twelve years.

Recently introduced cultivars

The number of cultivars will clearly change from time to time. Under-mentioned are some of the varieties appearing in the current issue of the Netherlands Register of Varieties.

Agrostis tenuis
Bardot: a fine-leaved grass that forms a very thick turf. It maintains its colour through the winter, and is fairly resistant to fusarium patch.
Tracenta: a grass with a fine leaf, holding its colour through the 'off season'. Its light green leaves can form a thick turf.
Holfior: although it can form a thick turf, it is somewhat susceptible to fusarium patch.
Highland: a fine-leaved variety with an excellent winter colour.
Contrast: a fine-leaved light green strain that can produce a thick turf.

Agrostis canina L.spp *canina* Hwd
Novobent: produces a thick turf, light green in colour. A stoloniferous species that can establish itself quickly.
Barbella: although a little susceptible to fusarium patch, it holds its colour well in winter and forms a good light, soft green turf.

Festuca rubra commutata
Highlight: a fine-leaved strain that can form a very thick turf. It is fairly resistant to disease, having among other things, little sus-ceptibility to Autumn rust.
Koket: has a distinct dark green summer colour, which it holds through-out the winter. Quite tolerant of drought conditions. It can form a thick turf, and is fairly resistant to disease.
Barfalla: a fine-leaved strain that can form a close knit sward, holding its colour well in the 'off season'.

Festuca rubra L. var *trichophylla* Gaud.
Dawson: a fine dark green coloured strain that can form a reasonably thick turf, but is somewhat liable to attacks of red thread.

Golfrood: because of its drought-resistant qualities, it can hold its colour and condition in these conditions. It appears to thrive better on heavy than on light soils. A fine-leaved strain, it holds its colour well in winter.

Festuca rubra L. var. *rubra*
Gracia: although it can form a thick turf, it is somewhat susceptible to the fungal disease red thread.
Novorubra: this strain can thrive on a wide variety of soil types, and because of its long rhizomes, it can quickly spread to form a reasonably thick turf.
Agio: a dark green strain, forming a moderately thick turf, somewhat susceptible to Corticium.
Bargena: a fine-leaved strain that can produce a moderate to thick turf, a little susceptible to red thread.

Festuca ovina L. var. *tenuifolia* (Sibth.) Dum.
Novina: a fine, dark-leaved strain that thrives on dry, acid soils.
Barok: a very fine, dark green strain.

Festuca ovina spp. *duriuscula* L.
Biljart: its colour both in summer and winter is a rich dark green. Very resistant to drought conditions, but in normal circumstances this strain cannot stand competition from other grasses. It is virtually completely resistant to red thread.

Poa pratensis L.
Fylking: a fine-leaved variety, highly resistant to leafspot disease and rust. It can form a compact thick turf under good fertile conditions.
Merion: a broad-leaved strain, resistant to leafspot, forming a thick turf that holds its colour well in the winter.
Baron: a thick turf forming variety that holds its colour reasonably well in winter.
Prato: a fine-leaved strain that is winterhardy and is quite resistant to hard wear.
Monopoly: a broad-leaved strain forming a thick turf that is suited to surfaces that are subject to hard wear. It does not withstand close mowing.

Lolium perenne L.
Pelo: a fine-leaved strain that is winterhardy, and quite resistant to hard wear.

Barenza: this variety can form a very good, hard-wearing turf, although it is a bit prone to attacks of rust.

Lamora: a hard-wearing turf can be produced with this strain.

Manhattan: although it is somewhat slow in growth, this moderately fine-leaved variety produces a very good turf when established.

Stadion: this variety can form a dense hard-wearing turf, with a high degree of resistance to disease.

Phleum pratense L.

Pastremo: although susceptible to leafspot, *Pastremo* can form quite a good thick turf.

King: this strain of Timothy can form a good, winterhardy turf, although it can be somewhat susceptible to leafspot.

Phleum nodosum L.

A very flat-growing strain which forms a reasonable turf. A little sensitive to drought conditions, although it stands well and is very winterhardy. Somewhat susceptible to leafspot.

Sport: a reasonably fine-leaved, flat-growing strain that can form a thick turf. Like the other cultivars of *Phleum nodosum*, a little susceptible to leafspot although very winterhardy.

CHAPTER EIGHT

Choice of seeds mixture and rate of sowing

It has already been pointed out that the number of grass species contributing to the herbage of a fine lawn is decidedly limited, and the same will be found for golf and bowling greens, and even golf fairways and sports grounds. The latter may be composed of comparatively large numbers of miscellaneous plants, but usually well over 70 per cent of the turf will consist of two or three species. On swards consisting of the finest turf, bent, or a perfect blend of bent and fescue, may account for almost 100 per cent of the herbage. The conditions imposed on a fine lawn are very uniform, though very exacting, as compared with a pasture or a meadow, but this very uniformity and definiteness permits the choice of a seeds mixture consisting of species most suitable in meeting the precise demands. In agricultural practice some 30 to 40 years ago it was not uncommon to include 20 species in a grass land mixture, but to-day rarely more than 8 or 10 are utilised, and there is a tendency to further simplification. Knowledge of seeds mixtures for fine turf purposes has advanced in a similar direction and it has been shown that the simpler mixtures, composed only of species suited to the definite requirements, are best. In fact, to include a large number of species in a lawn or green mixture is to invite eventual disaster, because the least desirable grasses may flourish exceedingly and crowd out or severely hamper those that are especially desired; colonisation in patches and unevenness through some plants failing to knit may also occur; and, finally, the inclusion of unnecessary species involves waste of money.

The seeds mixture must, therefore, be simple and it must consist of species capable of intermingling to form a uniform sward. Blending is most important, but will not be achieved if two markedly stoloniferous strains or species of grass are sown together, since the tendency will be for each to colonise large areas of ground, some of them consisting almost wholly of one and some of the other. The resultant effect of such a condition would be a network of patches, an effect found in greens sown with mixed strains of bent, or sodded with turf containing mixed strains. If, therefore, two or more strains or species are to be used in a mixture they should consist of strains or species that are not markedly stoloniferous. On the other hand, if a green of one species is desired, then it would appear essential that it should consist of a stoloniferous strain selected to suit the conditions, without the aid of other species, and planted as a pure culture, as is done in vegetative planting. A mixture for use in sowing a fine lawn (and these remarks also cover putting greens, croquet lawns and such-like), need only contain two or three species, and these should be selected from among the bents and fescues commercially available.

Experiments at St Ives have shown that the following simple mixtures satisfy the conditions, giving good intermingling and a uniform sward:

> 8 or 7 parts by weight Chewing's fescue
> 2 or 3 parts by weight Browntop

Chewing's fescue is non-rhizomatous and the browntop bent rarely forms more than short stolons. On better soils there is a tendency for the bent—the aggressive partner in this mixture—to oust the fescue, but by controlling the fertility this may largely be checked, since fescue is more tolerant of poorer soil conditions. An example of this may be seen on excavated lawns that have been sown with such a mixture. Here the bent tends to predominate in the deeper 'filled' soil, while the fescue assumes an ascendancy in the part 'drawn' and covered with less soil. Some lawn owners prefer the more leafy sward of bent while others prefer the wiry and bristly sward of the fescue. On golf and bowling greens, a turf of fescue is faster than one of browntop. If desired the mixture given above may be made more favourable to fescue by increasing the Chewing's fescue to 9 parts and reducing the browntop to 1 part; but even if only 5 per cent of bent is included in a mixture it often happens that the fescue will gradually disappear under the effects of keen mowing and the influence of systematic dressing. Creeping bent as the source of bent (*Agrostis*), is not suggested for the finest turf mixtures, though it may be used on coarser swards, because comparative trials have shown it to be less uniform than browntop, and there is the possibility of patches developing in the turf.

Good lawns can be formed from either Chewing's fescue or browntop sown alone, but, the bent seedlings being small, the rate of establishment of a pure bent lawn is apt to be slow, and so in practice it is better to sow a mixture, with the quick-growing fescue acting as a 'nurse' in the early stages. Some experimental work by Madden in New Zealand has shown the advantage of this practice in aiding weed suppression and giving better initial ground cover. The figures obtained by this worker are given in Table 8.1, and reference will be made later to Column 4.

TABLE 8.1
Area of ground covered by grasses and weeds

	Browntop —pure (1)	Chewing's fescue—pure (2)	Browntop and Chewing's fescue 1:2 (3)	Browntop Chewing's fescue, and rye-grass 1:2:2 (4)
	per cent	per cent	per cent	per cent
Bare ground	13·0	12·0	6·0	19·0
Browntop	56·6	1·8*	32·6	3·3
Chewing's fescue	—	62·6	51·8	18·2
Perennial rye-grass	—	—	—	53·7
Weeds	30·4	23·6	9·6	5·8
	100·0	100·0	100·0	100·0

* Volunteer (not sown).

In seasons when the seed of Chewing's fescue is unreliable as regards viability, the inclusion of Creeping Red fescue is advised in the following proportions:

3 parts Chewing's fescue
4 parts Creeping Red fescue
3 parts Browntop

The substitution of hand-gathered fescue (var. *glaucescens*) from sea marshes for the creeping fescue is permissible, especially if the latter contains any seed of rye-grass. Or, if desired, Aberystwyth red fescue strain S59 (certified) may be employed, since trials have shown that it blends well with the other fescues and the bent in a closely-mown sward. Only a sample quite free from rye-grass should be used for the finest swards. Part of the fescue may also be included as fine-leaved fescue, especially on rather acid or peaty soils, and in years when hard fescue is cheaper than Chewing's fescue, this species may be employed for making a cheaper non-rye-grass mixture, though the resultant turf is not so satisfactory. Trials have also shown that good results can be obtained when velvet bent is used with Chewing's fescue, in place of browntop, but there is the tendency one would expect from a creeping form of this type to dominate the sward rapidly to the exclusion of the fescue.

It may be argued that the above simple seeds mixtures are insufficient to meet the wide range of soils likely to be encountered in different parts of the country. It should be noted, however, that mixtures of these types have been satisfactorily employed under a wide range of soil conditions, but in any event the view is expressed that it is preferable when sowing a lawn to modify the soil to a medium loam consistency rather than 'juggle' with the seeds mixture in an effort to suit existing conditions. This has been stressed in the chapter dealing with the preparation of the site for sowing. For larger areas it may not be possible to modify the soil materially in this manner, but here the conditions are usually less exacting and a more comprehensive seeds mixture may be chosen; even so bent and fescue should be well represented in the mixture. Hard-and-fast rules in devising a seeds mixture for large areas can hardly be laid down, since local conditions and the purpose for which the sward is intended must always have a deciding influence, to say nothing of the funds available.

In spite of the findings of present-day turf research, many proprietary seeds mixtures for fine lawns and greens still contain as many as 8 or 10 species, and while there are no doubt widely-differing views on this matter, it is difficult to understand on what basis such mixtures have been compounded. In some instances there is little doubt that the mixtures are made up for the purpose of maintaining a standard catalogue price, and the occasional changes in the composition of these mixtures are designed to counterbalance the fluctuations in the market prices of the ingredients.

As is generally known, there are two types of seeds mixtures commonly used, namely rye-grass mixtures and those containing no rye-grass. It is usual to include some 50 to 60 per cent of ordinary commercial perennial rye-grass in many proprietary rye-grass mixtures, and this undoubtedly leads to rapid establishment and quick cover. If such mixtures contained in addition 40 to 50 per cent of bent and fescue there might be some chance of the lawn becoming established eventually, but as the mixtures usually contain only 1 to 5 per cent of bent and 10 to 20 per cent of fescue, these species are almost smothered out from the beginning. Then, as the rye-grass dies out under the influence of mowing, a bare open turf results, which forms a happy resting-place for weed seeds. The only advantage of such rye-grass mixtures is their cheapness and the fact that they form a quick cover. They do also, as is shown by the figures obtained by Madden in Table 8.1, result in slightly better initial weed smother, but the ultimate turf formed is sparse and not permanent.

Where it is desired to establish and maintain a rye-grass sward, for example on a sports ground, leafy pasture varieties should be used. These leafy strains are more persistent under the mower. They are less objectionable than the ordinary rye-grass as far as stalk production is concerned, though on light soils all strains are likely to be less leafy and more stalky.

The amount of rye-grass, mainly leafy, should be in the order of from 30 to 35 per cent, while fescue and bent should be well represented in the mixture. From 10 to 12 per cent of bent is a suitable amount to include. An endless series of mixtures can, of course, be made up by varying slightly the amounts of each ingredient but in practice it is the major constituents that determine the nature of the resultant sward.

Mixtures free from rye-grass, yet somewhat lower in price than those containing bent and fescue only, may be made up by including crested dog's-tail, smooth-stalked meadow-grass (when available), rough-stalked meadow-grass and hard fescue with reduced amounts of bent and red fescue, but while these are very useful mixtures they do not produce a sward approaching the standard of pure bent and fescue mixtures. They should be avoided if the finest turf is required, e.g. on golf greens, bowling greens, and first-class lawns. Rye-grass mixtures must not be sown if a fine lawn is desired, and even for first-class hockey grounds, cricket outfields, or golf fairways they are not to be preferred. The only occasion when they must be used for this type of sward is when consideration of cost definitely precludes a better article. Rye-grass mixtures are normally used for playing fields and on areas like football grounds where rapid re-establishment in the off-season' is required.

While it is impossible to lay down hard-and-fast rules in seeds mixtures for extreme conditions of soil, certain modifications are possible; thus, on very acid soils some of the red fescue may be substituted by fine-leaved fescue, and on dry sandy soil the proportion of fescue may be increased at the expense of the bent and smooth-stalked meadow-grass included. In shady situations it is usual to include wood meadow-grass and rough-stalked meadow-grass, while the latter species is also useful on moist rich soils where a fine turf is not needed. On acid peaty soils part of the fescue may also be substituted by wavy hair-grass. Crested dog's-tail is a useful species being tough and hard-wearing, but it should not be included in the finest mixtures except on chalk soils and in dry situations. Its greatest use is as a constituent of mixtures for sports grounds, playing fields, and the like.

The inclusion of clover in seeds mixtures for large areas is sometimes considered, and if desired, then wild white clover of indigenous strain should be used. On poor gravelly soils yellow suckling clover is sometimes useful, whilst on calcareous soils bird's-foot trefoil forms a drought-resistant legume to include as part of the mixture.

Leaving out considerations of cost, the seed rate to be used in sowing down new turf depends upon (1) the composition of the seeds mixture and quality of the ingredients; (2) the cleanness, tilth and fertility of the land; (3) the purpose of the sward; and (4) how soon the turf is required.

When sowing putting greens, bowling greens, and fine lawns with a fescue/bent mixture it should not be necessary to use more than 1 or, at the most, $1\frac{1}{4}$ oz per sq yd (32 to 40 g per m²), always assuming the seed is of good viability. For bent only, $\frac{1}{2}$ oz per sq yd (16 g per m²), is an ample seed rate, though as little as $\frac{1}{8}$ oz (4 g) has given satisfactory but slower results on clean land. Bent seedlings are small and rather slow to establish.

Experiments have been carried out in an attempt to cut down the seed rate in view of the high cost of fine seed. In one trial the bent and fescue were sown separately in opposite directions in narrow drills 3 in (7·6 cm) apart and while good turf was soon established in this way at a rate of about 40 lb per acre (45 kg per ha) no better result was obtained than with 40 lb (45 kg) of bent seed broadcast in the ordinary manner.

The only advantage of sowing fine grasses above normal rates is to obtain better competition against weeds, especially annuals. The disadvantages are greater cost and the risk of 'damping off'. A heavy seed rate is no substitute for a good seed bed.

As already indicated, sports grounds and playing fields are usually, on grounds of cost, sown with rye-grass mixtures. At one time, it was common to use as much as 5 to 6 cwt per acre (625 to 750 kg per ha), approximately 2 oz per sq yd (64 g per m²), of which 50 to 60 per cent was perennial rye-grass, thus giving the small amounts of finer grasses very little, if any, chance of establishment. To-day, rates of 2 cwt per acre (250 kg per ha) are commonly specified, but even this is too high. Roughly 112 to 140 lb per acre (125 to 157 kg per ha) of a balanced mixture should be regarded as a maximum. In experiments at St Ives designed to study several seeds mixtures (containing rye-grass) turf swards from sowings at 28, 56, 84, and 112 lb per acre (32, 64, 94 and 125 kg per ha) were compared. Turf from the 28 lb (32 kg) rate was inferior for the first eighteen months but at no time was there much to choose between turf from the other three seed rates. It was noted, as might be expected, that the check to annual weeds was greatest at the higher rates of seeding. There was little difference in density between turf sown at 56, 84 or 112 lb per acre (64, 94 or 125 kg per ha) and any small benefits of the higher sowings were not commensurate with the greater cost.

In practice, rates of from 56 to 85 lb per acre (64 to 95 kg per ha) of rye-grass mixture containing no more than 30 to 35 per cent rye-grass and a good allowance of finer bottom grasses have often been used with satisfactory results. Naturally when sowing at lower rates the seed must be of good viability; as always there must be a good clean seed bed and any plant food deficiencies must be made good by using a compound fertiliser containing nitrogen in advance of sowing.

Whenever mixtures containing rye-grass are used for turf it is important that the grass be regularly mown from an early age otherwise the rye-grass easily outgrows and may even smother the finer grasses sown in the mixture.

CHAPTER NINE

The purchase of grass seeds

A few years ago, the owners of small lawns used to rely for their supplies of seed upon ready prepared mixtures, bought from a seedsman. Many of these mixtures were put on the market under names borrowed from well-known sports clubs or stately mansions, the inference being that the seeds would give a turf equivalent in quality to that found at the place named on the packet. The result may or may not have come up to the standard expected. Reliable seed houses could be depended upon to supply good standard lawn mixtures, but there were also a number of not so reliable dealers. Although there were Seeds Acts in operation, there were no provisions in these Acts that required a merchant to conform to a standard of quality for lawn seed mixtures sold as such.

There were many examples of lawn seeds being sold by disreputable stores, with low purity analysis and high percentages of harmful weed seeds in the mixture. There were other examples of seed being sold as a bowling green mixture containing high proportions of chaff, weed seeds and unwanted grasses. Hay loft sweepings were often sold as seed mixtures, and one sample examined contained 44 per cent of rye-grass (only 53 per cent of this was viable), 50 per cent of chaff and 6 per cent of weed seeds.

To be good seed, a sample must fulfil certain requirements which may be summarised as follows;

1. it must contain a high proportion of viable seeds capable of strong growth,

2. it must be free from the seeds of weed capable of establishing themselves in the lawn,
3. it must be reasonably free from inert matter, such as chaff and dirt, and
4. it must represent the species or variety of that species shown on the label attached to the container.

The first three points are amenable to laboratory test but it is not possible by a laboratory test (though it might be possible after a time as a result of growing a sample) to give the final verdict on the last point. If deemed necessary, a sample of seed offered can be tested on payment of a fee at one of the Official Seed Testing Stations, and the report of the analysis, which is for private use only, will declare (i) the germination, i.e. the viability or percentage of numbers of purchased seeds that are alive; (ii) the purity, i.e. the percentage of the sample by weight which consists of pure named seed, dead and alive; and (iii) a statement of the chaff and weed impurities. A comparison can then be made between different lots of seed offered, for by a simple calculation the samples can be reduced to a common denomination by using for each the following formula:

$$\frac{\text{Germination per cent} \times \text{Purity per cent}}{100} = \text{Real value}$$

A comparison of the 'real value' and the price quoted at once shows which seed is the best value for money, but the 'real value' may be misleading unless due regard is paid to the nature of the weed impurities present. Minute amounts of weed impurities in fine turf seeds can be the means of introducing a tremendous number of weed plants to the area.

While the Seeds Act 1920 and subsequent amendments in 1961 and 1964 covered the supply of seeds sold to farmers, only the ambiguous conditions of the Trade Descriptions Act 1968 and amendments covered the sale of seed for amenity or non-agricultural use. There may be never-ending debates over whether the advantages outweighed the disadvantages when Great Britain joined the European Economic Community, but without doubt one of the advantages, at least to the groundsman, of joining the Community, is the implementation of the European Economic Community's Directives on seeds, which for the first time in the United Kingdom cover amenity or lawn seeds.

These regulations, the Fodder Plant Seed Regulations, 1974, came into operation on July 1st 1974 and were formulated to protect the consumer, and to improve the quality of the products. They regulate the marketing in Great Britain of seeds of fodder plants and revoke the regulations made under previous Seeds Acts. The regulations will be enforced by the Minister of Agriculture, Fisheries and Food in England and Wales, and by the Secretary of State in Scotland. They apply to seeds of the fodder plants such as *Agrostis canina canina, A. gigantea, A. stolonifera, A. tenuis; Festuca ovina, F. rubra; Lolium perenne; Phleum pratense; Poa annua, P. pratensis, P. trivialis* and others.

Seeds may be marketed only if they are of specified categories which attain minimum standards prescribed by the regulations, although the seller will be at liberty to claim that his products attain the higher standards that are laid down. Two examples of the higher voluntary standards are that the minimum percentage of purity of *Festuca rubra* is 95, and of *Lolium perenne* 98. The maximum amount of weed seeds allowed would be 0·5 per cent and the minimum percentage germination for *Festuca rubra* would be 75 and for *Lolium perenne* 80.

The sale of most amenity seeds would be restricted to varieties which had undergone testing in one or more countries within the European Economic Community, and found to be distinctly different to all varieties currently on a 'Common Catalogue', of varieties of kinds of agricultural plants published or to be published in the Official Journal of the European Communities.

Provision is made for the selling and labelling of the packages in which seeds are sold, and for the taking of samples for verification and enforcement purposes. Since July 1st 1976, all seeds mixtures that are sold in the United Kingdom to consumers are officially labelled with full particulars as to contents by weight.

The regulations also provide that sellers are deemed to warrant the correctness of certain particulars stated or implied in the sale of seeds, and since July 1st 1976, official certification of seed is obligatory in the United Kingdom for those species covered by the directive.

It would appear from the above, that 'good seed' indeed can be expected, in all its requirements.

CHAPTER TEN

Sowing seeds and treating the new sward

Having prepared a fine seed bed and satisfied oneself that fallowing has been adequate, sowing of the grass seeds may commence. It is important, however, again to stress the need for patience and care in dealing with the last stages of preparation, and the futility of going to a great deal of trouble with the soil and then sowing seed containing injurious weed seeds, or conversely failing to prepare the soil satisfactorily and then sowing an expensive seed. Either will bring poor results, if not failure.

Even though a very good seed bed has been produced, it is often advisable, especially on soils known to be poor, to carry out some pre-treatment, and the figures in Table 10.1 obtained by Madden in the

TABLE 10.1
Percentage of sward in grass, weed and bare ground (sward 6 months old)

	Quick-acting fertilisers	Slow-acting fertilisers	No fertiliser
Bare ground	8·0	17·0	32·0
Sown grasses:			
Browntop and Chewing's fescue	89·5	71·6	54·8
Weeds and clover	2·5	11·4	13·2
	100·0	100·0	100·0

course of experiments conducted in New Zealand, are of interest in this connexion. They show the advantage of using a quick-acting fertiliser mixture of nitrogen and phosphate as against a slow-acting mixture of these plant foods, or no pre-treatment at all. Sulphate of ammonia and superphosphate were used as the quick-acting fertilisers.

As a practical recommendation for small areas the following mixture may be raked into the soil 7 to 10 days before sowing:

$\frac{1}{2}$ oz per sq yd (16 g per m²) sulphate of ammonia
1 oz per sq yd (32 g per m²) superphosphate
$\frac{1}{4}$ oz per sq yd (8 g per m²) sulphate of potash

For large areas the dressing should be on the following lines:

from 1$\frac{1}{2}$ to 2 cwt (75 to 100 kg) sulphate of ammonia
from   3 to 5 cwt (150 to 250 kg) superphosphate
from $\frac{1}{2}$ to 1 cwt (25 to 50 kg) sulphate of potash

Such a mixture must, however, be used immediately after mixing. If it is to be stored, even for a few days, a conditioner must be included otherwise the mixture will set hard in the bags.

Pre-treatment with lime before sowing is not recommended unless there are obvious indications of high acidity and lime deficiency; this matter receives further attention in Chapter 19. Where there are no obvious signs of lime deficiency then the above general fertiliser will give the required fillip.

Discussion frequently takes place as to the best time of the year at which to sow seed, but generally speaking there are two suitable periods of the year—the spring and late summer or early autumn. Experience has shown that late summer sowing, about the second or third week of August in northern or colder parts of the country, and early September in the warmer and more southerly parts will achieve success. This time of sowing provides a longer period of suitable weather for fallowing the soil, because before spring sowing there may not have been sufficient moist, warm weather to ensure a good germination of weed seeds. Spring sowings usually contain more weed plants than autumn sowings. If the seedlings are well established in the autumn they are ready to go right ahead at the onset of spring weather the following year. Further, there is less likely to be winter kill of seedlings in the cold weather following an autumn sowing than through the effects of desiccation in summer drought after spring sowing. It is a mistake, however, to sow grasses late in September and even in October as is sometimes done, because under these conditions there may be poor germination and even failure through winter kill.

Fig. 8. 'Heeling' the soil before final preparation of the seed bed.

Fig. 9. Sowing seed using the grid system to ensure even cover.

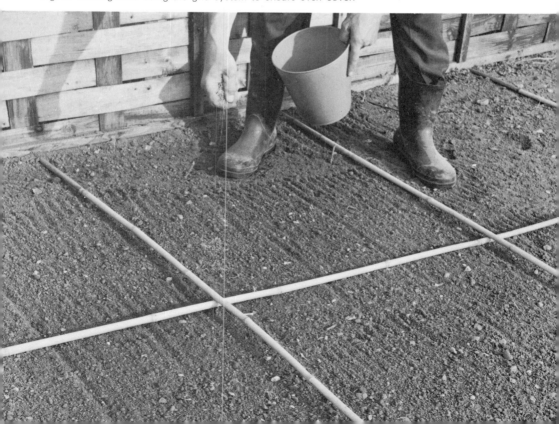

This is particularly true of bent seedlings, which are very small in the early stages and may be beaten down and gradually destroyed. Fescue, on the other hand, is more tolerant of late seeding and should be used predominantly for late sowings of fine seeds.

Broadcast sowing by hand is quite satisfactory provided certain elementary precautions are adopted. Uniform sowing is important because it results in a more satisfactory sward, and, of course, if the seedlings are regularly spaced they are better able to compete against any weed aggression which may take place. It is customary to divide the quantity of seed available into two lots of equal weight and sow in opposite directions. Greater evenness can be obtained, however, by dividing the area to be sown into a number of spaces and dividing the seed into double this number of equal small lots. Each space is then sown in cross directions.

On large areas some mechanical means of sowing is necessary, and perhaps the most popular method is to use the fiddle sower. Some of the small distributors made for applying fertilisers to turf can conveniently be adapted for sowing seeds. Thus, using a 36 in (90 cm) fertiliser distributor of the moving band type, it was possible to sow evenly as little as 40 lb of bent seed per acre (45 kg per ha). It was found advisable to test the machine on a floor or tarpaulin to check the setting. The spinning disc type distributor can be effectively used as a mechanical aid for sowing seed.

Sowing should take place on a still, quiet day, and always when the surface of the soil is dry. The seed should be sown on a raked surface, and then be very lightly raked in—a wire rake is useful—but deep covering is not to be recommended. Experiments have shown that the amount of added covering over newly-sown seed determines to a large extent the degree of establishment. Table 10.2 will make this clear.

TABLE 10.2
Percentage establishment per 100 viable seeds

	Seed raked in and lightly covered	Seed raked in and *not* covered
Browntop	11	39
Chewing's fescue	74	68
Fine-leaved fescue	54	52

These figures can be correlated with seed size, for when small seeds like bent are covered there is a tendency for the soil to cake over the surface and smother the young seedlings, so that establishment is prevented. With fescues, however, the seeds are larger and tend to lie on the surface, so failing to obtain the right conditions for germination and growth; when covered, therefore, rather better establishment is obtained.

In sowing pure bent, therefore, covering is not required, but with fescue there is an advantage in covering. In practice mixtures of fescue and bent are usually employed, and here a light covering at no more than 2 lb of fine soil or compost per sq yd (1 kg per m²) should be given. Where fescue alone is used from 3 to 4 lb per sq yd (1·6 to 2·0 kg per m²) may be applied. In large-scale sowings it is impracticable to cover with a special dressing.

After sowing the lawn, light rolling, if the surface is dry enough not to cling to the roller, may be done on light and medium soils, but on heavy soils it is preferable to omit this operation as caking of the surface reduces establishment. Leaving the soil somewhat rough after sowing provides some degree of shelter to young seedlings, especially bent.

The figures in Table 10.2 show also the low rate of establishment for bent, and illustrate the point that even if the seed germinates 100 per cent in the laboratory, not all the seedlings will make mature plants on the lawn.

On large areas, like playing fields or sports grounds, ordinary agricultural equipment should be used. The seed should not be drilled but broadcast on a harrowed surface, lightly cross-harrowed and flat rolled. Good results can be got by sowing after ring rolling, followed by cross-harrowing and flat rolling. The grass tends to establish in rows with this method.

In proximity to towns, trouble from birds (especially sparrows) is common on newly-sown lawns. A network of black cotton or strips of rag or tin or plastic tied to lengths of twine may be used as a scare. The seed can be treated with a repellent to prevent bird depredations.

Given good germinating weather, the seedlings should braird in from 5 to 10 days and will make rapid growth. It is at this time that great care is required in establishing a sward and the discretion of the lawn owner or greenkeeper must be fully exercised. If an early autumn sowing has been made it is probable that before the onset of wintry weather sufficient growth will take place to call for one cutting. This should be done when the grass is about 2 in (5 cm) high, using a keen well-adjusted mower, but before topping is carried out it is advisable to scatter any earthworm casts with a bamboo rod and to roll the lawn once or twice with a medium weight roller. The blade of the mower should then be set so that it removes about half the leafage; keen mowing must at all costs be avoided. Following an autumn sowing on lawns, top-dressing may be carried out with compost about February, and as spring advances the frequency and intensity of the mowing may be gradually increased. Spring fertiliser treatment may be required, but it is wise to 'nurse' the grass at this stage and to allow it to become well established before cutting too keenly.

Newly-sown grass is prone to 'damping off' diseases, especially when seeds are sown at the end of the autumn sowing period when moist, muggy conditions often prevail, and again if sown too early in spring before the soil has had time to warm up. Several fungi are responsible for 'damping off' diseases of turf grasses but the most common are *Pythium* spp. Reference is made to other species as well as to methods of control in Chapter 27 on fungal diseases of turf.

It should always be realised that 'damping off' is favoured by heavy sowings.

Even though great care has been taken in preparing a seed bed and in the choice of clean seed, it may happen that a number of weeds appear in the newly-sown turf; these will, however, usually be found to be annual weeds that have blown into the soil at the time of sowing, or have been introduced by careless use of contaminated top-dressing, or have even survived the fallowing period. There is no need for alarm about annual weeds though if the grass is weak and poorly established, plants like common chickweed (*Stellaria media*) may grow more rapidly than the sown grass, so tending to smother it before cutting can commence. Annuals like chickweed, redshank, fat-hen, mayweed, and groundsel gradually die out as a result of regular mowing, but if very plentiful their removal by hand picking is advised. It sometimes occurs that the amateur, seeing a number of annual weeds in his lawn, immediately jumps to the conclusion that the seedsman has sold him impure seed, forgetting or being unaware that the seeds of annual weeds are rarely found in good grass seeds because they are removed by the cleaning machinery. It is much more important for the lawn owner to concern himself with the removal of adventitious plants of perennial rye-grass, cocksfoot, or Yorkshire fog, introduced with the seed or more probably already present in the soil; these, especially the last species, tend to persist in the mature lawn in spite of the mowing. A frequent cause of difficulty in newly-sown turf is the presence of annual meadow-grass, but if the soil has been well fallowed the amount of this will be so small that it will be possible to remove it in the early stages.

Prior to 1939 there was introduced a method of sowing lawns in which the seeds are 'pre-sown'. That is, they are arranged in parallel rows between two sheets of a thin paper-like vegetable medium, obtainable by the yard (metre) in 2-ft (60-cm) widths. It was claimed that more uniform spacing of the seed, more uniform burying, less bird damage and better conditions for germination resulted from this method. Within two or three weeks of planting, the paper medium decomposes. Seeds mixtures for different purposes and qualities of turf were obtainable. The cost was rather more per square yard than using the seed in the broadcast manner but comparative trials failed to show any special advantages. The 'pre-sown' method took longer to lay down than the broadcast. Apparently the sheets are again being produced, but the method, while perhaps of value on small lawns, has obvious limitations, e.g. on windy exposed places, on undulating surfaces and for large areas.

During World War II, attention was directed to soil stabilisation, and it assumed particular importance when parking grounds and temporary or emergency airfields, made by seeding, were hurriedly required. It was found that treating newly-sown land with a cold bituminous emulsion permitted the earlier use of the surface for landing or for wheeled traffic. These results have led to the investigation of the method for peace-time purposes such as the establishment of recreation fields, roadside verges, embankments and even turf to be used for games like tennis and football.

A series of seeding experiments was described by Martin Sutton, and the subject dealt with by R. B. Dawson and J. R. Escritt who were responsible for experiments at St Ives. These experiments, carried out at three separate seasons of the year, showed in the first place that grass seeds germinate more rapidly when covered by the bituminous layer, a difference of 4 to 6 days against controls being noted according to species. It was also found that all grasses tested were able to establish through the 'stabilising' layer, but with some a small reduction in the 'take' took place. It has been claimed by some workers that weed germination is prevented by the bituminous layer, but this was not confirmed.

In other experiments at St Ives the emulsion was applied to established turf. This process involves applying sand to the turf, then the bitumen emulsion, a further dressing of sand, and rolling. Various rates of sand and bitumen have been tried. The grass soon grows through re-forming a complete coverage over the tough bitumen-sand layer. In some instances slight stimulation of the grasses was observed.

The toughened surface layer produced by sand and bitumen not unnaturally prompts the idea that it might increase the wearing qualities of golf tees, cricket wickets, tennis courts and football fields. Except for winter golf tees, the result of trials on such areas do not engender enthusiasm. The process is messy, there are several practical difficulties and the cost is not a small item. For those wishing to make a trial however, the procedure is as follows:

1. Treat the surface with sharp coarse sand (which must be damp) at 10 lb per sq yd (5·4 kg per m²).
2. Apply $\frac{1}{2}$ gal 30/35 per cent bitumen emulsion to each 1 sq yd (2·75 l to each m²) in the form of a spray.
3. After spraying, apply 1–2 lb coarse sand to 1 sq yd (0·54–1·08 kg to 1 m²).
4. Roll, using roller of about 2 cwt (100 kg).
5. Treatment should be done in spring or early autumn.

It has been suggested that the provision of a bituminous layer on a newly-sown playing field might permit its earlier use at, say, a new school. This is probably true, but whether the added cost justifies the end is another matter. Indeed the rate of establishment of a playing field could in many cases be speeded up more simply by better planning, by the adoption of good cultural methods and by using better seeds mixtures without much additional cost.

CHAPTER ELEVEN

Making verges and banks

The establishment and maintenance of grass verges is always a difficult proposition in a garden and unless it is properly carried out is best left alone, because nothing looks worse than a ragged edge with broken pieces and bare spots surrounding the bedding display. On the other hand, a neatly-kept verge shows off the floral display to best advantage. In making new verges it is important to allow sufficient width to take the mower conveniently, and the edges should be regular and arranged 2 to 3 in (5 to 7·6 cm) above the borders or adjacent paths. To get the best results a series of level pegs and narrow wood straight-edges should be used to find the right level and to enable the intervening space to be built up with soil. Whether the verge is to be sown or sodded makes little difference at this stage, though if sods are to be planted the level will be proportionately lower. A straight-edge should also be used at right angles to the length of the verge for the purpose of checking the level of the soil and smoothing it out. The verge should be made about 3 in (7·6 cm) wider than it will be finally; this makes seeding or sodding easier and when established the edge can be cut back to the width required. Wide verges are preferable to narrow.

In turfing a verge the sods should be laid carefully and truly and then lightly beaten and rolled. When the verge is well established and after the edges have been cut to the decided width, it is sometimes advisable to support the edges with iron strips. If the border and path are on a sloping grade the verge should follow the gradient also.

Where the verge edge has become broken or the width too narrow through trimming, a good repair can be done by knicking down the centre, severing the turf, and sliding it outwards to a new line. The bare centre area left is then turfed with new sods or filled with soil and sown.

The production of banks on lawns and sports grounds is a matter that requires careful consideration and planning. Where the scheme is one of formal arrangement, then it is necessary to secure the levels very carefully because the effect will be lost if there is a wavy margin to the bank. In less formal work the general level and arrangement should be decided, after which some undulations and irregularities are allowable. The upper and lower edges of the bank should first be determined by pegs and horizontal straight-edges, and the slope should then be checked by means of a further straight-edge placed up the slope which can also be used to regulate the depth of the soil. In deciding upon the angle of the slope consideration must be given to the fact that the bank will eventually require mowing and that suitable equipment will be needed. Generally speaking an angle of 25 to 30 degrees is satisfactory for mechanical mowing. A slope of 20 degrees makes foothold easier but of course the bank takes more room. Shallow banks (3 to 4 ft high (0·91 to 1·2 m)) may be made steeper (45 degrees) since they can be mown from the bottom with a hand (or small motor) mower. A less-severe slope helps to conserve moisture and prevent excessive baking in drought, while the general effect is more pleasing. The slope should be so graded that the upper edge is gently rounded to avoid skinning by the mower and the basal part should be tapered out in a gentle curve so as to permit uniform cutting at the foot.

In preparing the bank a good depth of soil is required, and this soil should be well dug, working sideways along the bank and turned uphill before chopping the clods down with the spade. If necessary, amelioration of the soil may be carried out as advised under the general construction of lawns. All general work and cultivation of the surface should be done in an uphill direction to minimise the tendency for the soil to roll down to the lower levels. Many banks suffer from a deficiency of soil on the upper edges and an excess at the base of the bank. Consolidation of the bank is rather important, so as to reduce erosion and to conserve moisture, and after testing the angle with a straight-edge, trampling and beating of the soil are required.

When banks are sown there is always some danger of the seed being washed away by heavy rainfall, and it is not uncommon to find that the upper edges are deficient, having too few seedlings, while the base of the bank is overcrowded. Seeding of banks is perhaps best carried out in the late summer because the grass can get well established before the winter, thus being in a better position to withstand drought the following season. The washing away of seeds on banks may be minimised by the device of placing horizontal laths at intervals along the slope, these being later removed when the young grass is well up. Although bare strips are left by this process they readily fill in and are soon lost. Another method is to cover temporarily with cheese cloth and good results can be obtained by covering with straw (held in position by strings and pegs) until the seedlings have rooted.

In turfing banks the sods should be laid from the base of the slope upwards, the size of turf depending upon its nature. Large turves are more difficult to handle so that 1 ft by 1 ft (30 cm by 30 cm) and 1 ft by 2 ft (30 cm by 60 cm) are usual. The work should be done in an uphill direction, the turf being gently beaten, the operator standing at the top or part way up the bank. The beater should consist of a piece of thick board to which a handle has been attached at an angle.

In constructional work, when an artificial mound has been produced on the flat and where the turf has been rolled back for the purpose, it is comparatively easy to unroll the long strips, which may be from 6 to 10 yd (5·4 to 9·1 m) in length, and put them into position quickly. As when turfing on the flat, the turf banks should be dressed with sand or sandy loam and compost, to facilitate knitting and establishment of the turf.

CHAPTER TWELVE

The vegetative production of turf

The vegetative method of producing turf has received very little practical attention in this country, but is worthy of consideration because of the comparative ease with which uniform turf can be produced. It may, therefore, be of interest, especially to those of an experimental turn of mind, to try out the method. Usually, vegetative turf production is done with creeping grasses but it can be carried out quite easily with non-creeping species, using their shoots or tillers and dibbing them in at intervals of 2 to 3 in (5 to 7·6 cm). These shoots rapidly tiller-out to form thick plants, and with top-dressing soon make a turf. Another way is to obtain some sods of, say, Browntop (*Agrostis tenuis*), and to tear or shred them up into separate shoots and scatter these on the prepared surface. After light top-dressing, roots are made and tillers produced, and then by occasional mowing and top-dressing a continuous sward soon develops. Thus a square-foot (0·09 m²) sod of *A. tenuis* made 40 to 50 sq ft (3·71 to 4·64 m²) of excellent uniform turf.

Some years ago, a number of new greens were prepared on the St George's Hill and Wentworth Golf Courses, rough turves and stolons of a slightly rhizomatous *Agrostis* being broken up and scattered on the prepared soil, and gradually worked down into an excellent sward.

Vegetative turf production is usually carried out with species of grass which form extensive surface runners or stolons. In this country Creeping Bent (*A. stolonifera* var. *compacta* Hartm.) and Velvet Bent

Fig. 10. A plant of *Agrostis canina* showing extensive stolon formation.

Fig. 11. *Left*: Planting stolons: September.
Fig. 11. *Right*: Same area: next June.

(*A. canina* L. subsp. *canina*) have been used experimentally. Although it is rather more cumbersome than the production of turf from seeds, the method is so simple and can so easily be carried out in practice that it is astonishing that no nurseryman has seriously taken up the growing of stolons on a large scale in this country.

The method involves three separate operations: (i) growing a crop of stolons, (ii) planting out these stolons, and (iii) working them down, when established into a turf. The two species of *Agrostis* referred to above form extensive runners in August and September—in the former species they may be from 24 to 30 in (60 to 75 cm) long, and in the latter species from 12 to 18 in (30 to 45 cm). Both species are very variable, but the forms with which experiments have been done are leafy types that are vigorous and produce a dense, fine turf. They are shy seeders and the best way of producing a crop of stolons is to plant, in spring, separate shoots or small tufts of the selected grass or 1 in sq (2·5 cm sq) pieces of turf, about 2 ft (60 cm) apart in each direction, and assuming the soil is reasonably fertile a vigorous production of stolons result. One square foot (0·09 m^2) of turf broken up and planted out will grow a crop of stolons sufficient for planting out several thousand square feet of prepared soil. At the end of August or the beginning of September these runners are pulled off the parent plant, chopped into short lengths about 2 in (5 cm) long and scattered lightly like chaff on the prepared soil bed. The speed of turf formation depends largely upon the number of short lengths of stolon scattered upon the prepared ground. Spacing can be increased or decreased according to the amount of material available, but one or two pounds (0·45 to 0·90 kg) of stolons of creeping bent is enough for 10 sq ft (0·92 m^2) of lawn, or a sq ft (0·09 m^2) of stolons of creeping bent is enough for 10 sq ft (0·92 m^2). A very light covering of soil is then necessary followed by light rolling with a wooden roller, after which roots and shoots develop at the nodes, followed by tillering out of these young plants. It is of course, important in dry weather to keep up the supply of moisture. As soon as the shoots are established, gradual working down can commence.

Stolons of both the above grasses planted in September, produced excellent turf by June, and could have been used as a putting green. The turf of both species is fine in leaf, dense and remarkably uniform throughout. One advantage over seeding is the greater uniformity that can be obtained, because, given time, thousands of square feet of turf can be produced from the division and sub-division of a single selected plant.

Another way of planting is to take the complete stolon and plant in rows from 4 to 6 in (10 to 15 cm) apart, but excellent results can be got by planting small bundles of shoots from 2 to 3 in (5 to 7·6 cm) apart.

For the sake of completeness and for the help of readers abroad information is included below upon vegetative turf production in other countries with other species of grass.

In the United States the production of golf greens and lawns vegetatively is common, many clubs and firms growing supplies of recognised varieties of bent for turf production.

Unfortunately some of the American varieties of creeping bent have earned ill-repute because of their tendency to form a nap or grain, which makes putting on golf greens uncertain, as the speed depends upon whether the ball runs along or against the nap. The strains of creeping bent and velvet bent with which the experiments referred to above were carried out, do not show the same tendency to nap as the American creeping bents. They are more leafy and finer in texture but require careful top-dressing and planting in suitable soil.

In the southern states of North America, i.e. approximately south of latitude 38°, it is unwise to risk planting bent, but in these warmer southern States a variety of grasses may be used for vegetative production of turf. Thus suitable species propagated vegetatively in Florida, as described by Enlow and Stokes are Bermuda Grass (*Cynodon dactylon* L.), St. Augustine Grass (*Stenotaphrum secundatum* Walt.), Carpet Grass (*Axonopus compressus* (Siv.) Beauv.), Centipede Grass (*Eremochloa ophiuroides* (Munro) Hack.), and St Lucie Grass, a non-rhizomatous variety of Bermuda. In the southern part of Kansas Bermuda grass is used for lawns, whilst in the west Buffalo Grass (*Buchloë dactyloides* (Nutt) Engelm.) propagated vegetatively resists extremes of temperature and drought.

The *Cynodons* are cosmopolitan, and varieties and species are also extensively used for vegetative turf production in other countries, the names adopted being: Bermuda in USA, Kweek in South Africa, Neguil in Egypt, Dhoob or Doob in India, Serangoon in Malaysia. Kikuyu (*Pennisetum clandestinum*) and Durban Grass (*Dactyloctenium ægyptium*) are both used vegetatively in South Africa.

Tropical grasses have been introduced into the southern states of North America, and species like *Zoysia* (Korean or Japanese lawn grass), and Blue Couch (*Digitaria didactyla*) from Australia, are propagated vegetatively.

In the hotter parts of Australia Bermuda grass and blue couch are extensively propagated by stolons, and these species, as well as others like *Zoysia* and species of carpet grass and *Paspalum*, are used for producing lawns and for the various parts of golf courses in Malaysia.

While it is granted that the production of turf by vegetative means is easier in tropical than temperate climates, nevertheless the method has been so successfully adopted in the semi-temperate parts of the United States that there appears to be room for considerably more attention to the subject of turf-making by stolons in this country.

Finally, brief mention may be made of the production of a sward with a non-gramineous plant—Camomile (*Anthemis nobilis*). It occurs as almost a pure stand in large patches in some of the royal parks. Propagation may be carried out by splitting a turf and planting the shoots 1 to 2 in (2·5 to 5 cm) apart, when it will form a sward. It does not appreciate close mowing.

PART THREE

Maintenance of established turf

CHAPTER THIRTEEN

Grass mowing and its effects

Most lawns are mown in a haphazard manner but if the best results are to be obtained it is essential that mowing be carried out systematically and with circumspection. There is something more in mowing than just keeping the place tidy or disposing of the leafage produced; mowing must be controlled in accordance with the purpose for which the turf is intended, and frequency and intensity have an influence on turf density, weed infestation, earthworm activity, and yield of clippings. The return or removal of the cuttings also affects the equilibrium of the plant population composing the sward.

Nearly all lawn and sports turf is mown nowadays with some type of cylinder mower—a machine that has introduced a new and potent factor into modern lawn maintenance. No doubt the cylinder mower has made fine lawns possible, but the effects are different from those brought about by scything and grazing, the older methods of keeping down growth. Under the influence of the cylinder mower the grasses are perpetually 'over-pruned' and nothing is returned to the soil as in grazing. As a result the flat rosette weeds (e.g. dandelion, cat's-ear, daisy, etc.), the mat weeds (like yarrow, pearlwort and selfheal), and the clovers spread below the cutting blade and by their crowding smother and reduce the tillering capacity of the grasses. If the sward is 'let up' to the scythe or the grazing of stock the competition against these bottom-growing plants is much greater. Further, in a mixed sward containing finer grasses, rye-grass and clovers, that is being grazed, the fine grasses (bent and fescue) are less palatable than the rye-grass and clover and so suffer much less defoliation. Under grazing these fine grasses are at an advantage as compared with rotary mowing, whilst under the scythe the difficulty of cutting them also acts in their favour.

It is a common complaint that seaside golf greens, for example, are no longer composed of fescue, and mowing is undoubtedly an important, though not the only, factor involved in their decline. The greens on some of the old-established links were at one time kept short by occasional scything but mainly by rabbit nibbling. Rabbits are remarkably selective in their grazing, choosing the softer-leaved and lusher grasses like rye-grass and the meadow-grasses, as well as the clovers, whilst leaving the fescues relatively unharmed. In some Wiltshire experiments Thomas has shown that the effect of enclosing rabbits on an area of pasture reduced the agriculturally useful grasses (*useless* for fine turf) from 32 to 7 per cent in 15 months. They reduced the clover from 51 to 4 per cent. The moss and weeds increased, it is true, but grasses such as bent and fescue, the agriculturally useless grasses (*useful* for fine turf) remained almost unaffected and actually showed a 3 per cent increase.

The transition of meadow and pasture to a fine turf may be seen on many golf courses, the rough containing taller-growing hay species, the fairways approximating to a well-grazed pasture, while the greens contain in the main turf grasses like bent, fescue and annual meadow-grass. The change from pasture to lawn has been critically studied by Harrison and Hunt who found that regular mowing and dressing of a section of pasture to form a lawn led to a reduction of rye-grass and clover combined from 75 per cent in the pasture to 6 per cent in the lawn, and an increase in bent from 14 to 83 per cent, which provided a very uniform surface.

The effects of mowing fine lawns may be studied experimentally from at least two angles—the intensity of the cutting and the frequency—and as these two aspects have been studied separately and in combination at St Ives during recent years, some references to the results may be included at this point.

Intensity

A sward sown with Browntop was divided into two strips each 100 sq yd (80 m²) in area, and whilst the frequency of mowing each was the same, the intensities were different, namely, $\frac{1}{8}$ in (3 mm) and $\frac{3}{8}$ in (9 mm) height. The cuttings were removed and weighed on a dry matter basis, observations being made on various other points. Dealing firstly with the yield, and calculating that on the short mown plot as 100, then the relative yield from the long mown plot lay between 75 and 97, according to season, as in Table 13.1.

TABLE 13.1

	Year 1	Year 2	Year 3	Year 4
Duration of cutting season in weeks	20	31	27	39
Short cut, $\frac{1}{8}$ in (3 mm)	100	100	100	100
Long cut, $\frac{3}{8}$ in (9 mm)	75	96	97	87

The longer mown turf has therefore yielded consistently less grass clippings. Botanical analysis in Year '3', after the experiments had been in progress two full seasons, showed the presence of 17·6 per cent of annual meadow-grass and 6·3 per cent of weeds on the long cut, whilst under the short cut the respective figures were only 0·5 per cent and 2·1 per cent—showing that keen mowing is controlling weeds and annual meadow-grass. On the other hand, moss was more common on keenly-mown plots than on long. Counts of shoots or tillers made on each strip showed that close cutting, irrespective of other treatment, gave a denser turf than long cutting, in the proportion of 100 shoots on the short to 56 on the long. As an example of the density of the turf on the short-cut plots the area receiving sulphate of ammonia had 53 shoots per sq in (6·4 cm^2) as against 39 under the same manurial treatment but mown long. Observations on cast formation by earthworms, which may be taken as an indication of earthworm activity, have shown approximately three times as many on the long cuts as compared with short cuts. The explanation of this may lie in the heavier withdrawal of plant nutrients and soil bases on the more intensively-mown area, leading to a soil condition less suitable to earthworm activity.

Frequency

Two swards made respectively from New Zealand bent and Chewing's fescue were subjected to a system of weekly and thrice-weekly mowing for a period of 24 weeks. They were cut to the same intensity and were treated in all other respects in an identical manner. The weekly produce from each plot was weighed on a dry-matter basis and pooled in four-weekly lots. The data showed that under both systems of cutting and on the average for the season the fescue yielded 10 per cent more clippings than the bent. Moreover in the early part of the season the fescue yielded almost twice as much herbage as the bent.

It has been shown by grass land workers that the yield of leafage is inversely related to persistency, and the result of this experiment suggests that Chewing's fescue may not be as persistent as bent. This is found to be true in practice. Further, the fact that the yield of fescue is so much heavier in spring also leads to the supposition that the persistency of this grass is being undermined, it being known that species that produce heavy yields in spring are adversely affected if defoliated at that time.

A comparison of the yields under the two frequencies of mowing shows that both swards yielded consistently less total produce when mown thrice weekly than when mown once weekly. There was also a correspondingly reduced withdrawal of nutrients from the soil where the three cuts were given, and of course a more suitable sward resulted. Increasing the cuts to say six per week would no doubt show a further reduction of total yield and in fact mowing of intensively managed turf is rapidly becoming almost a daily operation.

Frequent and intense defoliation has the effect of leading in time to deterioration of the turf, but this can hardly be due to the withdrawal of the plant foods since analysis of the produce shows that less is removed under frequent mowing than less frequent. More probably it is due to the direct weakening effect on the plant, the root ranges being shortened and so placing the grass at a disadvantage. Thus in a bent sward the root weight was reduced from 100 to 86 by trebling the frequency of mowing.

Hunt has investigated the effect of frequency and intensity of clipping on perennial rye-grass as affecting leaf yield and root development. The figures for roots are illuminating. Clipping at 1 in (2·5 cm) height from April to August, every 30 days, gave 23·25 g of root while at $\frac{1}{2}$ in (1·25 cm) height the weight was 4·08 g. Plants cut every 10 days at 1 in (2·5 cm) height gave 2·01 g and at $\frac{1}{2}$ in (1·25 cm) only 1·2 g by the month of May. After this month a decline in root weights took place.

The decrease in yield of top growth and roots (a common finding in practice) is not easily accounted for, but is probably due to a reduced assimilating power and to the reduced carbohydrate reserves of the plant being a limiting factor under intensive defoliation. Again, weak roots cannot forage for nutrients in the soil and the plants are more readily affected by dry weather.

Intensity and frequency combined

In a third experiment both factors, intensity and frequency, have been studied in combination on a series of 64 plots during a mowing season of 29 weeks in one year. Table 13.2 shows the relative yields of grass clippings on a dry-matter basis.

TABLE 13.2

Height of cut a week	Mown once a week	Mown thrice a week
$\frac{1}{8}$ in (3 mm)	100·0	88·8
$\frac{3}{8}$ in (9 mm)	92·4	75·3

Weekly mowing, irrespective of height, produced greater yields of clippings than thrice-weekly mowing. Keen mowing, irrespective of frequency, yielded more clippings than longer mowing. Most clippings were removed from the areas mown short at less frequent intervals, while least clippings came from the area mown frequently at the longer height. Thus from the point of view of the grass plant it received most defoliation, perhaps mutilation, when mown keenly at low frequency, while least permanent damage was done to the plant when cut less keenly at three times the frequency.

Practical considerations

The practical interpretation of the results of these experiments is that mowing should be done regularly but not too keenly. Unfortunately many lawn owners and other concerned with sports turf do just the reverse, they cut their turf weekly or fortnightly and to ensure as long an interval as possible before it needs attention again, they mow as keenly as their machines will let them. Nothing could be more damaging to a sward than such a spasmodic system of mowing, and no doubt this maltreatment often accounts for the thin swards, open to weed invasion, which are all too frequently to be found. It may be argued, especially on large lawns, that more frequent mowing is impossible, as time does not permit, but this difficulty may largely be surmounted by modern methods of mechanisation, which, instead of releasing labour for other work, should be used to enable the turf to be cut more often without any greater expenditure of time. Advertisements for machines designed to speed up mowing often stress the increased leisure or time that will be gained for other work, but such enticements do a disservice to the lawn since time saved should be used profitably in mowing two or three times as often with the blade of the machine slightly raised.

Mowing should therefore be controlled and should be given careful thought, taking into consideration all the relevant facts. The degree of frequency must in practice be largely governed by the amount of growth, which is in turn related to the weather conditions, season of the year, and fertility of the soil. For example, the time taken to mow a certain playing field varied from 8 to $9\frac{1}{2}$, 12, 13, 17, and 20 hours.

All practical men know they can make a nicer job of mowing when the grass is dry, and they know further that wet mowing is a longer process owing to the need to stop more frequently to clean the machine and to heavier 'going'. A timing test showed that a job that took 45 minutes in dry weather required 60 minutes in wet.

Ribbing of the grass by the mower blades is a point of importance. If the turf is ribbed it is a sign that the cutting has been too long delayed or the cutters set too tight or that the revolutions of the cutting cylinder are too few—in other words the machine is incapable of doing better.

It is a mistake to allow the grass on a fine lawn to become long in winter; it should be topped in open weather—but not cut keenly to summer level—when thought necessary. Many lawn owners allow their turf to grow 3 or 4 in (7·6 or 10 cm) long in spring before mowing, a process both damaging to the grass and apt to open up the sward. In dry weather in summer the blade should be raised. Cutting should, if possible, be avoided during cold east winds, or discolouration of the leaf tips is likely to result.

The problem of deciding whether to allow the clippings to return to the turf or whether to remove them in the box is one that often causes trouble to the amateur. It must be said at once that there is no hard-and-fast rule, but during a drought the cuttings should be returned to act as a mulch, while if the turf is cut when wet the mowings should be removed, as otherwise they cling together in unsightly patches. An experimental area was divided into two strips; on one the cuttings were always removed and on the other they were always allowed to return irrespective of weather conditions. After several seasons some striking differences emerged and these have a bearing upon the mowing of large areas like golf fairways where the mowings are always allowed to fly, the gang mowers having no boxes. In the experimental plots there were regularly more worm casts on the plots to which the cuttings were returned—possibly a reflection of the greater amount of organic matter which this strip received. This sward also contained more annual meadow-grass (*Poa annua*) to the extent of

26·0 per cent of the herbage as against 6·0 per cent when the cuttings were removed. Boxing the clippings therefore helps to control this species. Further, the turf to which the cuttings are returned is consistently softer, spongier, and lusher than the other turf, though in dry weather it is moister and more drought resistant. On the other hand, the turf to which the clippings are returned is greener in winter and there is no moss invasion as compared with the other strip, where moss is prevalent. These differences were brought about by *regular* return or removal of the cuttings, but they indicate the trend.

The return of the grass mowings to the turf conserves plant food, since the contained mineral matter is replaced by decomposition of the clippings, but against that the requisite plant foods may be easily and cheaply applied in the form of fertilisers and manures.

Cutting of the lawn should always be done neatly and in parallel strips but the direction of these should differ at each cut, following the points of the compass, because this leads to a better control of strong shoots of rye-grass or runners that tend to form on the surface. The control of plants like rye-grass may be facilitated by regular brushing or drag matting, and every lawn should be switched to remove sticks, pebbles, worm casts, or other débris before putting the machine over.

Sometimes lawns and sports fields regularly cut with motor or gang mowers develop a series of wave-like ridges, sometimes quite pronounced, about 8 to 12 in (20 to 30 cm) apart and at right angles to the direction of mowing. In minor cases the grass only is affected, but in serious cases there is ridging of the soil itself. This 'corrugated' or 'washboard' effect is most pronounced in wet weather, being rarely seen in dry and is probably associated with rhythmic movements set up in the motor unit. It may be remedied by a change in the direction of mowing (diagonal or at right angles) and by cross rolling.

Mowing is not the simple operation of removing excess growth, as many imagine, but a process having far-reaching effects and therefore worthy of the most careful study and control.

CHAPTER FOURTEEN

The choice of a mower

There is today a wide range of lawn mowers for all purposes, and the main considerations in purchasing a new machine are (i) the money available, and (ii) the size and nature of the area to be cut.

While there are four basic methods of cutting grass, cylinder mowing is the most acceptable and widely used, because the cylinder mower leaves the best possible finish on turf due to the clean cutting action of the cylinder against the bottom blade, like a pair of scissors.

The 'cuts per yard (metre)' of a machine will determine the finish that a cylinder mower will give to an area of turf. 'Cuts per yard (metre)', which remains constant at whatever speed the mower is used, means the number of times a knife in the cutting cylinder passes over the bottom blade while the machine moves forward one yard. The greater number of knives in the cutting cylinder, the greater the 'cuts per yard (metre)' and the smoother the finish. The lesser number of knives in the cylinder, the fewer cuts per yard (metre) and 'ribbing' may be quite apparent.

Among the hand machines on the market, there are two main types: (a) roller machines in which the cutters are driven by chain from the land rolls, and (b) side wheel machines in which the cutting cylinder is driven from the wheels. A 12 in (30 cm) side wheel machine with five blades may be obtained, and while capable of a lot of useful work, it cannot be expected to give the fine finish given by a multi-bladed roller type machine, which not only will put a better 'finish' on the surface, but will rib less and will enable mowing to be done up to the very edge of the area. The production of hand mowers is limited, and in the main, their use is confined to the small garden.

A wide range of powered machines is available, and many improvements in design and performance have been made in recent years. In some models the land roll and cutting cylinder are engaged by separate clutches, and the machines may thus be used as a roller with the cutting cylinder out of operation. Some models are fitted with mechanically actuated centrifugal clutches so that on opening the throttle, the machine glides forward. Powered machines are on the market in a variety of sizes and makes, able to cope with all conditions. Table 14.1 shows some of the widths and types of machines with their capacity per hour and other details;

TABLE 14.1

Size of cutting width	Blades in cylinder	Cuts per yard/metre	Cutting performance sq yd/m per hour	Suitable for
18/20 in 45/50 cm	10	106/135 per yd 148 per m	1,200/1,330 yd² 1,000/1,100 m²	Bowling greens Golf greens
18/20 in 45/50 cm	6	64 per yd 70 per m	1,200/1,330 yd² 1,000/1,100 m²	Up to 1 acre Up to 0·4 ha
24 in 61 cm	5	60 per yd 65 per m	1,920 yd² 1,600 m²	Up to 4 acres Up to 1·6 ha
30/36 in 76/91 cm	6	60 per yd 65 per m	2,500/3,000 yd² 2.070/2,500 m²	Up to 12 acres Up to 4·8 ha

A number of electric and battery driven mowers are available. They are usually small width models and mainly used in the domestic market.

Mowing of large acreages is done by gang mowers drawn by a tractor or towing unit. The mowers are used in multiples, usually up to nine, and can be fitted with either pneumatic tyres or studded steel wheels. The nature of the ground will usually determine the speed at which the mowers are operated, and a normal speed for average conditions would be about 6 m.p.h. (10 km/h). A high standard of finish can be obtained when the machines are adjusted and operated correctly. Some makers build a heavy duty unit in which the cutting cylinder has less blades and greater diameter, thus permitting long or very tough grass to be cut.

The hydraulic linkage of a tractor can be used to facilitate transport over short distances, while various methods have been devised where road transportation of the gang units over longer distances is required, for instance when a number of school or public playing fields are maintained by a single outfit.

Fig. 12. A mower of an 18 or 20 in (45 or 50 cm) cut, suitable and able to give a very fine finish on turf areas of up to 1 acre (0·4 ha) in extent.

Fig. 13. A mower with a 24 in (61 cm) width cut. Height of cut can be easily adjusted, from $\frac{5}{16}$ to 1 in (8 to 25 mm).

Fig. 14. A versatile mowing machine designed not only to keep trim roadside verges and long grass areas, but can also be quickly converted to a cylinder machine.

Fig. 15. A highly manoeuvrable piece of equipment with power driven cutters enabling a high standard of mowing even under adverse conditions.

Figs. 16–17. Quintuple gang mower for mowing large areas where regular cutting is possible and a good finish essential.

Table 14.2 shows the cutting width and performances of a number of combinations of units:

TABLE 14.2

Number of units		3	5	7	9
Width of cut		7 ft 0 in 2·10 m	11 ft 6 in 3·5 m	16 ft 0 in 4·9 m	20 ft 6 in 6·2 m
Acres/Hectares cut per hour	4/5 m.p.h. 8/9 km/hr	3 1·21	5 2	7 2·83	9 3·64
	7 m.p.h. 11/13 km/hr	4 1·62	7 2·83	10 4·4	12 4·85
	10 m.p.h. 16/19 km/hr	6 2·43	10 4·05	14 5·66	18 7·28

Fully hydraulic gang mowers have been on the market for some years now, and can be completely attached to the tractor, making the mowing unit extremely mobile and manoeuvrable. All the cutting units lift up or down hydraulically, handled in seconds by finger tip control from the tractor seat. As the cutting cylinders are powered by small hydraulic motors, cutting can be carried out in even adverse conditions. A good finish can be obtained, cuts per yard (metre) being variable between 20 to 75 (22 to 77), depending on the tractor gear selected. Under average conditions, and operating at a speed of about 5 m.p.h. (9 km/hr), the machine with five units will cut 5 acres (2 ha) in an hour.

Rotary mowing does not give such a fine finish as cylinder mowing, and rotary mowers are mainly used for the cutting of rough or long grass areas. Mowers are available that have a variety of cutter assemblies, i.e. discs with detachable knives, cutter bars with detachable knives and solid cutter bars. The action is to 'flick off' the grass rather than cut through it, and there is no bottom blade to the mower. The machines are generally light to use, although tractor drawn and 'ride on' models can be obtained, and will cut close up to obstacles. Electric versions with this rotary action are also available, and a similar machine is obtainable which rides on an impeller-generated cushion of air.

Flail mowers are used for clearing long, tough grass and scrub on areas which are completely unsuitable for conventional mowers. The grass is not cut with this machine, but as the name implies, is flailed and chewed to a mulch. Specially toughened steel flails, mounted in pairs along a large diameter steel shaft, rotate at high speed and chop off the grass. Both pedestrian controlled and tractor mounted models are available.

Having chosen a sound machine to suit the particular purpose, it is desirable that it should be kept in a worthy condition. Small faults often lead to further damage and perhaps a major breakdown. The first cut of the season is best taken high in case any débris has been overlooked. The mower should not be bumped over kerbs or steps as this may knock up the bottom blade against the cutters or result in a broken casting. Tight setting of the bottom blade onto the cutting cylinder, or over low cutting, will lead to excessive wear. The handles should be held firmly so as to control the machine, but should not be held too rigidly. Held too tightly, there may be a tendency for weight to be put on to the handles and then the cutter may be held off contact at the front, giving thereby a poor finish.

A steady walking pace, cultivating the knack of merely steering, is ideal for pedestrian controlled motor mowers, and they should not be flogged by mowing beyond their capacity. Where the grass is long, overloading can be avoided by topping it first. The introduction of centrifugal clutches on many mowers has lessened the risk of over-loading the transmission by 'letting in the clutch with a bang'. Even with a centrifugal clutch, at the moment of setting off, the load on the transmission can be eased by momentarily depressing the handles of the machine. Operating gang mowers at excessive speeds is a common cause of deterioration. All mowers require systematic and regular lubrication of all bearings and working parts.

After use, mowers should be brushed or washed down, then dried, wiped over with an oily rag, and the blades of the cutting cylinder covered with a light film of oil. Regular cleaning affords an opportunity to examine for loose or lost nuts and bolts. Most professional users make a point of having their equipment checked thoroughly in preparation for the cutting season, paying particular attention to re-grinding cylinders and fitting new bottom blades, and indeed, most owners of machines used on the domestic lawns would do well to follow this procedure.

CHAPTER FIFTEEN

The preparation and use of top-dressings

Top-dressing of intensively-managed turf is almost as essential as mowing, and should form one of the regular operations of maintenance. Top-dressing refers to applications of materials low in manurial value, but having considerable bulk, and not regarded as fertilisers. The general purpose of top-dressing is to assist in preserving or restoring the level of a stretch of turf; to ameliorate the physical texture of the soil; to encourage the grasses to tiller; and in some cases to provide a particular type of surface, for instance, a cricket pitch. It has often been claimed that top-dressings are valuable as a vehicle for spreading relatively small amounts of concentrated fertilisers. If some thought is given to this claim, it will be realised that fertilisers should be applied at a specific rate per square yard, while the top-dressing will be applied at a variable rate per square yard, dependent on the levels of the area. It would appear then to be impossible to apply a fertiliser combined with a top-dressing, and to fulfil the conditions needed for a successful operation. The use of a carrier, for instance sand, to aid the distribution of relatively small amounts of concentrated fertilisers is an accepted turf maintenance practice.

The top-dressing of golf and bowling greens for example, is a well established practice. Examination of old-established greens often shows layer and layer built up of annual dressings of sand and compost going back over a long period. It is just as important that some top-dressing should be carried out on ornamental lawns.

Perhaps the commonest and most useful form of top-dressing for

Fig. 18. The compost heap, showing layers of soil and manure, and a rotary screen.

use in lawn and green upkeep is compost, a term which has rather a wide range of application. Usually it refers to a mixture of soil and decayed vegetation. Decomposed farmyard manure would be a useful addition to the mixture, but supplies of this are not easily obtained. The best soil to use for such a mixture is a friable loam containing 10 to 15 per cent of clay, and not more than 20 per cent of coarse sand. Such soil is friable, crumbles well and mixes easily with other materials. It is often found that, in preparing compost, the soil ingredient has been entirely or largely omitted. However the inclusion of some soil in a mixture is as important as including a suitable form of organic matter. The use of organic matter alone in the form of leaf mould or fresh manure (when available), often leads to ill results in the form of a spongy surface, tendency to water-logging and disease. It is appreciated that the making of compost to include soil may be difficult for the small lawn owner, and also that there may be the danger of introducing weed seeds. This can be got over by exercising some foresight and spreading out the soil to be used in a shallow layer and allowing weed seeds to germinate—although many of the weed seeds found in garden soil are from plants that do not establish in turf, e.g. chickweed, shepherd's purse and mayweeds—and of course any that do establish themselves can be easily eradicated by the use of selective herbicides.

Various forms of organic matter may be used in preparing a compost, such as old turf, leaf mould, grass cuttings and any farmyard manure that may be obtainable. Grass cuttings and manure may both be a source of weeds, which may, however, be largely destroyed if the heat of fermentation is sufficient.

Finished compost does not depend for its value upon its fertilising ingredients since it rarely contains more than one per cent of nitrogen and even less phosphoric acid and potash, but while the percentage of these materials is low, it should be realised that the rate of application of the material may be heavy. Compost is of primary importance on account of its physical properties, though there is evidence to show that root development is favoured by its use. It also helps to conserve moisture by acting as a surface mulch.

In practice, a good compost heap is best built up with alternate layers of soil (9 in (23 cm) deep) and organic matter (3 to 4 in (7·6 to 10 cm) deep), the heap being allowed to stand for a period of about 12 to 18 months to ensure good decomposition. It may be turned half way through this period if desired. The material is then cut down and screened. Sharp sand may then be added. For most purposes a $\frac{3}{16}$ in (4·8 mm) mesh is adequate, but for finer turf a $\frac{1}{8}$ in (3·1 mm) mesh should be used, and when large quantities have to be handled a rotary screen is essential.

By decomposing waste vegetation with the assistance of a chemical accelerator, excellent supplies of rotted organic matter equivalent to farmyard manure can be produced either for including in compost heaps or, after more prolonged decay, for direct application to turf.

Compost heaps and prepared material should always be protected from the elements. A heap exposed to rain loses nitrogen, while screening is made difficult if the material is saturated with moisture. It is a good plan for a new heap to be in the course of construction at the time the old one is being brought into use, so that a continuous supply is available.

The dangers and anxieties of using soil and manure containing weed seeds in compost piles are less serious with the advent of selective weed-killers, but they can readily be overcome by the process of sterilisation by heat. There are three main methods by which this may be carried out, namely by baking, by steaming, and by electricity. The baking process is usually carried out in a shallow brick trough below which run flues from a furnace situated at one end. The heat thrown up under the base of the trough raises the temperature of the material. A suitable type of baking plant is the 'Reaseheath' pattern, but experience has shown that the trough is too long if heating throughout is to be satisfactory without charring at the furnace end. The plant can be much improved by shortening the length and increasing the width ('Wilmslow' plant), or the same length may be used by introducing a false bottom with wider air space over the furnace. These sterilisers hold approximately 3 tons. Turning of the material is advisable to ensure that the material at first on the surface becomes adequately heated. There is also the 'Holmes' or vertical type of baking plant, but loading of this is more difficult.

For steam sterilising a vertical boiler and a grid of perforated steam pipe is required. The grid is placed in a shallow pit ànd compost to a depth of about 20 in (50 cm) placed over it. The capacity is about 1 ton, and steam at 40 to 60 lb pressure (275 to 413 kN/m²) is passed through. The temperature is quickly raised and by this means 1 ton may be sterilised in approximately half an hour. Baking requires longer. Small portable low pressure steaming plants may be obtained for garden use, and take from one to several cwt (50 kg plus) of material. The John Innes Horticultural Institution has designed a useful brick-built low-temperature steaming plant.

In the third method a current of electricity is passed through the material, the resistance of which raises the temperature. The consumption is from 1 to $1\frac{1}{3}$ units per cu ft (0·02 m³), depending on the nature of the soil. Sterilisers of various capacities are made, from small ones (30 to 40 lb and 1 cwt sizes (13 to 18 kg and 50 kg)), useful to the amateur gardener, to larger outfits holding $\frac{1}{3}$, $\frac{1}{2}$ or 1 ton (355, 508 or 1,016 kg) of compost. The process is complete in 60 to 75 minutes.

In another type of commercial electric steriliser, the current does not pass through the soil, six $1\frac{1}{2}$ kW plate type resistance heaters assembled in three banks provide the heat. Having a capacity of about 5 cwt (254 kg) it is claimed that sterilisation is completed in about $1\frac{1}{2}$ hours for a power consumption of approximately 11 units.

It is often said by those concerned with the preparation of compost that sterilisation destroys some of the properties of the material. The effect is to destroy fungal spores, some bacteria, earthworms, weed seeds and insect pests, and it has been shown that this is complete at a temperature of 71°C, if it is maintained for 30 minutes. On the other hand, it has been shown that nitrifying and other bacteria are not destroyed at this temperature, so that the material benefits from the process, which is in effect, pasteurisation. In practice it has become usual to raise the temperature up to about 100°C.

Work by Monteith in the United States has shown that compost heaps can be successfully treated with the tear gas chloropicrin (trichloro-nitro-methane) for the destruction of weed seeds. Over 90 per cent of all weed seeds were destroyed. No toxic effects remained after a week or ten days. The properties of tear gas are such that this method is not likely to become popular.

Other chemicals can be useful as soil sterilants. Methyl bromide, a gas at normal temperatures and pressure, almost odourless and colourless but highly toxic, should only be used by contractors' staff who have experience in its usage. It is considerably cheaper than steam sterilisation done by contract. Lengths of perforated tube are placed over the area to be fumigated. Polythene sheeting is then used to cover the area, and tightly secured to prevent the gas escaping. After the gas has been applied, the covers are retained in position for about five days. After thorough aeration, the soil can be used about 3 days after the removal of the covers. Dazomet is another of the chemicals used as soil sterilants.

The valuable experiments by Lawrence and Newell on the preparation of composts for potting purposes have shown that lime or chalk should not be added before sterilising. Storing of compost for a period before use is always recommended, but these workers have shown that the check to growth associated with newly-sterilised materials can be avoided by addition of superphosphate afterwards. They recommend that the ingredients (e.g. sand and loam) should be separately sterilised, followed by addition of such materials as granulated peat and fertilisers. The effects of preparing composts in various ways were studied on a variety of plant seedlings but not upon grasses. It is, however, the usual practice in greenkeeping and lawn management to add the fertilisers for the turf to the composts after sterilising. There is therefore no necessity to remedy deficiencies in the compost.

The time and expense expended in the sterilisation of soil compost may not be considered worthwhile in view of the wide variety of herbicides, fungicides, pesticides and vermicides available.

The amount of compost to use will depend on conditions. A considerable amount more will be needed on an uneven surface, than on one which is relatively level, and an average rate will be about 2 tons per 1,000 sq yd (940 m^2). The distribution of compost on turf is not difficult provided reasonable care is taken that the material is friable and the surface to which it is being applied is dry and has been mown short. It is usually applied broadcast by shovel, and although

Fig. 19. Working in top-dressing with a Trulute.

the use of distributors has been suggested, this does not work well in practice. Relatively large amounts of top-dressing have to be applied, and the material is very seldom in a dry enough condition for distributor operation.

Many of the secrets of good composting lie in the after-treatment of the dressed turf. The material should always be worked in by means of a lute, the back of a rake, chain mat or drag brush, the object being to work the friable material among the bases of the grass shoots. The process also leaves more of the material in the hollows, so improving the surface level.

For those who are unable to prepare compost in the accepted sense of the word, using manure, there are various ways in which the organic matter may be supplied. Spent hops, leaf mould and various types of sedge peat are available for top-dressing mixtures. The various types of sphagnum peat, e.g. ground peat moss, are inclined to lead to a spongy surface when used alone, but in the absence of other forms of organic matter they may be used to the extent of 10 per cent of a mixture with soil and sand. However, it is always advisable that these materials should applied with sand and a small amount of soil. Repeated dressings of peat alone may lead to a surface that is impervious to water and that dries out readily in drought. The above mentioned materials may be used in various proportions to suit the conditions, but a useful proportion is one part of medium loam soil, two parts of sharp sand, and one or two parts of the organic matter. Disintegrated dried sewage sludge is also a material that can be obtained in certain districts, and used for top-dressing purposes.

Autumn top-dressing by means of sand is also important, particularly on heavy soils. Sand chosen for the purpose should always be sharp and gritty, and a good average pit sand should contain at least 60 per cent of particles passing through a 0·5-mm* and over a 0·2-mm sieve. Sand containing much material greater than 2 mm or more than a few per cent below 0·2 mm should be rejected. In coarse sand for wetter soils about 20 per cent passing through a 2-mm and over a 1-mm sieve is permissible. Ten cwt (500 kg) to, say, 500 sq yd (470 m²) is a usual rate on heavy soil and it should be worked into the surface, preferably while growth is still active. There is generally a good deal of controversy as to whether inland sand or a sea sand should be utilised, but no hard-and-fast rules can be laid down. Inland sands are often free from lime, whereas sea sands almost invariably contain lime; from 1 per cent up to as much as 60 per cent of calcium carbonate. The use of sea sand containing a high amount of shell will act in the same way as a dressing of lime, and experiment has shown that it will favour the softer-growing types of grasses and earthworm activity. It would, however, be foolish in seaside districts where sea sand can be obtained for the carting, to import inland sand from a distance. The use of sea sand is sometimes justified on turf that has become too lime deficient when a small dressing of calcium carbonate is beneficial to correct this.

Sand acts in two ways: it dries the surface and leads to increased tillering of the plants, so giving a greater turf density. Sanding, which is a winter and early spring job, can be abused like any other dressing,

* 1 mm = 0·0394 in

and applications should not be so heavy as to smother the grass or to give a thick layer in the soil. Should this happen there will be a tendency in future years for the turf to form a cleavage plane at this point.

Charcoal gives excellent results as a top-dressing, and has the advantage that it can be bought carefully graded. For wet places, $\frac{1}{8}$ and $\frac{1}{4}$ in (3·2 and 6·4 mm) mesh is useful, while $\frac{1}{16}$ in (1·6 mm) mesh is more suitable on firmer, well-established turf. There is often a marked deepening of the colour of the grass following an application of charcoal, doubtless due to the presence of a small amount of absorbed nitrogen. The rate of application is from $\frac{1}{2}$ to 2 lb per sq yd (0·25 to 1 kg per m²).

Whatever the top-dressing used, it is important that it should be worked into the turf after application using some form of harrow. On small areas a chain mat or a drag brush may be used, and on large areas, a tractor drawn chain harrow or bush harrow.

Fertilisers and their practical use

To the majority of lawn owners, manuring or fertilising is the first essential to betterment of the turf, but there is an unfortunate tendency to ignore other factors and so fail to obtain the maximum benefit and best value for money spent. Thus, unless surface drainage is correct and the soil is open and friable there will be a poor response, while the water supply during drought must be adequate if the fertiliser applied is to be effective. A thin sward, poor in colour, with moss and weeds encroaching, in all probability requires manurial treatment, but other factors must also be taken into consideration in deciding upon the course to adopt.

It is common knowledge nowadays that growing plants require nitrogen, phosphorus, potassium, and calcium (usually referred to as nitrogen, phosphoric acid, potash, and lime) to maintain a healthy growth and development. In addition, however, elements such as sulphur, magnesium, manganese and boron are required, but they are normally present in the soil in sufficient quantity, so that only rarely is there any response from their addition to the soil. Fertiliser treatment aims at maintaining the supplies of nitrogen, phosphate, and potash which are liable to fall short of requirements.

Turning from the general to the particular, if these elements are to be applied to grass the amounts and forms of application must be chosen with due regard to the soil and the purpose for which the grass is intended. Thus, the efforts of the farmer to increase the bulk of herbage, improve the chemical analysis of the crop, and favour lush grasses and clovers, are diametrically opposed to the aims of the turf owner, who is unconcerned with analysis, does not want too much bulk, and certainly does not wish to encourage clovers.

The finer grasses, the bents and fescues, are found growing naturally on poor, infertile and often acid soils that are low in phosphates and potash, and evidently in the uncultivated state these grasses are able to exist in the presence of small amounts of these manurial elements. On the lawn, however, these grasses are growing under very different conditions and rather better supplies of plant nutrients are required.

Of the three elements, nitrogen is removed by the growing grass in greatest quantity, and it is this ingredient that gives the most striking and visible response as regards vegetative growth or leaf production. When a pile of clippings is removed from a lawn it is not always realised how much plant food is being taken away. Approximately 80 per cent of the weight removed is moisture, a figure that is lower in dry weather, whilst the remainder consists of the organic matter built up by the grass plant through photosynthesis together with the ash derived from the minerals absorbed by the roots. This ash contains the phosphorus, potassium, calcium, magnesium and other minor minerals. In some experiments carried out at St Ives the clippings mown off two bent and fescue swards were collected, dried and weighed throughout the season, and analyses were carried out upon the dry produce. Half of each sward was subjected to monthly dressing with nitrogen as sulphate of ammonia, whilst the other half was left as a control. The differences in yield, analysis and withdrawal of nutrients on an average basis, between species and treatments, is strikingly shown in Tables 16.1 and 16.2.

The figures show that Chewing's fescue makes greater demands upon soil nutrients than the bent, and that with both species the withdrawal of nutrients is greater after fertilising with nitrogen. The application of sulphate of ammonia, when compared with the controls, gives a higher percentage of nitrogen in the clippings and a slightly lower lime content, but phosphate and potash, while greater in the bent, are lower in the fescue.

No phosphate or potash was used on these plots so that all the amount of these elements found in the clippings has been derived from the soil—a striking feature being the relatively high amount of potash removed and presumably formed from the degradation of the felspar in the particles of this boulder-clay soil. Where the nitrogen has been given the percentage of calcium is lower, so that in spite of the increase in yield the total amount of calcium removed is increased comparatively little.

TABLE 16.1

Mean analysis of two turf grasses under a regular system of mowing

Species	New Zealand Bent		Chewing's Fescue	
Treatment	Control	S/A	Control	S/A
	per cent	per cent	per cent	per cent
Nitrogen	3·23	4·65	3·29	4·29
Phosphate as P_2O_5	0·89	0·96	0·92	0·84
Potash as K_2O	2·56	2·70	2·27	2·03
Lime as CaO	0·95	0·62	0·79	0·59
Mean yield, lb per acre	1,200	2,100	1,840	3,000
Mean yield, kg per ha	1,340	2,352	2,066	3,360

TABLE 16.2

Mean yield of plant nutrients in lb per acre

Species	New Zealand Bent		Chewing's Fescue	
Treatment	Control	S/A	Control	S/A
Nitrogen	38·6	97·6	60·5	128·7
Phosphate as P_2O_5	10·7	20·2	16·9	25·2
Potash as K_2O	30·7	56·7	41·8	60·9
Lime as CaO	11·4	13·0	14·5	17·7

It is commonly asserted by lawn owners and greenkeepers alike that frequent mowing results in increased loss of soil nutrients, but actually the more often a lawn is cut the less nitrogen, phosphate and potash is taken from the soil. This is shown in Table 16.3, in which

TABLE 16.3

Relative amounts of Nitrogen, Phosphate and Potash removed from two species under two systems of mowing

(Uptake from Chewing's fescue mown weekly being expressed as 100.0)

Nutrient	New Zealand Bent		Chewing's Fescue	
	Mown weekly	Mown thrice weekly	Mown weekly	Mown thrice weekly
Nitrogen (N)	91·6	80·9	100·0	85·6
Phosphate (P_2O_5)	94·3	84·3	100·0	90·0
Potash (K_2O)	93·8	80·6	100·0	81·3

the relative amounts of nutrients taken up by two species under two systems of mowing are compared.

The poverty-stricken appearance of fine lawns that are constantly mown is often due not so much to impoverishment as to repeated defoliation, i.e. mutilation of the grass, and here the first step to improvement would be raising the blade of the mower.

As already pointed out the main plant food removed in the clippings is nitrogen, and as nitrogen favours leaf growth it is necessary to supply this element periodically, and the form in which it is applied is of considerable importance. Lesser amounts of phosphate and potash are removed from the soil, and while some of the requirement is satisfied by compost dressings and some by soil degradation it is nevertheless necessary that occasional use be made of fertilisers containing these nutrients. While such dressings may be applied · with advantage, especially on poor soils, their continued heavy use may well lead to a poor sward with a gradual reduction of the finer bent and fescue grasses.

The presence of nitrogen in the soil in a form available for plant growth is thus a most important factor, and there is a complex cycle of changes that will determine the form and fate of naturally-produced nitrogen as well as that added in fertilisers. Living in association with leguminous plants certain bacteria are found in small nodules attached to the roots, these having the power of fixing atmospheric nitrogen and releasing a portion of it for the use of the plant. With the breakdown of these nodules and the roots, the available nitrogen in the soil is increased and consequently the growth of adjacent plants is improved. This is the explanation of the improvement in the vigour that has been observed to follow the invasion of poor turf by clover.

In addition there are certain soil bacteria that are able to fix atmospheric nitrogen in the soil and convert it to their own use, after which, on the death of the organism, it is released. Other bacteria in the soil are concerned with nitrification and convert ammonium compounds to nitrites and nitrates. Then there are bacteria responsible for the decay and breakdown of organic plant residues as applied in compost or derived from decaying roots and leaf clippings. They also decompose the remains of soil organisms, releasing in these processes ammonium compounds that are again oxidised to nitrates by the nitrifying bacteria. The whole process is a series of linked reactions to which the grass is attached as the principal remover of nitrate for building up protein matter.

The cycle of changes is further complicated by certain bacteria that (in conditions of bad aeration or water-logging) cause the reduction of nitrites and nitrates to ammonia, and by other bacteria that are capable of oxidising organic matter and giving off free atmospheric nitrogen. Fortunately, in soil the activity of the latter group is small, and they are mainly associated with dung heaps, where considerable losses of this element may result.

Finally, there is the loss of nitrate in the drainage water, and this is apt to occur before the nitrate is taken up by the plant. The linking up of the various changes may best be shown in the diagram.

Nitrogen Cycle in Soils

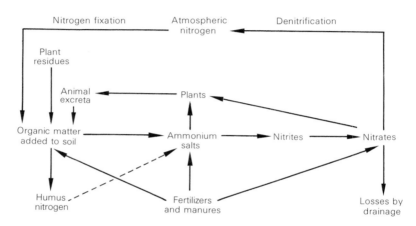

It was once believed that green plants could only take up nitrogen in the form of nitrate, so that ammonia had to be oxidised to nitrite and then nitrate by bacterial activity before becoming useful to the plant. Evidence has accumulated that plants can take up some of their nitrogen directly as ammonia without the intervention of bacteria. Certainly from observations on bent and fescue grass plots at St Ives the rapid visible response from ammoniacal fertilisers suggests that this is so.

Combined nitrogen for use by growing plants may be applied artificially as a fertiliser in various forms, as also can the phosphatic and potassic manures, and it may be well to describe some of these and their uses in lawn upkeep and greenkeeping.

Nitrogenous fertilisers

Amongst the fertilisers in this group there is a wide range of materials; some are natural or manufactured while others are derived as waste

Fig. 20. Weed eradication. *Right*: untreated turf. *Left*: Weeds eradicated by sulphate of ammonia and iron treatment.

matters often from industrial processes. Undoubtedly the most extensively used nitrogenous fertiliser for turf is sulphate of ammonia, which was formerly a by-product in the coke and coal industry but is now very largely produced as a synthetic product from atmospheric nitrogen and hydrogen combined at high pressure. Sulphate of ammonia so produced is a whitish odourless crystalline salt, soluble in water and sold with a guaranteed analysis of 21 per cent of nitrogen. It is always advisable to purchase the quality known as 'dry neutral' which has less than 0·025 per cent of free sulphuric acid.

The extensive use of sulphate of ammonia for fine turf probably began with the pioneer American investigations of Piper and Oakley, who showed that it was possible to start with a weed-free turf and maintain it thus by systematic dressings of this fertiliser. This finding has been amply confirmed by many experiments carried out during the past years. It has long been known that sulphate of ammonia tends to make the soil acid. The repeated applications in the American trials led to an increase in the acidity of the soil, so that the tendency was to account for the non-appearance of weeds by this induced acidity. It is important to draw a distinction between the maintenance of freedom from weeds in turf and their eradication by sulphate of ammonia in a turf that is already weed infested. The two aspects are quite different and sulphate of ammonia has undoubted value for the second purpose though the reasons for the decline of the weed population must be sought in various directions. This subject will be reviewed later.

Sulphate of ammonia is one of the most popular turf fertilisers, though like many other materials that give good results it can be abused, and much harm can also result from faulty application. The rate of dressing should not exceed 3 lb per 100 sq yd (1·6 kg per 100 m²). The nitrogen in it is quick-acting and leads to a vigorous growth of grass and so to a denser and thicker sward. The nitrogen in sulphate of ammonia is retained in the surface layers of the soil so that there is no likelihood of it being lost in the drainage water, which is likely when nitrate of soda dressings are given.

Another quick-acting nitrogenous fertiliser is nitro-chalk, which appeared on the market as a synthetic product. It is made by blending together ammonium nitrate and calcium carbonate to give a granular compound, which is comparatively easy to distribute though best spread on fine turf with a carrier of compost. Half the 21 per cent of nitrogen is present in the form of ammonia and half as nitrate, while 35 per cent of nitro-chalk is calcium carbonate. For use on acid turf nitro-chalk has advantages, though on putting greens the sudden stimulus to growth is inclined to encourage diseases, and plot trials show that long-continued and regular use encourages worm and weed invasion.

Another synthetic nitrogenous fertiliser is known as calcium cyanamide which has the same nitrogen as sulphate of ammonia and mechanical condition has been improved by granulation. There is approximately 20 per cent of free lime. It has advantages on acid soils but its use is limited because of its alkalinity.

Nitrate of soda containing 15·5 to 16 per cent of nitrogen is very rapid in action and forms a useful plant stimulant. The material is crystalline or granular, but the purchase of nitrogen in this form is more expensive than as sulphate of ammonia. Nitrate of soda is a valuable source of quick-acting nitrogen for rapidly 'bringing on' turf, but continuous use tends to injure the soil tilth and leads to caking in dry weather. On experimental turf plots continued use has led to worm and weed invasion and to a soft spongy turf, particularly in wet weather. The turf in these trials, while undoubtedly more drought-resistant than plots receiving an equivalent amount of nitrogen as sulphate of ammonia, is more susceptible to disease. If nitrate of soda is applied immediately before heavy rain, losses of nitrate are easily incurred.

Nitrate of lime (13 per cent nitrogen) takes up moisture readily in storage and is seldom used in practice. It gives results on turf similar to those obtained from nitrate of soda.

There are various other nitrogenous compounds available, many of them being waste products. One of the best known in turf maintenance was perhaps soot, but with the change over of heating methods from coal to oil, and solid fuel in many areas, the supply of soot is somewhat limited. It is a variable commodity containing anything from 2 to 11 per cent nitrogen. Its application to turf must be made with circum-spection because of its unsightliness, and in practice the best plan would be to mix the soot with compost and to apply it when rain will wash it quickly into the soil. The darkening in soil colour following the use of soot is advantageous since it tends to give a warmer soil.

A common fertiliser is dried blood, obtained in raw form from slaughter-houses. The material is prepared by the precipitation of the protein matter, which is then dried to brown flakes giving a product somewhat variable in composition but usually contains about 13 to 14 per cent of nitrogen. Dried blood is quick-acting, the nitrogen contained being almost as quickly available as that in sulphate of ammonia. Trials have shown that blood encourages rather than reduces weed infestation. In its favour it may be said that dried blood is useful on sandy soils, is safer to use, and gives a more drought-resistant turf than sulphate of ammonia. Being of a friable and dry nature it is often included in proprietary mixtures.

Hoof and horn meals depend for their value as turf fertilisers upon the fineness of grinding. Containing 12 to 14 per cent of nitrogen they form a source of slow-acting nitrogen but should not be used where a rapid response is required.

Leather waste containing as much as 6 per cent of nitrogen is sometimes used in mixed fertilisers as a means of increasing the nitrogen content, but it is relatively unavailable and can only be regarded as a drier and conditioner for mixing purposes. Turf plots treated with 'de-tanned' leather indicate similar effects to those with dried blood.

Mention may be made of other by-product materials such as waste shoddy derived from the textile industry, which may contain from 5 to 14 per cent of nitrogen. The material is only very slowly decomposed in the soil and so its main use for turf purposes is as a bulking agent, though it may also be used in compost heaps that are to remain untouched for several seasons, or for digging into seed beds.

The waste-product nitrogenous manures described above are all of animal origin or wastes from factories and towns. There are other materials, of vegetable origin, which are quite useful for the treatment of turf. Thus castor meal with from 4·0 to 6·0 per cent of nitrogen when applied judiciously to turf gives quite good results; if used excessively it is apt to encourage earthworm activity. It is a useful material for application to light, sandy soils. Malt culms, derived from the rootlets of germinated barley in malting, contains 3 to 5 per cent of nitrogen, but, being useful in feeding-stuffs, only damaged material should be used as an organic fertiliser on turf. It may be used as a straight dressing at 1 or 2 oz per sq yd (34 to 68 g per m²) or mixed in a compost heap to decompose before application. Spent hops containing about 3·5 per cent of nitrogen may, when finely ground, be used for direct application or in the compost heap. Finely-ground peat, which has been extensively advocated in recent years for turf upkeep, contains about 1 per cent of nitrogen and forms a useful ingredient of compost mixtures; the nitrogen, however, is relatively unavailable.

Various organic wastes such as feathers, greaves, hair, rabbit flick, slaughter-house refuse, fish waste, brewery and distillery wastes and pomace, from the cider industry, are sometimes offered for turf purposes, but all these materials are unsuitable for use unless they have passed through a preliminary period of decomposition in the compost heap. Supplies of seaweed, sold as proprietary liquid fertilisers, are readily available, and are used mainly as fertilisers for outfields. Many lawn owners, managers of playing fields and golf courses, pay high prices for some organic materials, which, with a little trouble, they could easily prepare themselves by building into compost heaps such materials as the above, as well as grass clippings, shoddy and similar waste materials.

Phosphatic fertilisers

Phosphates serve several important functions in the soil. They tend to encourage earlier development of the young plant, and as has been shown, favour the development of roots in turf; they also counteract the forcing action of nitrogenous manures used alone, and in agricultural crops, improve the grain and the feeding value of fodder. In greenkeeping perhaps the best-known phosphatic manure is raw bone meal, which has long enjoyed a position of high esteem for turf purposes. A good-quality bone meal contains about 4 per cent of nitrogen and 20·5 per cent of insoluble phosphoric acid, and it is generally described as a phosphatic manure even though it contains this appreciable amount of nitrogen. The mechanical condition of bone meal is an important point to note when purchasing bone meal since many samples on the market are too coarse for application to turf. It should be finely gristed but not too dusty.

Another phosphatic material derived from bones is steamed bone meal or steamed bone flour, which is obtained by extracting the gelatine from the bone meal, thus giving a reduction of the nitrogen percentage and increase in the phosphoric acid, a usual analysis being 0·75 per cent of nitrogen and 27·5 per cent of phosphoric acid. On account of its lower nitrogen content, steamed bone meal is not so effective as bone meal on turf, but it is, of course, a valuable source of phosphoric acid and is often in a finer state of division than bone meal. It is often used as a conditioner in compound fertilisers. Bone charcoal, prepared for use as a decolouriser, may often be obtained under the name of spent bone char. This material is black in colour and contains from 1·5 to 2 per cent of nitrogen and from 28 to 35 per cent of insoluble phosphoric acid.

Superphosphate differs from most other phosphatic fertilisers in that the phosphoric acid is soluble in water as distinct from that in bone meal, basic slag, and rock phosphate, which is insoluble in water. The full name for this material is superphosphate of lime, but it is important to avoid the error of assuming that the lime referred to behaves like true lime or limestone. Besides the calcium phosphate present in it the other lime compound is gypsum and superphosphate of lime does not correct soil acidity. The usual grade to-day contains 18 per cent of soluble P_2O_5. The material is made by the interaction of mineral phosphates and sulphuric acid, and is a development of the original manufacture of superphosphate from bones by Lawes. Although the phosphoric acid in superphosphate is soluble in water, when applied to soils it rapidly becomes insoluble but, being in a very fine state of division in the soil it gradually becomes available to the growing plant. Superphosphate has proved to be exceedingly valuable when considered as a fertiliser for turf with a marked improvement being shown in the density of the turf and its resistance to drought, the latter no doubt being a reflection on the improved root development. Superphosphate, when applied in neat form to turf, is apt to scorch the herbage, and it should therefore only be given when mixed with sufficient carrier. On calcareous soils superphosphate is found to be superior to bone meal.

Among the insoluble forms of phosphatic manures mention must be made of basic slag, a product derived from the manufacture of steel. In purchasing basic slag it is important that the fineness of grinding should conform to the accepted standard, and at least 80 per cent of the material should pass through the British Standard test sieve, mesh

No. 100. Basic slags are sold on their content of phosphoric acid, which ranges from 6 to $18\frac{1}{2}$ per cent, but there are also differences in solubility as determined by the accepted test with citric acid, the high soluble group having 80 per cent or more soluble, while the other has 40 per cent or less soluble. The activity of the phosphate is related to the value for the solubility so that a good slag is one with a high soluble phosphoric acid content. It contains some free carbonate of lime and other compounds capable of neutralising acidity and it may be said that 1 cwt (50 kg) of basic slag is equivalent to approximately $\frac{2}{3}$ cwt (34 kg) of lime. Basic slag is not much used in turf management and perhaps this may be attributed to its well-known reputation for encouraging clover. The general improvement of pastures following basic slag dressings is very largely due to the increase of leguminous plants. Old turf composed of bent will respond readily to dressings of slag, but there is a danger that by using it worms, as well as clovers which may be latent as small plants, may be encouraged. The alkalinity of slag makes it particularly useful on peaty and acid soils and in many instances very acid turf would undoubtedly respond to its use. Where turf conditions indicate a trial with slag, the dressing should not exceed 5 to 7 cwt per acre (620 to 870 kg per ha).

Finally, mention must be made of mineral or North African phosphate, which contains from 25 to 39 per cent of phosphoric acid, and is important from the point of view of relative cheapness.

The phosphoric acid contained is insoluble and slow-acting except possibly under acid conditions. Ground mineral phosphate has comparatively little value in turf management generally but comes in useful for special circumstances e.g. golf fairways which are acid. In such circumstances a useful response may be obtained from the phosphoric acid and also from the small amount of lime usually contained.

Potassic fertilisers

It will be remembered from the figures given for the amount of potash removed in the clippings from certain experimental plots that potash was the second in respect of the amount removed. The role of potash is associated with the manufacture of carbo-hydrates by the green leaf, and is linked with nitrogen in controlling growth, but obvious reponses to potassic fertilisers are seldom obtained, though swards receiving potash tend to remain greener during the winter months and in drought than those not receiving it. Various potash fertilisers are available but, since in turf management potash is normally applied in fertiliser mixtures, only the high-grade compounds need to be considered.

These are sulphate of potash containing 50 per cent of K_2O and muriate of potash containing 40, 50, or 60 per cent of K_2O. The former is preferred for fertiliser mixtures but the latter may be used provided the mixtures are to be applied fairly quickly. Potash fertilisers have not been used extensively in lawn and green upkeep, and most proprietary mixtures for dressing lawns are usually low in this plant nutrient. Perhaps this is due to the fact that potassic fertilisers when applied to agricultural grass land favour the growth of clover. On the other hand high nitrogenous manuring as required for turf production involves the uptake of high amounts of potash, and it is possible that improved turf, freer from disease, would be obtained if potash were used in greater quantity, especially on light soils.

Concentrated fertilisers

In this group may be placed such materials as urea, ammonium phosphate, ammonium nitrate, potassium nitrate, and triple superphosphate. Urea, a highly concentrated nitrogenous fertiliser, contains somewhere in the region of 46 per cent nitrogen. If urea is applied to turf it can give an almost instantaneous response, but there is also a high risk of scorch. However, if urea is mixed with formaldehyde, then the urea-formaldehyde compound formed, containing about 36 per cent nitrogen, is quite slow in action and can be applied without danger of scorch.

Ammonium phosphate is manufactured in two forms, but only one is produced on a large scale, namely mono-ammonium dihydrogen-phosphate, which contains theoretically a percentage of 12·1 per cent of N and 61·7 per cent of P_2O_5. The commercial form contains less phosphoric acid.

As a source of ammoniacal nitrogen and water-soluble phosphoric acid mono-ammonium phosphate can only be compared with a mixture of sulphate of ammonia and superphosphate. It is important to know that while the latter contains calcium in the form of gypsum and calcium phosphate, no such calcium is present in ammonium phosphate. It has been shown in experiments that ammonium phosphate has equivalent weed-killing effects to sulphate of ammonia, and is also valuable for producing root development on browntop and certain fescues. Ammonium phosphate plots have a tendency to be lighter in colour, but denser, than those receiving sulphate of ammonia. They are not quite so dense as those receiving sulphate of ammonia and superphosphate. Ammonium phosphate has an undoubted value in lawn upkeep, and it is to be hoped that more use will be possible in the future. A suitable rate of application would be 4 lb per 100 sq yd (2·1 kg per 100 m^2).

Ammonium nitrate and potassium nitrate are seldom encountered but triple superphosphate is becoming fairly common. A typical sample may contain 47 per cent water-soluble phosphoric acid so that triple superphosphate may in effect be regarded as three times as concentrated as ordinary superphosphate.

Miscellaneous fertilisers

For convenience quite a number of materials of interest in turf upkeep may be grouped under this heading. Of these poultry manure is one of the most familiar. When properly prepared the material is friable and bulky, but it cannot be regarded with favour for regular use on turf because it tends to encourage weeds and worms. Undried poultry manure should not be directly applied to turf but may be incorporated in the compost heap.

Under the heading of miscellaneous materials one may include various forms of sewage. Dried sewage has some value as a fertiliser, but usually the material is looked upon as a useful top-dressing material to be used either alone or as a major constituent of some compost substitute mixture. Dried sewage should preferably be free from lime or at any rate contain only a very small amount. Some industrial sewages may contain harmful constituents, but these seldom reach the market.

Fish guano is another material that is sometimes used for turf dressings, or as an ingredient of proprietary mixtures. It is variable in quality and analysis, and often has an objectionable odour.

Little need be said about Peruvian guano, which at one period had a high popular reputation for turf, since it is now almost unobtainable. It should always be bought on the basis of the analysis. When available the price is high.

Various types of guano are made from market and town wastes, and some of them are valuable for turf purposes.

At times ground cocoa husk or shell is offered. Spent mushroom manure is sometimes procurable and both this and the cocoa husk can be applied direct to turf or composted.

A list of fertilisers and their analyses will be found in Appendix One (p. 290).

Granular fertilisers

Nowadays much use is made of granular fertilisers, usually compounded from sulphate of ammonia, superphosphate and muriate of potash, the proportions being varied for different crops. (Nitro-chalk is one kind of granular.) Some of these compounds are suitable for big areas of turf and when broadcast the granules fall between the grass shoots, thus minimising scorch. A useful type contains 8 per cent nitrogen, 12 per cent P_2O_5 and 8 per cent K_2O for use at 3 to 4 cwt per acre (360 to 480 kg per ha), but where more nitrogen and less phosphate is required one containing, say, 12:7:7 may be used at the same rate.

Slow release fertilisers

For a long time in turf culture there has been a need for a slow release nitrogenous fertiliser. Although the organic materials, such as hoof and horn, do go some way towards achieving this, they are quite expensive and are in short supply.

Ureaform, as mentioned previously, comes under the category of slow release, and other materials are on the market with the granules of plant foods being enclosed in a film of sulphur. Another range of fertilisers are available under a proprietary label, based on Isobutylidene diurea (IBDU), a by-product of the Japanese plastic industry. It is to be hoped that an efficient slow release material can be developed, as in those mentioned above there is a tendency for a considerable early release of nitrogen with, consequently, somewhat disappointing results.

CHAPTER SEVENTEEN

The evaluation, purchase and compounding of fertilisers

Most amateur lawn owners think of fertilisers in terms of proprietary compound mixtures containing the three main plant foods, and ideas of fertiliser costs are often based upon the prices paid for these preparations. Unless the lawn owner is only concerned with a small area or wishes to avoid a little additional trouble he can mix compound fertilisers for himself or, alternatively, submit a formula to a reputable merchant with the request that the compound be made up. Hard-and-fast formulæ are difficult to lay down in view of the varying soils, price and turf requirements.

Complete proprietary mixtures vary widely in analysis according to the views of the supplier; thus examination of the declared analyses of a number shows a variability of the nitrogen from 2 up to 32 per cent, of the phosphoric acid from 1·0 up to 16 per cent, and of the potash from 0·5 to as much as 12 per cent. It is customary in such mixtures to include the nitrogen in more than one form in order, it is stated, that it should become available by degrees. This involves the use of organic nitrogen-containing compounds. Phosphate may also be included in different forms. In support of this custom it is argued that if all the nitrogen is included in an inorganic form such as sulphate of ammonia, much of it will be lost in the drainage water, though it is a well-established fact that ammonia is held in soils and the losses are very small. Phosphate is rarely lost in appreciable quantity in drainage waters.

A simple method of manuring intensively-managed turf is to apply a complete fertiliser in spring, and to follow with several dressings of a nitrogenous fertiliser such as sulphate of ammonia during the season.

Compound manures

A generalised basic compound fertiliser should contain:

                5 to   7 per cent nitrogen
               10 to 15 per cent phosphoric acid
                2 to   4 per cent potash

Such a mixture may be used in spring at 2 oz per sq yd (67 g per m²) if further nitrogen is to follow. A mixture falling within these limits could be compounded by mixing together the following materials:

    15 parts by weight sulphate of ammonia
    15   dried blood
    40   fine bone meal
    25   superphosphate
     5   sulphate of potash

This mixture, it will be seen, derives its nitrogen from the first three ingredients and it is present in both inorganic and organic forms. The phosphate also is present in two forms. It must not be assumed that this mixture is generally applicable under all·conditions, but it is included here as a guide as to how mixtures may be compounded. It is impossible to prescribe for all conditions, and there will be times when such a mixture would be unsuitable, and where some other recipe would be more desirable. Further, there is a choice of materials available for compounding mixtures of this type, so giving a number of products having the same final analysis of plant foods.

The use of sulphate of iron in conjunction with mixtures such as the above is now usual, and 10 per cent may usefully be added, some of the other ingredients being proportionately reduced.

Mixing

Certain fertilisers do not mix satisfactorily. For example, ammoniacal manures should not be mixed with materials containing free lime, such as basic slag or certain rock phosphates, because free ammonia is likely to be lost. Sulphate of ammonia mixes well with superphosphate, bone and fish meals, nitrate of soda and potash manures. Compound mixtures of sulphate of ammonia and superphosphate, especially if potash salts are present, are inclined to set hard on storage, but the addition of bone flour or castor meal as a drier will largely prevent this.

Mixtures containing nitrate of soda are apt to become moist and sticky unless a drier is added.

A complete table showing the compounds that may be mixed and that may not be mixed is given in Appendix Three (p. 292).

In preparing a mixture the method adopted depends on the quantity concerned. If the amount is relatively small no difficulty should be encountered in ensuring intimate intermingling. Where large lots are involved it is advisable to spread separate layers of the ingredients one upon the other and then to throw the heap up into a conical pile, later digging this down and passing it through a screen. Small quantities are best handled at a time, and it is advisable to allow the freshly-mixed material to stand in a heap for a few days to 'cure', when it can be broken down, screened and bagged, after which it will not easily set. For those without adequate facilities for mixing it is better to send a recipe to the merchant to mix on his premises.

When mixing materials it is important that all lumps should be eliminated, and the mixture should be in good fine powdery condition so as to facilitate even distribution. Even distribution is most important when treating turf, as a lump of, say, superphosphate would scorch the grass, and as regards nitrogenous manures a lack of uniformity in colour will result unless the material has been spread evenly. It should be realised that when fertiliser is applied to turf, there is practically no lateral spread of the effect, so that a heavy local dressing will only cause improvement of the area immediately surrounding it. Only fine-ground qualities of hoof and bone meals should be used.

Materials that have to be stored should be kept in a dry place, or they are likely to become lumpy. Nitro-chalk is apt to absorb moisture. Even some of the raw materials used for preparing mixtures, e.g. sulphate of ammonia and nitrate of soda, are liable to lose condition, though the granular nitrate of soda and the dry neutral sulphate of ammonia show a great improvement on the old materials.

It must be said that mixing 'at home' is virtually outdated. Apart from possible inadequate facilities, the labour needed to mix and bag the mixture is scarce and expensive. There may be some saving in the cost of the materials themselves to offset the increased labour charges, and this would be one of the factors to be taken in account. Proprietary brands of fertilisers come in a great variety of types, catering for all sorts of turf and for all sorts of seasons and also come in convenient size bags for handling.

The purchase of manures

The Fertiliser and Feeding Stuffs Act requires that the seller of compound fertilisers shall make a written statement of the percentages of the plant food present under the following heads:

> Nitrogen (N)
> Soluble phosphoric acid (Sol. P_2O_5)
> Insoluble phosphoric acid (Insol. P_2O_5)
> Potash (K_2O)

This holds good with the exception of a sale of two or more articles that are mixed at the request of the purchaser before delivery and also to sales of quantities less than 56 lb (25 kg) if taken from a receptacle upon which the analysis is prominently displayed. The Act applies to fertilisers only and not to materials mixed together and sold under a branded name as 'lawn food'. All too often with lawn fertilisers statements such as 'equal to ammonia', 'total phosphate of lime', 'sulphate of potash', are used in addition to the figures required by law. Should the above be the only statement made then it is illegal. This can only be regarded as a device to enhance the apparent value. Thus, a well-advertised proprietary fertiliser containing 1·5 per cent of nitrogen might be much more attractive to some customers if sold as containing 7·2 per cent sulphate of ammonia, though both figures convey the same information.

The analysis of a compound manure, such as already given, may readily be calculated by multiplying the proportion of each constituent in the mixture by its percentage content of nitrogen, phosphoric acid or potash and dividing by the total weight. Thus, in the mixture already given the percentage of nitrogen derived from the sulphate of ammonia may be calculated by multiplying the 15 parts of sulphate of ammonia by 21 and dividing by 100: i.e. $15 \times 21 \div 100 = 3\cdot15$ per cent of N.

This may also be done for the other ingredients, giving a final analysis as follows:

15 parts by weight	sulphate of ammonia (21% N)		= 3·15%	Total
15	dried blood (14%N)		= 2·10%	N =
40	fine bone meal	$\begin{cases} (3\cdot75\% \text{ N}) \\ (20\cdot5\% \text{ Insol. } P_2O_5) \end{cases}$	= 1·50% / = 8·2%	6·75% Insol. P_2O_5
25	superphosphate (18% Sol. P_2O_5)		= 4·5%	Sol. P_2O_5
5	sulphate of potash (50% K_2O)		= 2·5%	K_2O

Valuation

Other things being equal, the value of an artificial fertiliser depends upon the quantities of the principal manurial ingredients present, and by using the percentages of these and the price paid a simple system of comparative valuation may be carried out.

If the price per ton of a straight fertiliser containing one form of plant food be divided by the percentage of the plant food present, the deduced cost is described as that of a 'unit'. By a study of such unit values it is possible to select the most economical manure and to protect oneself against fraud when buying basic or special manures.

The unit price of nitrogen, and other plant foods, varies with the commodity, thus it is highly probable that a unit of nitrogen derived from nitrate of soda will be higher in cost than that from sulphate of ammonia. Similarly, in organic fertilisers like dried blood, the cost per unit would be higher again, owing to the special value placed upon the material for use in compound fertilisers for turf. Unless some special outstanding merit attaches to the nitrate of soda and dried blood for a particular purpose, then obviously sulphate of ammonia would be the best 'buy' of the fertilisers mentioned.

A difficulty is encountered when calculating the unit value of insoluble P_2O_5 in a material like bone meal, containing $3 \cdot 75$ per cent of nitrogen in organic form as well as 21 per cent of P_2O_5. It is necessary to assign a value to the nitrogen content, deducting this from the cost per ton and leaving the remainder as the value of the insoluble P_2O_5. By simple mathematics the unit price of the P_2O_5 can be easily determined.

The unit prices of fertilisers are not fixed. They vary with the market price of the materials, which are found published in various agricultural and trade journals.

While it is relatively simple to calculate the values of 'straight' fertilisers, it is quite difficult to do this with compound ready-mixed fertilisers. Although as stated previously, the percentage of plant food must be given by law, no statement is required as to the actual fertilisers contained. It is therefore difficult to evaluate say, the nitrogen content, which may have been included in more than one form for some special purpose. Evaluation on units of plant food can readily be done, some allowance being made on the assumption that perhaps half the nitrogen is in an organic form, and half inorganic. A unit value can then be calculated on the current prices—using dried blood and sulphate of ammonia for instance—and applying this to the compounds being compared. In matters of doubt, an independent authority should be consulted.

As regards mixtures offered in ready-made form the valuation in arithmetical manner is not always a complete safeguard. Although the full amount of plant foods shown in the analysis may be present these may be of little value because of slow availability or unsuitable form. Thus, by incorporating ground-leather waste into a mixture, the percentage of nitrogen can be made to look high, but this material is likely to be so slow-acting as to be of little value. It is true that the purchaser receives his nitrogen as advertised, but it is questionable whether the turf will receive its nitrogen this year or next or only 5 or 6 years hence. Purchasers should not be misled by the claim that a manure has a value not indicated by the analysis.

Materials like dried blood, rape meal, and guano have some action in improving both the physical condition and water-holding capacity of soils. They cannot therefore be valued solely as plant food, but the quantity used can have very little appreciable effect in improving the physical properties of the soil. In lawn upkeep any substantial change in the physical condition of the soil is best carried out by the deliberate use of compost containing organic matter, or by the use of special top-dressing rich in this material.

As stated above high amounts of organic fertilisers may be present in a compound manure but be worth very little owing to the fact that they become available so slowly. The growing plant absorbs its nitrogen in the form of nitrates, i.e. by a rapid process, and the material is very largely used up; but the nitrogen in many materials is not readily available and must be converted to nitrate in the soil. Some materials like sulphate of ammonia, dried blood, rape meal, and guano pass through this change rapidly, but there is always some loss in the process. The risk of loss varies according to the amount of change necessary. It is often stated that quick-acting nitrogen as in sulphate of ammonia is rapidly lost and that organic slow-acting nitrogen is held better, but the reverse is more likely to take place. Of course a rapidly available material may be applied at the wrong time of year when grass cannot respond, so that it is largely wasted, but it is true to say that very slow-acting materials requiring a long process of change involve losses. Slowness of availability may detract from value instead of adding to it, thus 100 lb (45 kg) weight of nitrogen or phosphoric acid or potash that will not become effective until some remote date is less valuable than the same quantity that can be brought into action during the current season.

Organic forms of fertilisers for turf have the advantage that they are safer to use in the hands of the inexperienced, and being more bulky than inorganic, they are easier to spread. For use by the amateur, therefore, they have a somewhat enhanced value, but the price they command, even with this allowance, is out of proportion to their real manurial value.

However, with the increased use of granulated fertilisers, the danger of wrong application of inorganics has been lessened, the granules being free flowing, being easily seen, and being less liable to disturbance by windy conditions during application.

Storage

The majority of proprietary brands of fertilisers are sold in plastic bags weighing about 56 lb (25 kg), and while withstanding damp conditions very well, these bags can easily be punctured or split. When storing, they should be stacked flat, to a height of about ten bags on a layer of duck boards or wood to keep them from contact with a damp earth or concrete floor.

The subject of fertilisers, their valuation and use in turf upkeep has been discussed in this account in some detail because experience has shown that most lawn owners, greenkeepers, managers of sports grounds and golf courses, are largely 'in the dark' and often pay prices far in excess of those that should be charged when the fertilisers are regarded as suppliers of plant food.

CHAPTER EIGHTEEN

Sulphate of iron

A brief reference has already been made to the use of sulphate of iron in conjunction with compound fertiliser mixtures, but as the function of sulphate of iron is not that of a fertiliser, it is necessary that its properties should receive separate consideration. Sulphate of iron has been well known for many years to horticulturists, among whom it is known for its ability to improve the colour of flowers and of the leaves of certain plants. Sulphate of iron certainly improves the colour of turf but is more particularly of value for controlling disease and weeds, especially moss.

Sulphate of iron has long been used as an ingredient of lawn sand mixtures and it appears to have been first advocated about 1913 for regular use on turf by Dr C. M. Murray in South Africa, who advised its systematic use in conjunction with sulphate of ammonia. Afterwards it was extensively adopted in this country, first as an auxiliary in weed eradication, and secondly as a means of combating the chlorotic appearance of grass sometimes observed to follow the use of quick-acting nitrogenous fertilisers, such as sulphate of ammonia.

In its crude commercial form sulphate of iron ($FeSO_4 . 7H_2O$) is obtainable as large blue-green crystals containing 45 per cent of water ($7H_2O$), in chemical combination as water of crystallisation, and 20 per cent of iron (Fe). In this form the material is unsuitable for use on turf, though crystals as fine as castor sugar are obtainable from some sources. It has become customary, however, to use the sulphate of iron in the 'exsiccated' or 'calcined' form, which is produced by heating the coarse crystals and driving off a proportion of the combined water. After grinding, the resultant material is a fine near-white powder having the consistency of flour. In the baking process it is necessary to avoid oxidation to ferric oxide.

Supplies of calcined sulphate of iron on the market are very variable; in some only one molecule of water has been removed, 41 per cent of water still being present, whilst in a well-calcined material $5\frac{1}{2}$ molecules have been driven off, so leaving a product containing about 16 per cent of water. An average quality contains 30 to 35 per cent of water, i.e. $4\frac{1}{2}$ to 5 molecules. Little information exists as to the relative merits of crystalline sulphate of iron and the various grades of the calcined form, but preliminary treatments have not shown any marked difference in the effects. Sulphate of iron, efficiently calcined, being in a fine state of division, distributes well and mixes easily with other materials. It is preferred to any other form.

Early experiments at St Ives have shown that when sulphate of iron is regularly used with sulphate of ammonia there is a more rapid diminution of weeds than with sulphate of ammonia alone. The end result may be the same, but weed-killing is more rapid, and the sulphate of iron imparts a beautiful deep green colour to the turf. Blackman also records a slightly greater weed reduction with sulphate of ammonia plus sulphate of iron as against sulphate of ammonia only, and he obtained similar results with the double salt, ferrous ammonium sulphate. Similar results with the double salt were also obtained in trials at St Ives.

In some experiments comparing sulphate of ammonia with light and heavy rates of sulphate of iron on plots sown with a mixture of bent and fine-leaved fescue, it was found that the heavier dressing resulted in a decrease of the bent and a proportionate increase of the fescue.

Sulphate of iron helps to induce soil acidity, and although it has been claimed that the sulphate assists utilisation of phosphate all the evidence so far indicates that it has the effect of immobilising phosphate in the soil, converting it into insoluble and relatively unavailable compounds. Plot trials have shown that long-continued use of sulphate of iron with sulphate of ammonia may lead to a thin, open, brownish-black turf slow to respond to rain or artificial watering. Where equivalent amounts of sulphate of iron and sulphate of ammonia are given with the addition of phosphate, this condition does not develop so readily. Sulphate of iron also has a tendency to make the soil dry and crumbly. It has a marked inhibitory action on fungi that causes turf disease and is sometimes used to prevent or control fusarium patch disease.

Sulphate of iron confers weed-killing properties on certain fertilisers, which, used alone, do not have this effect. Further reference will be made to the matter under weed control, where the properties of sulphate of iron as a moss killer will also be discussed. The sulphate also has a definite inhibiting action on earthworm activity. Thus, in some trials, 10 oz (283 g) of sulphate of iron applied in small amounts over four seasons reduced the worm casts from a range of 24 to 48 per sq yd (0·94 m²) to 2 to 24, while an application of 13·5 oz (382 g) over the same period had reduced the range of casts to 1 to 4 per sq yd (0·94 m²).

The place of sulphate of iron in modern turf upkeep is now well established, but it requires careful usage if the best results are to be attained, since over-application leads to lack of vigour and poor drought resistance. In fertiliser mixtures sulphate of iron should amount to about $\frac{1}{6}$ oz per sq yd (6 g per m²) or 50 lb per acre (56 kg per ha). For treatment of fusarium patch disease the rate of application is $\frac{1}{2}$ oz in 1 gal to 2 sq yd (16 g in 1·5 l to 2 m²). When used as a weed-killer the amount of sulphate of iron may vary according to circumstances and its use in lawn sands receives attention in Chapters 21 and 22. For spot treatment of individual weeds stronger mixtures are more appropriate, for example, equal parts of sulphate of ammonia and sulphate of iron.

CHAPTER NINETEEN

Lime and the preservation of soil acidity

In this country soils tend to become progressively more acid owing to the natural losses of calcium compounds into the drainage water. These losses are increased by the use of certain types of fertiliser and in addition, of course, lime is a constituent of the grass clippings (see Chapter 16) which are often removed in the box. As the soil becomes progressively more acid so bacterial activity is reduced. As a result a mat of fibrous matter consisting of semi-decayed leaves, stems, and roots, usually begins to form and gradually accumulates until it may be several inches thick. Even on chalk downs where lime is close at hand the accumulation may occur in course of time, and much old grass land in all parts of the country has developed this surface mat. Lime deficiency can be induced artificially as has been done on the Rothamsted Park grass plots or on the older turf plots at St Ives by using sulphate of ammonia in regular applications. The condition is more difficult to attain on calcareous soils but relatively easy on siliceous or sandy soils.

Much of the turf found on old-established sports grounds, golf courses, park lands and garden lawns is of this acid matted type. Such acid turf contains the desirable grasses (bent and fescue), some Yorkshire fog, scarcely any crested dog's-tail or perennial rye-grass, and very few weeds. It is characterised by low fertility and low pH.* The miscellaneous plants which exist, for example, heath bedstraw,

* pH. A scale for measuring acidity. The neutral figure is 7·0. Lower figures (from neutral downwards) indicate progressive degrees of acidity, higher figures (from neutral upwards) indicate progressive degrees of alkalinity.

wood-rush, cat's-ear, and creeping hawkweed, do not appreciably detract from the turf unless their proportions become very great. Under acid matted conditions worm activity in turf is either eliminated or very much reduced. Further, such turf provides a dry resilient sward during the winter months, though it has the disadvantage of being susceptible to drought and when once dried out re-wetting by rain is often very slow.

With these facts in mind it is not surprising that the inducement of acidity was at one time regarded as essential for good weed-free turf, especially as American experiments had pointed to the fact that weed-free turf could be maintained in such a state by withholding alkaline materials and treating the turf regularly with those leaving an acid residue, such as sulphate of ammonia and ammonium phosphate. Although these tests were not concerned with eradication it was argued that artificial inducement of acidity would lead to the elimination of weeds and coarse grasses. Actually, however, the elimination of coarse grasses is partly a function of the cutting factor and their failure to stand up to repeated keen defoliation. Whereas it is quite true that certain weeds can be eliminated by the use of materials tending to leave an acid soil, the induced acidity is only one factor operating against the weeds present. The evidence indicates that acidity is important as far as control of weed invasion is concerned, though indirect effects like iron and aluminium toxicity may be of more importance than acidity as such.

Apart from this aspect it is important to consider the question of maintaining the soil in an acid condition where this state already exists, and many cases are known where matted turf containing excellent grasses but perhaps lacking in vigour and density has been ruined by the destruction or reduction of the acidity through liming or by using basic slag or other material containing lime. The effect of this is shown in a gradual invasion of weed species, such species as daisy, selfheal, dandelion, chickweed, pearlwort, and plantains being the most likely to appear.

Acid matted turf is relatively free from earthworms, but indiscriminate liming of it leads to a rapid increase in numbers and activity, and instances are known where beautiful acid matted turf, clean and dry in winter, has been reduced to a sea of mud as a result of an injudicious application of lime. It is true that limed turf is more drought resistant than unlimed turf, but it is much softer and as there is little or no mat there is no 'spring' in the turf.

The effects of liming may clearly be seen on many old-established tennis courts where lines of worm casts and weeds coincide with whitening marks; the effect of the whitening persists for a long time.

From the above it must not be assumed that lime is always taboo. The requirements of turf used principally for robust winter games are obviously different from those of bowling greens and of putting greens, and even here conditions can become too acid for satisfactory growth. Nevertheless, liming must only be done judiciously after very careful consideration of the various factors involved. On acid matted turf it is better first of all to try the effects of a general fertiliser containing nitrogen, phosphate, and potash, or a dressing of nitro-chalk at, say, 2 cwt per acre (250 kg per ha). If, however, the turf is exceedingly sparse, with wood-rush, moss and sorrel, or highly acid, then it may be that light liming should precede the application of fertiliser. If this is done the rate should not exceed for a start 5 cwt to the acre (625 kg per ha) (about 2 oz per sq yd (62 g per m²)) of ground carbonate of lime. In the usual product about 80 per cent should pass through a 100-mesh sieve, though recent work shows that a slightly coarser material serves the purpose. Burnt or quick-lime and hydrated lime are not so suitable, since both scorch the turf, the former rather severely. When there is doubt it is much preferable to take advice on the matter, since an estimation of the 'lime requirement' may be carried out in the laboratory. A test commonly used will show the amount of lime required to bring the soil up to a desirable pH—even for agricultural purposes complete neutrality is not necessary.

Often systematic use of the hand-fork on small areas or mechanical spiker on large areas of matted turf will bring about a marked improvement without the use of lime. The process punctures the mat and loosens the soil, thus aiding water penetration and encouraging root development. The full effect of the mechanical process cannot be obtained, however, unless it is accompanied by suitable dressings of fertiliser.

A scientific discussion of the lime status of soils is outside the scope of this book and is a matter requiring further investigation in relation to turf culture. It may well be found that weed and worm inhibition are more directly associated with the amount of exchangeable lime and bases in the soil, or with the toxicity of active iron or aluminium under acid conditions, and only indirectly with the acidity or pH. However, the evidence to date points to the advantage of preserving the acid matted turf if naturally present. If it is to be retained, and worm and weed invasion prevented, lime should be withheld except under special circumstances. When the soil is not acid, the attempt to induce acidity may be made by the periodic use of peat, lime-free sand, good compost, and by careful choice of fertilisers, though under some soil conditions the attainment may prove difficult. It is unwise to attempt to induce the desirable acid condition quickly by using excessive quantities of quick-acting fertilisers like sulphate of ammonia, although there are circumstances when direct acidification can be undertaken with advantage. Typical of this is the use of finely-ground sulphur at 1 oz per sq yd (32 g per m²) or 300 lb per acre (340 kg per ha) on golf fairways lying on heavy soil fairly well supplied with lime.

CHAPTER TWENTY

The weed problem and some common species

Most lawn owners, gardeners, and greenkeepers are more interested in methods for the eradication of weeds or the control of invasion than in studying the species, their propagation and the reasons for their persistence in turf. Nevertheless, some general knowledge of the factors involved and the species found in turf is a necessary prelude to a study of control. It is not to be wondered that so much interest is taken in weed eradication, since it is a problem that is decidely acute on many lawns, sports grounds and other turf areas.

In the popular mind a weed is a 'plant growing out of place', but no exact definition can be given. Often a weed regarded as an enemy in a lawn or green is a friend of the farmer, for instance, clover or even ribwort plantain, which sometimes forms a useful plant in sheep pastures. Similarly, rye-grass and cocksfoot, the valued grasses of the farmer, are regarded as weeds in turf for fine lawns, bowling, or golf greens, though rye-grass would be acceptable on a playing field or football field.

Weeds may broadly be classified into three groups, according to the duration of their lives; namely, annuals, biennials and perennials, but at times they merge one into the other. Only a few annuals cause trouble in established turf, though some like groundsel, chickweed, and fat-hen may appear in newly-sown grass. Since they depend for their continuation upon the setting of seed, such annuals speedily die out under regular mowing. Some annuals however (e.g. annual meadow-grass and parsley-piert) are more persistent, since they are able to adapt themselves to seeding even when the turf is being keenly mown.

A biennial weed is one that requires two years to complete the life cycle; in the first year germination of the seed and vegetative growth take place, while flowering and seed formation do not occur until the second year. Very few biennials occur in turf, conditions again being against seed formation. Wild carrot and spear thistle are perhaps the exceptions. The vast majority of weeds in turf are perennials having no definite term of existence and capable of constantly spreading and increasing. The most aggressive turf weeds belong to this class.

A list of common weeds of turf and of those less commonly found is given below, and the popular and botanical names have both been included. It will be noted that two grasses are included:

Weeds commonly found in turf:

Bulbous buttercup	*Ranunculus bulbosus* L.
Creeping buttercup	*Ranunculus repens* L.
Upright buttercup	*Ranunculus acris* L.
Cat's-ear	*Hypochæris radicata* L.
Creeping soft-grass	*Holcus mollis* L.
Daisy	*Bellis perennis* L.
Dandelion	*Taraxacum officinalis* Web.
Mouse-ear chickweed	*Cerastium vulgatum* L.
Certain mosses	
Pearlwort	*Sagina procumbens* L.
Broad-leaved plantain	*Plantago major* L.
Buck's-horn plantain or starweed	*Plantago coronopus* L.
Hoary plantain	*Plantago media* L.
Ribwort, ribgrass, or narrow-leaved plantain	*Plantago lanceolata* L.
Selfheal	*Prunella vulgaris* L.
Sheep's sorrel	*Rumex acetosella* L.
Wild white clover	*Trifolium repens* L.
Wood-rush	*Luzula campestris* L.
Yarrow or milfoil	*Achillea millefolium* L.
Yorkshire fog	*Holcus lanatus* L.

Weeds less commonly found in turf:

Bird's-foot trefoil	*Lotus corniculatus* L.
Celandine	*Ranunculus ficaria* L.
Chickweed	*Stellaria media* Cyrill.
Cinquefoil	*Potentilla reptans* L.
Coltsfoot	*Tussilago farfara* L.
Common erodium	*Erodium cicutarium* L'Her.
Dove's-foot geranium	*Geranium molle* L.
Fat-hen	*Chenopodium album* L.
Field chickweed	*Cerastium arvense* L.
Germander speedwell	*Veronica chamædrys* L.
Hardheads	*Centaurea nigra* L.
Hawk's-beard or smooth crepis	*Crepis virens* L.

Heath bedstraw	*Galium saxatile* L.
Creeping or mouse-ear hawkweed	*Hieracium pilosella* L.
Knotweed or Knotgrass	*Polygonum aviculare* L.
Marsh penny-wort	*Hydrocotyle vulgaris* L.
Musk erodium	*Erodium moschatum* L.
Parsley-piert	*Aphanes arvensis* F & S.
Ragwort	*Senecio Jacobea* L.
Salad burnet	*Poterium sanguisorba* L.
Sea erodium	*Erodium maritimum* L.
Sea milkwort	*Glaux maritima* L.
Sea pink or sea thrift	*Armeria vulgaris* Willd.
Sea plantain	*Plantago maritima* L.
Shepherd's purse	*Capsella bursa-pastoris* DC.
Silverweed	*Potentilla anserina* L.
Spurrey	*Spergula arvensis* L.
Creeping thistle	*Cirsium arvense* Scop.
Dwarf or stemless thistle	*Carduus acaulis* L.
Tormentil	*Potentilla tormentilla* Leck.
Thyme-leaved speedwell	*Veronica serpyllifola* L.
Wall or field speedwell	*Veronic arvensis* L.
Water chickweed or blinks	*Montia fontana* L.
Yellow suckling clover	*Trifolium minus* Relb.

In addition to the plants listed above there are various miscellaneous weeds found under the special conditions obtaining on seaside, down-land or peaty turf, whilst occasionally garden escapes occur as lawn weeds.

To the lawn owner the chief complaint about weeds in the turf will be the neglected and untidy appearance they impart to the sward. On sports turf they can, in addition, influence the game but apart from this and the æsthetic aspect, weeds affect the neighbouring grasses by competing for room and crowding and shading the grasses from light; they also rob the grasses of soil nutrients and water, so contributing to the progressive deterioration of the turf. Chemical analysis of weeds has shown that they absorb nitrogen, phosphoric acid and potash in relatively large amounts, so that they cause an unnecessary drain on the soil. In dry weather they deplete the water reserves in the soil and thus hasten the onset of drought conditions. The relatively large area of bare ground left when a large weed like a plantain is removed, shows the intense smothering effect of a weed so closely appressed to the ground. Add to this the similar crowding of the underground parts or root stocks of weeds and grasses occupying the same turf, and the great need for checking weed infestation on turf must be appreciated to the full.

On looking through the list of commoner weeds already mentioned it will be realised that most of these species occur in turf in all parts of

Fig. 21. *Ranunculus bulbosus*: Bulb buttercup.

the country, on every class of soil, and in swards designed for every purpose. They are ubiquitous. The reason for this may be sought in the mowing factor, which constantly operates irrespective of soil, climate, altitude, management, and even manurial treatment. In explaining the spread and general distribution of these common weeds it is important to realise that it is *because* of the intensive mowing that the weed problem in turf assumes such magnitude.

The weeds that survive and become most aggressive in mown turf are those that can, by their habit of growth, not only escape the mower blades but can also, despite cutting, increase either vegetatively or by production of flowers and seeds below the cutting level. Rosette or flat weeds such as daisy, dandelion, the various plantains, and cat's-ear, all grow closely appressed to the ground, so escaping punishment from the mower. Moreover, a single plant occupies a large proportion of ground as compared with a single grass plant in a turf. Daisy, ribwort plantain and cat's-ear, throw out shoots that develop into daughter plants still closely pressed to the ground, so building up the original crown into a closely-packed colony. Under conditions of really keen mowing, e.g. on putting greens, and bowling greens, these weeds do not normally form seeds but it is a common experience to see daisies flowering and seeding on lawns, golf fairways, and sports grounds, and even ribwort plantain seed heads that have escaped decapitation. On seaside turf huge areas of starweed (buck's-horn plantain) are not uncommon, and this is due to the constant mowing and to the weed being able to set quantities of seed well below the level of the keenest cutters.

While the weeds mentioned above are aggressive in turf because of their habit of budding off daughter plants and because of the relatively large size of their leaf blades compared with those of mown grasses, certain other weeds by reason of their habit are still more powerful in the competitive struggle. These are the mat weeds, creeping buttercup, wild white clover, selfheal, yarrow, silverweed, pearlwort, and mouse-ear chickweed, to which should be added the gramineous weeds, Yorkshire fog and creeping soft-grass. The weeds in this category have the ability to adjust themselves to turf conditions by developing much shortened stems and leaves—thus escaping defoliation—but in addition they can spread rapidly by vegetative means. White clover, creeping buttercup, mouse-ear chickweed, and silverweed produce overground runners that force themselves in among the grass shoots, later rooting at the nodes and sending out new shoots. Yarrow, selfheal, and creeping soft-grass increase, however, by a system of underground stems, ramifying in the soil and sending up new shoots.

In addition to the above, certain weeds trail over the surface and do not root at the nodes, e.g. knotweed, garden chickweed, and various speedwells. Perhaps the worst of the weeds mentioned above is pearlwort, the universal distribution and persistence of which in fine turf is due to its very low moss-like growth, to the fact that it can spread by vegetative growth, and to its capacity also of being able to form seed despite keen mowing. It is therefore a plant singularly well adapted to existence in fine turf.

Not only do weeds directly smother grass but their presence makes the grass grow more upright, less closely appressed to the ground, and consequently it is more seriously defoliated than need be.

Continuous keen mowing of the growing sward and occasional cutting in the winter are essential on putting greens, and keen mowing for at least six months per annum of bowling greens, croquet, and tennis lawns. This intensive cutting has a weakening effect on the grass, and when it is accompanied by the continuous ground-floor competition set up by rosette and creeping weeds, leading to smothering or reduced shoot (tiller) production, is it to be wondered that faulty or inadequately managed turf should progressively deteriorate? The removal of ground-floor competition by mechanical, chemical or other means is always the first step to improvement of neglected turf.

The establishment of weeds in turf may take place by two methods— the introduction of seeds, or of portions of the actual plant, and the dispersal may be assisted by a number of factors, such as some fortunate coincidence or the aid of special adaptations of the seed or plant itself. During high winds the seeds of many plants are carried a long distance, and it is not uncommon even for portions of plants like rhizomes to be transported in this way. Such weeds as dandelion, cat's-ear, groundsel, thistle, and numerous composite plants have seeds equipped with a plume as an aid to wind distribution. The seeds of other plants are provided with hooks that readily catch in the clothing, or in the coats of animals. Birds are known to be active agents in spreading seed, and common turf weeds like ribwort plantain, mouse-ear chickweed, creeping buttercup, dandelion, and others, have been found in viable condition in the crops and droppings of many birds. In the construction of new lawns and greens, weeds are often introduced by the use of soil transported from elsewhere, as this may contain either dormant weed seeds or lengths of root stocks of such grasses as creeping soft-grass. Small seeds like pearlwort are readily spread by being transported on the feet of human beings or animals, or through adhesion to implements. On areas where the cuttings are allowed to fly, the scattering of daisy heads and plantain seeds usually accounts for their rapid increase. Badly-prepared compost is another source of weed infestation, and the sowing of impure seed may be a cause of much future labour. Improper fallowing of land before sowing is a frequent cause of infestation of new turf, and even if the soil appears to be free from weeds there may still be present, buried in the soil, the seeds of plants capable of establishment in turf, which have been lying dormant for a long period of time.

CHAPTER TWENTY-ONE

Weed inhibition and weed eradication

The aim of the groundsman or greenkeeper is to grow good turf suitable for the sport or pastime for which the area is to be used. Control of weed growth is therefore an essential part of turf management, for apart from their unsightliness, weeds present a positive obstruction to the sporting activities. Their means of control in earlier days relied mainly on applications of lawn sand and the skilful use of fertilisers such as sulphate of ammonia. Severe weed infestations were often overcome by hand weeding, and the skilled drew a sharp distinction between weed inhibition, by which they meant the prevention of invasion into an already weed-free turf, and weed eradication, which would be necessary once weeds were allowed to become established.

The discovery of the first of the now firmly established range of synthetic growth regulators, referred to as Selective Herbicides, has simplified the eradication of weeds in turf, but their use must never be considered as a substitute for good turf management.

Good turf management should concentrate on maintaining grass vigour and weed inhibition, and the success of this programme will eventually determine the amount of chemical weed control required.

Factors that have to be considered are:

(i) Site preparation; if a new turf has been established from clean seed on a well-prepared seed bed, it may be maintained in its weed-free condition, mainly by the sensible use of fertilisers.

(ii) Soil type; this will determine the natural flora liable to thrive. Heavy, badly drained soils will not support desirable grasses, therefore

Fig. 22. A compact complete outfit for aeration, scarifying and brushing of smaller areas of turf.

Fig. 23. A general purpose tractor mounted aerator.

Fig. 24. A heavy-duty tractor mounted aerator.

an efficient drainage system prior to sowing or turfing is essential. Similarly, after the sward has been established, aeration and the use of porous top dressings will be necessary to maintain grass vigour.

(iii) Fertiliser programme; a balanced nutrient programme should be considered using fertilisers which will help to maintain weed-and worm-free conditions. Applications using sulphate of ammonia or ammonium phosphate discourage both, but nitrate of soda, although also a source of nitrogen, has the opposite effect.

(iv) Soil pH; desirable grasses for good turf prefer acid conditions, and grow well in a pH range from 5·5 to 6·0. Excessively low pH soils will require liming, while the use of acid fertilisers will tend to reduce pH values.

(v) Top-dressings; the use of top-dressings is a useful method to build up soil fertility and produce an even playing surface, but top-dressings must be considered as a possible source of weed invasion.

(vi) Mowing; close mowing tends to encourage weeds such as pearlwort. If the mowing surface is uneven, bare or thin areas may appear because of scalping. Weeds can readily be established in these areas. The use of gang mowers, where necessarily the cuttings are left to fly, can encourage the spread of weed seeds.

(vii) Scarification; this simple operation does much to control the growth of creeping weeds.

(viii) Aeration; slitting and spiking all are operations that reduce the amount of soil compaction. Compacted soils can reduce grass vigour and encourage weeds such as knotgrass.

(ix) Earthworm control; soil brought to the surface in the form of worm casts, can contain viable weed seeds, but can also prove to be ready-made seed beds for wind-blown weed seeds. Worm casts rolled flat by mowing equipment or trodden flat by the traffic of players, tend to kill off existing grass, and this is in many cases is colonised by weeds.

(x) Pest and disease control; areas of turf damaged by attacks of pests or disease, are liable to be infilled with weeds.

The use of selective weed-killers

The weed-killing effect of the sulphates of ammonia and iron is in part, at least, due to their corrosive action on the foliage of the weeds. 'Hormone' type weed-killers, to which the term 'selective' has now been affixed, have quite a different effect. Their absorption by susceptible plants causes great physiological disturbances resulting in ultimate destruction. The popular description 'hormones' for the

Fig. 25. Weed eradication with selective weed-killer. *Left*: treated. *Right*: untreated.

Fig.26. Swelling of creeping buttercup stems and increased growth after applying MCPA weed-killer. *Left*: untreated. *Right*: treated.

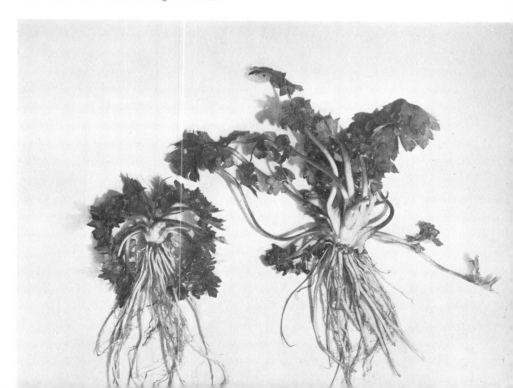

chemicals on which these weed-killers depend is less correct than the term 'plant growth regulators'.

In the early 1930's research workers became extremely interested in compounds showing growth-regulating effects on plants and isolated some such compounds from natural sources. Later a whole range of related synthetic compounds was produced and these new substances have found many practical applications as, for example, for promoting the rooting of cuttings or for 'setting' tomatoes and other fruit. Research showed that, while very small doses of these various chemicals produced more or less desirable effects, rather larger (although still very small) doses would kill plants. This was followed by the observation that, since some plants are more easily killed than others, a selective effect can be obtained by suitable adjustment of the dose given. As a result of considerable programmes of experimental work by a number of research workers of I.C.I., of Rothamsted and of various centres in the USA, two particularly active compounds in this respect were discovered, namely 2,4-dichlorophenoxyacetic acid (2,4-D) and 4-chloro-2-methylphenoxyacetic acid (MCPA). These chemicals in suitable doses exert selective phytocidal action through which many dicotyledonous plants are killed while many monocotyledonous plants, including grasses, are resistant and thus survive.

Much of the early work on these chemicals was done during World War II, and thus emphasis was first placed on their value for agricultural purposes, such as weeds in cereals. Subsequent work on turf areas rapidly proved the value of these synthetic growth regulators.

MCPA and 2,4-D have for many years been established as an essential part of the maintenance of weed-free amenity turf. On the whole, results obtained from both are very similar, but the spectrum of control was limited. Daisies, dandelions, buttercups and plantains were all easily eradicated, but clovers, trefoils and yarrow proved resistant.

Further discoveries over the years have led to the development of additional compounds, the most notable of these being 2-(4-chloro-2-methyl phenoxy) propionic acid (mecoprop or CMPP), since it was found that this material gave good control of many 2,4-D/MCPA resistant weeds, and mixtures of 2,4-D/CMPP became commercially available as the first broad spectrum selective weed-killer for use on turf. The range of chemicals for use on amenity turf, together with their application rates is:

Single materials:
  MCPA 20/40 oz per acre (1·40/2·80 kg/ha)
  2,4-D 16/32 oz per acre (1·12/2·24 kg/ha)
  Mecoprop 32/48 oz per acre (2·24/3·36 kg/ha)

Mixtures:
  2,4-D 12/24 oz per acre (0·84/1·68 kg/ha)
      plus one of the following:
  Mecoprop 24/36 oz per acre (1·68/2·52 kg/ha)
  Dichlorprop 32 oz per acre (2·24 kg/ha)
  Fenoprop 16/32 oz per acre (1·12/2·24 kg/ha)
  Dicamba 2/4 oz per acre (0·14/0·28 kg/ha)
  Ioxynil 9 oz per acre (0·63 kg/ha)

All the above compounds are insoluble in water, and are prepared commercially as one of the following forms:

  (i)   Sodium/Potassium Salts.
  (ii) Amine Salts.
  (iii) Esters (water mixing oils).

The dosage rates listed above, however, are the equivalent amounts of active material required. These vary since esters tend to be more active than amines or alkali salts, while at the same time the amount of chemical required to control different weed species also varies.

Commercially the marketing of selective weed-killers is now extremely complicated, and although straight formulations of 2,4-D and Mecoprop are readily available, many mixtures referred to as broad spectrum weed-killers are being marketed. Once the problem weed species have been determined, reference to the weed charts issued by many companies allows the best preparation to be chosen, which should be then applied strictly according to the manufacturer's instructions.

The initial effects of growth regulators are seen in discolouration and in curling and twisting of the stems and leaves of weeds which often become brittle. The plants finally wither away as though by bacterial rotting.

In general, mature grasses of all kinds are not unduly affected when sprayed with selective weed-killers at the normal rates required to remove the common run of weeds, though there is usually slight discolouration which may be more marked in hot dry weather. For this reason and others it is better to avoid treating with selective weed-killer during such weather. Applications of selective weed-killers are apt to be rather more drastic and harmful on newly-established turf whether from seed or sod and great care must be observed if they are to be used at all in the first few months in the life of a new sward.

The effect of selective weed-killers on the germination of grass seeds is important where renovation with grass seed may be necessary after weed removal. In the case of 2,4-D there is little visible effect even when the seeds are sown on soil which has been treated the same day but it is clear that with other materials, under dry conditions at any rate, the germination of grass seed may be adversely affected if this is sown within a period of 3 to 4 weeks after the date of weed-killer application.

With regard to dilution, trials have shown little difference in efficiency as between a given amount of selective weed-killer applied in 6, 12, or 100 gal of water per acre (67, 134, or 1124 l per ha), except possibly where low-growing weeds are protected by grass. In the latter case higher volumes would seem to have a better chance of success, and manufacturers usually recommend 20/30 gal of water per acre (225/337 l per ha).

Most effective results are usually obtained in late spring and early summer and of course applications at this season have the advantage that grass will fill in better than it will later in the year. It has been found that the use of fertilisers in conjunction with the weed-killers is advantageous and everything so far points to best results being obtained when fertiliser is applied about 10 to 14 days before the anticipated date of applying weed-killer. With good timing of this type the disappearance of weeds and growing in of grass takes place simultaneously. It should be noted that with spring applications weed-killing can well follow the ordinary routine spring dressing of fertiliser.

The mowing factor seems of comparatively little importance in relation to selective weed-killing. Experiments conducted by American workers showed that, provided a short time was allowed for absorption of the chemical, mowing could follow treatment without adverse results while efficiency was not affected by mowing before treatment. Experience in this country is consistent with this and recommendations are usually to treat within a short period after mowing so that a day or so can elapse before further mowing is necessary.

Research and experience have combined to show very clearly the need for not allowing any trace of growth-regulating chemicals to reach crops for which they are not intended. They affect a number of common plants and shrubs adversely and so wind drift and other means of contamination should be avoided at all times. Even the vapour from some of the formulations may be deadly to plant life, and all precautions should be taken to prevent these selective weed-killers reaching garden and glasshouse plants. In particular any tackle used for their application should be most thoroughly cleansed before being used for any other purpose connected with plant growing. In general the use of plant growth regulators is attended with little or no risk to human beings and animals.

Some users have found that dusts are easier to use than sprays since they can be applied directly by hand or by fertiliser distributor of suitable type. In view of the difference in efficiency, however, liquid preparations are usually preferred. After suitable dilution they may be applied by small hand sprayers, by knapsack sprayers (especially useful with a horizontal lance attachment) or by mechanical spraying tackle of various kinds and sizes. Quite a number are available, ranging from hand-pushed wheelbarrow types to self-propelled and to tractor-drawn or tractor mounted, the pump being operated from the power-take-off. When small confined areas are involved extra dilution and the use of a watering can has much to commend it. Selective weed-killers may also be used for spot treatment of isolated weeds. Dust formulations may be applied in small quantities to individual weeds, or sprays applied by a small hand sprayer, or, again, diluted solution may be applied by means of a simple 'dropper'.

Weed control chart

This chart has been prepared from results obtained under normal field conditions.

Group 1—weeds normally controlled by a single application.
Group 2—weeds normally controlled, but more than one application may be necessary.
Group 3—no useful effect, even with repeated applications.

Name of weed	2,4-D Fenoprop	2,4-D	2,4-D Mecoprop	Mecoprop	Ioxynil & Mecoprop
Bird's-foot Trefoil *Lotus corniculatus*	2	3	2	2	2
Bulbous Buttercup *Ranunculus bulbosus*	2	2	2	2	2
Creeping Buttercup *R. repens*	1	1	1	1	1
Cat's-ear *Hypochaeris radicata*	2	1	1	2	2
Chickweed *Stellaria media*	1	2	1	1	1
Mouse-ear Chickweed *Cerastium vulgatum*	1	2	2	1	1
Cinquefoil *Potentilla reptans*	2	2	2	2	2
White Clover *Trifolium repens*	1	3	1	1	1
Coltfoot *Tussilago farfara*	3	3	3	3	3
Crowfoot *Ranunculus acris*	2	2	2	2	2
Daisy *Bellis perennis*	2	1	1	2	2

Name of weed	2,4-D Fenoprop	2,4-D	2,4-D Mecoprop	Mecoprop	Ioxynil & Mecoprop
Dandelion *Taraxacum officinalis*	2	1	1	3	3
Dove's Foot Cranesbill *Geranium molle*	2	3	2	2	2
Field Woodrush *Luzula campestris*	3	3	3	2	2
Hawk's-beard *Crepis virens*	3	1	1	3	3
Heath Bedstraw *Galium saxatile*	2	2	2	2	2
Knapweed *Centurea nigra*	3	2	3	3	3
Mouse-ear Hawkweed *Hieracium pilosella*	2	1	1	2	2
Parsley-piert *Aphanes arvensis*	3	3	3	3	2
Pearlwort *Sagina procumbens*	2	1	1	2	2
Broad-leaved Plantain *Plantago major*	2	1	1	2	2
Hoary Plantain *Plantago media*	2	1	1	2	2
Sea Plantain *Plantago maritima*	2	1	1	2	2
Ragwort *Senecio jacobea*	3	2	2	3	3
Ribwort *Plantago lanceolata*	1	1	1	1	1
Selfheal *Prunella vulgaris*	2	2	2	2	2
Silver Weed *Potentilla anserina*	2	2	2	2	2
Sorrel *Rumex* spp.	1	1	1	1	1
Speedwell *Veronica* spp.	3	3	3	3	3
Starweed *Plantago coronopus*	1	1	1	1	1
Thistles *Cirsium* spp.	2	2	2	2	2
Yarrow *Achillia millefolium*	1	3	2	1	1

Fig. 27. Lawn:
spraying.

Fig. 28. Lawn:
weed control.

Methods for control of some common weeds

Clover
Least trouble is experienced from this weed when the turf is regularly supplied with nitrogen, especially if this is in the form of sulphate of ammonia. White clover can be eradicated from turf by repeat dressings of the sulphate alone or mixed with sulphate of iron as in the 3:1:20 mixture. Blackman has attributed the reduction of clover following the use of ammonium compounds to the toxicity of the ammonium ions absorbed by the plant from the soil.

Today eradication of clover is nearly always attempted with selective weed-killers based on either Mecoprop or Fenoprop. Under good conditions, i.e. warm growing weather, a high degree of control can be obtained with sprays but the weather is not always co-operative. In practice it is best to arrange for repeat sprayings, preferably following nitrogenous fertiliser treatment, on three occasions between May and August. Creeping stems of white clover should always be raked up and mown off even if no chemical method of eradication is contemplated. Tap-rooted yellow suckling clover should be treated on the same lines, but may also be hand picked on small areas or 'spot' treated with lawn sand mixtures.

Yarrow
Perhaps the most resistant weed of turf, this species can be controlled by selective weed-killers based on Mecoprop, or a mixture of 2,4-D with Mecoprop, Dichlorprop, Fenoprop or Dicamba, though complete eradication may take more than one season. Brushing and raking up the leaves before mowing is helpful.

Plantains
All the plantains—broad-leaved, hoary, ribwort, buck's-horn and sea—are resistant to lawn sands but very susceptible to selective weed-killers which should be used for their control. The buck's-horn plantain or starweed, so common on seaside golf links, should be dealt with by all-over spraying with selective weed-killer, but as it often forms nearly a continuous covering previous manurial treatment to encourage intermingled grasses is wise, otherwise much bare ground can easily result.

Cat's-ear and dandelion
While these weeds can be dealt with by a variety of ways, spraying with selective weed-killer is advised. Cat's-ear is very susceptible. A

single treatment is not likely to eradicate all dandelions so repeat treatment may be needed.

Mouse-ear chickweed
Regular raking before mowing is helpful. The weed is controlled by using selective weed-killers based on Mecoprop or any of the 2,4-D mixtures.

Pearlwort
Perhaps this is the greatest scourge of highly managed turf, and develops so insidiously that unfortunately it is often allowed to grow into dense patches before steps are taken to deal with it. Modern selective weed-killers based on Mecoprop or Fenoprop applied at high volume rates will control it. Best results can be obtained if treatment can be given under suitable weather conditions in the months between May and August.

Veronica spp (Speedwell)
There are several species of Speedwell, but Veronica filiformis is the most serious problem in turf. Control can be achieved if applications of selective weed-killer based on Ioxynil with Mecoprop are used, preferably in the early spring before the flower heads have formed.

Weeds of sea marsh turf
By and large these can be disposed of with the selective weed-killers.

Annuals
Few annuals will resist for long the effects of constant mowing. Thus in new-sown turf annuals like groundsel, fat-hen, red-shank, garden chickweed, and spurry seldom persist, though on rich soil they can by sheer numbers and heavy growth easily threaten the existence of a new-sown turf. Gentle raking and light mowing should be done at regular intervals.

There are, however, several annuals that can prove a nuisance on established turf, for instance parsley-piert and knotweed. Usually found on light soils, parsley-piert is resistant to most selective weed-killers, but control can be expected by using the Ioxynil and Mecoprop mixture. Regular brushing and raking before mowing is important, while a strong thick growth of grass should be encouraged by manurial treatment.

Knotweed occurs on heavy land subject to puddling through use under wet conditions. It is a common weed of football fields as it is of

Fig. 29. Bent turf containing patch of Yorkshire fog.

farm gateways. Eradication is difficult. If well established in summer, repeated harrowing before mowing is important as well as hand pulling, but chemical control can be obtained using a selective weed-killer based on 2,4-D and Dicamba. The plant with its straggling stems is a prolific seeder so that soil where it has been growing is always heavily charged with seed. While spraying may dispose of one crop a succession is likely from seed in the land.

Yorkshire fog and creeping soft-grass
Patches of either of these grasses are often found in fine turf. Where the patches are small they should be removed and new turf inserted before they have time to enlarge, whilst systematic slashing and raking followed by re-seeding will do much to thin out the patches and generally reduce them to smaller proportions.

Grass growth control

Much interest has been shown in the possibility of reducing grass growth chemically, and so the amount of mowing. Maleic Hydrazide has been advocated, and is now marketed under various trade names.

Reduction in growth is quite marked, but because of direct and indirect damage, Maleic Hydrazide cannot be advised for the fine turf of lawns and greens. Where a degree of discoloration is acceptable, for instance where there is a lower standard of requirement, then the material can be useful. Roadside verges, rough areas in cemeteries, areas of waste land, and other areas where conventional mowing is difficult or costly, may be considered for treatment.

CHAPTER TWENTY-TWO

Moss

Perhaps one of the commonest weeds of neglected turf is moss, a name which is used promiscuously to cover all species. It is commonest in the autumn and winter months when the growth of grass is least and when atmospheric humidity and soil moisture are naturally greater.

True moss should not be confused with pearlwort (*Sagina procumbens*), a low-growing plant that superficially resembles it. In Scotland the word 'fog' is often applied to moss as known in England, and this term must not therefore be confused by Scottish readers with the term 'Yorkshire fog' as applied to species of *Holcus*.

Moss spreads in turf by a variety of methods that are singularly effective in ensuring colonisation of new ground. Most species produce small capsules above the leafy part of the plant which contain the dust-like spores so easily dispersed by wind, rain-splash or the action of machines. These spores germinate after alighting on a suitable substratum and produce a branched filamentous growth of simple structure (the protonema) that is the first stage in the development of the moss plant as we know it. Generally the spore sends out filaments in two directions, one remaining green and creeping along the surface of the ground, whilst the other loses its chlorophyll and forms an underground filament (a rhizoid). These filaments remain one cell in thickness. The protonema develops rapidly and may even form a tangled green felt. Small buds arise from it, developing young shoots of the adult moss plant. The rhizoids perform the same function as roots, absorbing moisture and minerals, and by developing buds or gemmæ give rise to

Fig. 30. Moss.

new aerial stems. Some of the rhizoids may also reappear on the surface to form secondary protonema.

Moss plants have a definite reproductive or sexual phase in their life history, but as it is very inconspicuous it need not be dealt with here. The various means of propagation combine to facilitate the very rapid spread of moss, and under suitable conditions the rapid colonisation of turf is hardly to be wondered at in view of the diversity of methods available.

There are many popular views as to the occurrence of moss, but it is safe to say that its presence in turf cannot be attributed to any one factor. Such factors as bad aeration, bad drainage, low fertility, high acidity, and in fact general neglect, may be predisposing causes. Popularly, moss is most often attributed to bad drainage, but it is perhaps true to say that more moss appears in turf on light, well-drained soil than under heavy wet conditions. While high acidity may favour moss it is often found under very alkaline conditions. A spongy loose surface on a green or lawn often favours the spread of moss, while undulations which are skinned by the mower soon become colonised by it. It often appears on those portions of greens that have worn thin or dried out during the growing season. Another common cause of moss prevalence is insufficient top-soil, often noticeable on lawns and greens that have been constructed from hillsides and where insufficient top-spit has been returned to the surface.

These are some of the factors covering the occurrence of moss, but it is probable that the various species respond in different manners to the varying conditions.

Examination of moss-ridden turf has shown the following species to be of common occurrence:

> *Barbula convoluta* Hedw.
> *Brachythecium rutabulum* B. & S.
> *Bryum argenteum* Hedw.
> *Bryum capillare* L.
> *Ceratodon purpureus* Brid.
> *Eurhynchium prælongum* Hook.
> *Hypnum cupressiforme* Hedw.
> *Polytrichum juniperinum* Willd.
> *Pottia truncata* Lindb.

In addition the following two species are occasionally found:

> *Campylopus flexosus* Brid.
> *Dicranum scoparium spadicium*, Boul.

Perhaps the commonest of the above species are *Ceratodon purpureus*, which has a deep velvety-green appearance, and *Hypnum cupressiforme*, which has a yellowish golden appearance rather like the golden cupressus.

The modern approach to the control of moss is best considered as a balance between cultural treatments to overcome conditions encouraging moss development, and chemical control which although extremely effective, can only be temporary in terms of length of control.

Cultural control

In treatments aimed to create conditions where moss will find difficulty in thriving, attention should be particularly made to the following points:

(i) Improvement of surface drainage; maintenance operations should seek to reduce excessive moisture remaining on the surface of the turf.

(ii) Removal of thatch; the build-up of dead organic matter forms a spongy layer that encourages water retention, and at the same time reduces the vigour of the grass.

(iii) Reduction of compaction; spiking and slitting, done as a regular maintenance procedure, improves aeration and water movement through the soil. Where thatch is present, scarification to reduce the mat of dead vegetation will also be necessary.

(iv) Reduction of shade; if possible, any obstacles that reduce the light intensity should be removed. For instance, the judicial lopping of trees casting shade, or the reduction in height of a hedge could greatly reduce shade without unduly affecting the amenities of the site.

(v) Improved grass vigour; by the use of a balanced fertiliser programme on impoverished soils, and by the liming of excessively acid soils, the grass may show an improvement in vigour. However, care is essential when applying lime to turf, as too much may encourage weed growth and invite attacks of fungal diseases such as *Ophiobolus*.

(vi) Careful use of irrigation; with modern irrigation systems now taken for granted, over-irrigation is now quite common. Most turf areas when first designed were never intended for the application of high water rates as applied by these modern systems. Irrigation is necessary in dry periods to sustain grass vigour, but excessive irrigation, unable to drain freely will have the reverse effect.

(vii) Care in mowing; turf is best mown regularly and mowings boxed off. The height of cut will be determined by the sporting activity for which the turf is being grown, but should never be lower than necessary. Mowing too closely, again, reduces grass vigour and in uneven areas tends to scalp high points, thus removing the grass completely.

(viii) Adequate pest, disease, and weed control; healthy vigorous grass will tend to eliminate competition, but areas damaged by pest or disease, or populated by weed growth will naturally tend to be replaced by moss growth.

Chemical control
Where chemical treatment to control moss is necessary, two approaches are possible:

(a) The use of lawn sands; a mixture of sulphate of ammonia and sulphate of iron together with sharp sand. This mixture is activated by moisture, the existing moss being burnt off, which can then be removed 10/14 days after treatment by scarification. Treatment is best carried out during the early spring when the grass is re-commencing growth and the soil is moist. Lack of rain after treatment will necessitate the use of irrigation equipment. Moss control is quick using lawn sands, but not long lasting, and re-infestation can rapidly occur. Commercial preparations are readily available, and should be applied strictly according to the manufacturer's instructions, but a typical mixture of:

> 3 parts sulphate of ammonia
> 1 part calcined sulphate of iron
> 10 parts sharp sand

can be prepared and applied at the rate of 4 oz per sq yd (135 g per m^2).

(b) The use of mecurous chloride (Calomel); this can be used alone, or as in some of the proprietary mixtures as a Mercurised Lawn Sand. Calomel used alone takes some time to act, and is usually applied as a wettable powder in the form of a coarse spray. Although the initial control of existing moss is slow, it will give a more long lasting control, preventing re-establishment for up to twelve months. Calomel can be mixed with sulphate of ammonia, sulphate of iron, and sand to make a Mercurised Lawn Sand for spring and summer application, and with sulphate of iron and sand for autumn and winter use.

Thus applications can be made at any time of the year, but best results are usually obtained from autumn or spring applications. Care should be taken that a Mercurised Lawn Sand containing sulphate of ammonia should not be applied in the autumn or winter, because this would have the effect of introducing nitrogen to the soil at an unsuitable time of the year.

Most mercury-based moss killers are marketed as proprietary products, and should again be applied strictly according to manufacturer's recommendations, but result usually in 20 per cent mercurous chloride being applied at the rate of $\frac{1}{2}$/1 oz per 20 sq yd (21/42 g per 20 m^2), depending on the degree of infestation.

As with most items of sports ground maintenance, the cost of moss killing can be high, often because of the large areas involved. Correct management of turf, to make a good healthy, thick sward becomes of economic importance.

CHAPTER TWENTY-THREE

Mechanical operations in turf upkeep

Until recent years rolling was almost the only mechanical operation given to turf apart from mowing, but nowadays the range of operations is much wider. Mechanical operations on turf may be grouped according to whether they deal with the surface (e.g. rolling, raking, brushing, and pricking), or the sub-surface (e.g. forking and spiking). One might perhaps also include mowing in the first group but it has already been dealt with in a previous chapter.

Surface operations

Rolling

That most lawns, greens, and sports grounds suffer from over-rolling is fortunately now being realised more and more, so that the tendency is to reduce the amount of rolling and to open up the ground after its ill effects. Most swards receive sufficient compression from the feet or from the rolling action of the modern roller type of mower, but on little-used turf or where a side-wheel machine is used, some rolling will of course be necessary. On no account should the roller be used when the surface is wet or the grass so thin that the roller rides upon the surface of the soil.

Perhaps the amateur uses his roller mostly for the purpose of removing irregularities, so that he may avoid skinning during cutting. Irregularities, apart from those following bad laying of turf or by churning up of the surface on sports grounds, are usually attributable to the activity of earthworms which during the autumn and winter season throw up casts, so leaving a surface that cannot be properly mown the following spring. The improvement of such a surface is best attained firstly by the removal of the earthworms and then by regular top-dressings to fill up the depressions. In modern practice it is customary for most of the trueing process to be done by top-dressing to fill up the hollows and not by rolling to compress the lumps. Final light rolling to put a 'face' on the turf then follows.

The amount of rolling given to a turf must be determined largely by the purpose for which the turf is intended. Thus a cricket wicket which requires a true non-resilient surface must be rolled more frequently and heavily than a golf green, where some degree of resiliency is desirable. For most practical purposes on lawns, a 2-cwt (100-kg) roller is sufficient. For sports grounds, rollers of greater weight are used. Where occasional light rolling is necessary (say on seedling turf) a wide wooden roller weighing about 1 cwt (50 kg) is satisfactory. Not only does over-rolling result in a bad physical condition of the soil but it leads to the formation of a hard caked layer, especially in dry weather and creates conditions more favourable to such weeds as broad-leaved plantain and knotweed.

Newly-sown turf must never be heavily rolled, or the young plants will be seriously hampered. Rolling should be more frequently carried out on light land than on heavy, and after frosty periods an occasional roll on a dry surface is beneficial in re-consolidating the turf and aiding the start of new growth in the spring. Moderate rolling with due regard to weather and moisture content of the soil is all that is necessary for general lawn purposes.

Raking, Brushing, and Harrowing

The value of raking as a means of renovating matted or neglected turf is well recognised but often forgotten even by those who are most anxious to improve their turf. Where it is very matted, raking the turf is the best preliminary to further treatment, because it pulls out the tangle of dead leaves from around the base of the grass shoots. Raking also fulfils the function of punishing small weeds and pulling out the runners of creeping plants like clover. Providing moss has not become too thickly felted, raking facilitates subsequent operations for control. Often in neglected turf creeping types of grass form a 'nap', which can be much reduced by this simple procedure. Raking also assists the entrance of air, moisture, and mineral matters, and enables fertiliser to be utilised more advantageously by the sward.

A garden rake with well-sharpened teeth is effective, but there are on the market various patterns of wire rake that are very valuable for surface treatment. Where raking is to be carried out as a routine operation for checking weeds like chickweed and clover, or preventing the formation of a nap, there is a modified wire rake, supported on wheels with which the operator can vary the pressure of the prongs on the turf. Various moss rakes are also available. Quite an effective tool can be made by driving a row of nails through an old wooden hay rake from which the teeth have been sawn off. A lath screwed down over the nail-heads prevents them being forced out.

Another surface treatment consists of scarifying with brushes containing steel-wire bristles or spring-steel teeth, this operation fulfilling the dual purpose of tearing out decaying organic matter and of brushing up the shoots of the grasses so that they meet the mower.

For large lawns and greens powered scarifiers are now available at various prices. The principle is a high-speed reel fitted with flat blade-like knives adjustable for depth of working.

Drag brushing is an operation of value in producing fine turf, but commonly neglected. It is particularly useful after the turf has been dressed with fine compost, because pulling the drag broom across the turf causes more top-dressing to be left in the hollow than on the humps, so leading to truer conditions. This operation also helps to drag up the shoots of chickweed and similar shallow-rooting weeds so that they may receive greater punishment from the mowers.

Coir or steel-link mats are also effective for working in top-dressings and trueing the surface. Under wet conditions, however, a coir mat is inclined to cause 'balling' up of the dressing and the steel-link mat is most widely used. For pulling up low-lying shoots of grasses the wire rake and drag broom are more effective.

The amount of spike harrowing that can be given to fine turf is strictly limited, although there are excellent small harrows on the market for the purpose. Vigorous harrowing of turf is often not practicable unless it is being broken in from old pasture, but there are machines that are provided with sets of small knives that slit the turf and so let in moisture and fertiliser dressings. By using a tool of this type the mat of fibre is opened up yet retained and there is little interruption in the use of the turf. Machines with knives of this type are also remarkably effective for punishing creeping weeds such as yarrow and clover, and marked reductions in the amount of these weeds have been noted following their practical use.

On less closely-mown turf, e.g. sports grounds and race tracks, the grass land harrow should be used in spring to tear out dead matter and smooth the surface. Rakes and stiff drag brushes, specifically designed for turf, are available for tractor haulage or for attachment to the hydraulic linkage—an arrangement that greatly facilitates manipulation on confined areas.

Switching
This operation is carried out with a 15 to 20 ft (4·5 to 6 m) bamboo cane, strong steel-wire or glass-fibre tip mounted in a suitable handle. It is very useful in dispelling dew before mowing, in scattering worm casts, and working in dressings, while it is also beneficial in giving partial control of certain turf diseases.

Pricking
Matted or over-consolidated turf also benefits from other forms of surface treatment such as shallow pricking by means of rollers studded with spikes. The commonest type consists of an elm or steel roller into the surface of which spikes from 1 to $1\frac{1}{2}$ in (2·5 to 3·7 cm) long have been inserted. They are arranged diagonally around the rollers and are capable of producing a large number of shallow holes. Better penetration is obtained by pushing such an implement than by pulling, but usually the lack of weight coupled with solidity of the turf prevent more than $\frac{1}{4}$ to $\frac{1}{2}$ in (0·63 to 1·27 cm) penetration. By rocking the implement backwards and forwards maximum penetration of the spikes can be obtained, but the hole produced is oval and not circular. Such an operation is remarkably effective in rejuvenating neglected turf, and as a preliminary to fertiliser treatment and top-dressing.

A modern version is motorised to give forward motion. By holding the machine against the pull of the motor a tilthing effect can be obtained for re-seeding, etc.

Pricking is a useful aid when artificial watering is necessary, since each hole acts as a small reservoir and aids the penetration of the water.

While pricking in this manner is effective for aerating the immediate surface of the turf it does nothing to affect the sub-surface layers which are often consolidated by excessive rolling or trampling. Deeper penetrating tools must be used for this purpose.

Sub-surface operations

Forking
This is best carried out in the autumn and winter months when it is least likely to cause inconvenience, and on golf greens a portion of the surface is left unforked for a time to maintain play. Unfortunately forking is often imperfectly carried out, but more of it could advantageously be done, especially on heavier soils or on greens where a

Fig. 31. A comparison of two turves. *Left*: from unforked turf. *Right*: Taken from immediately around a fork hole.

Fig. 32. The development of new roots in a tubular fork hole.

Fig. 33. Lawn: Aeration, hollow tining.

Fig. 34. Luting off the cores—hollow tining.

thick mat of fibre has developed. The compressing action of a player's foot on turf is quite considerable, and amounts to approximately 7 lb per sq in (4·4 kg per 10 cm²), which means a pressure of about 1,000 lb per sq ft (5,000 kg per m²) and is equivalent to a $4\frac{1}{2}$ cwt (225 kg) roller 3 ft (91 cm) wide making a contact of about 2 in (5 cm). Forking is one of the best means of relieving such compression. Until recent years when special forks with tapered and collared tines appeared, forking has always been carried out with an ordinary garden fork or a graip fork either by inserting it straight into the soil to the full length of the prongs and drawing it out on the same line, or secondly, by exercising leverage after insertion. Prising up of the turf in this way is at times found beneficial, but is apt to break the roots and leave an uneven surface, especially if the ground is stony. On light or medium soils straight in and out forking is usually sufficient as it breaks up compacted layers or pan, much as sub-soiling in agriculture.

In 1919, William Paul of Paisley introduced the first hollow tine fork. This implement (and others like it) removes cores of soil and turf, and has been widely adopted in lawn and green upkeep. The fork, though slower to use than a solid one, leaves a wider and more permanent hole, and on heavy soils and matted greens the removal of this core is especially beneficial because it enables top-dressings of more suitable material to be worked in. Hollow tine forks must be used with care on light sandy soils because there is a tendency for the sides of the hole to collapse before filling has taken place, thus leaving a pitted uneven surface. It should be inserted to a depth of at least 6 in at 4 in centres (15 cm at 10 cm centres).

Several modifications of the hollow tine fork have been put on the market, and in one of them the tines revolve, so aiding penetration, while in another the tubular tines have been replaced by a set of spiral tines, which remove about a quarter the amount of soil taken out by the tubular fork. Another variation is a fork with bayonet-shaped tines with which a deep pear-shaped slit may be made below the surface, yet leaving only a small slit upon the surface.

Besides relieving consolidation, forking has other important functions, and it has been found to be beneficial in combating drought. Thus in a certain experiment turf forked one year was found to be more drought resistant than an adjacent unforked area the following season when a drought was experienced. The soil on the forked plot in the dry period contained 14·6 per cent of moisture, whilst that on the unforked plot contained only 6·6 per cent. The grass on the forked plot was more vigorous and revived at a greater rate when rain fell.

Forking is also beneficial in helping rain penetration after drought, but often the soil is too hard for anything but surface pricking. This as well as deeper spiking should continue after a drought breaks and as the soil begins to soften. This is most important where there is a thick mat of fibre. Matted turf is apt to act like a sponge, so preventing water penetrating to the soil below. An unforked turf receiving rain and artificial watering contained 9·8 per cent of moisture, whereas the soil on an adjacent plot that had been hollow tine forked and that received the same amount of water contained 15·7 per cent of moisture. This turf was much greener in colour. Forking also favours root development, new fibre roots forming around the sides of the hole and running into the lower levels. No doubt this partly accounts for the increased drought resistance of forked turf. Quantitative estimations show that forking also improves the resiliency of turf even though no leverage has been exerted. Preliminary experiments have given no conclusive data that forking influences nitrification or the relative changes of the ammoniacal and nitrate nitrogen in the soil, though future work may reveal some connexion.

Spiking
The value of pricking and forking being so generally recognised, it is only natural that engineers and others should endeavour to produce machines capable of carrying out the work with greater ease and higher speed. Hand forking is not only hard work but it is also slow work, and as a result several types of spiking machine have appeared on the market to meet these objections. The difficulty in designing a suitable machine capable of spiking turf to a depth of 4 to 6 in (10 to 15 cm) is that as the machine moves forward the tine in being withdrawn tears the turf, so leaving a ragged slit with a raised lip, instead of a circular more or less vertical hole. Any machine designed on a rotary system has this disadvantage, and although in some instances a torn hole would not cause any inconvenience, in most circumstances on fine turf it is important that the hole should be made cleanly and without tearing. To surmount this difficulty spiking machines have been evolved with tines fixed to swivelling bars. This enables the tines to strike the turf vertically and to leave the soil on the same path as the machine moves forward. In one of these machines the penetration is secured by the addition of heavy weights, whilst in another the penetration is achieved by the adoption of a principle that in reality gives a hammer-blow action sufficient to drive the tines into the turf. In effect there is a high penetration-to-weight ratio.

No spiking machine for deep penetration is much use in dry weather when the soil is hard or very compressed, and to get over this difficulty the best machines are planned so that they may be fitted with shorter tines until the soil conditions become soft enough to enable longer tines to penetrate. Flat or chisel-shaped tines are finding much favour especially for summer use in fine turf.

The production of machines to speed up hollow tine forking has received attention, and various models exist. Hand operated hollow tine machines, incorporating the hammer-blow principle and spring tensioned swivel bars, are capable of removing cores about 3 in (7·6 cm) long without tearing the turf. Although substantially deeper penetration could be obtained by increased weight, these machines have reached a compromise between weight and power. Greater weight would be found impractical for continuous hand operation while power propulsion would greatly increase cost.

The machine can be called multi-purpose. The spiking unit is easily removed, and other lawn implements (brush, wire rake, slitter, roller) can be substituted.

The machines referred to above are all hand operated, but naturally much ingenuity has been exercised by engineers in devising wholly powered spikers. Various principles have been tried, and there are now several machines currently on the market. These involve a much higher outlay than hand equipment. In one larger machine, the tines (solid or hollow) are power driven into the turf and give clean holes 3 or 4 in (7·6 to 10 cm) deep as a continuous process. It is very often used for contract work. In another self-propelled type, when operated, the machine rides on its tines, the land wheels being raised. Penetration is caused by its own weight. It gives clean holes about $3\frac{1}{2}$ in (8·8 cm) deep (solid and hollow tines are available). A recent addition on the market is a machine using 'spoons' to loosen the soil beneath the turf and to scoop out cores of soil. The soil which has packed around the core has room to expand, and openings are made from the surface to allow water and air to enter the soil.

Spiking units for attachment to power units already in use for other purposes, like mowing, have also been devised and follow the general principles of hammer action and swivel bars.

While these and self-propelled machines are indeed valuable in turf maintenance they do not solve the problem of dealing with larger areas like sports fields, race tracks, and the like. Spiking is becoming more and more a routine on such areas as a means of relieving compaction, aiding surface moisture penetration and facilitating the recovery of turf that has taken heavy wear and tear. Tractor-drawn units on the gang principle have been evolved. In one form the tines are mounted on the corners of hexagonal plates; these are free to rotate

and the whole outfit is sufficiently mobile and flexible to follow undulations of the land. The tines, both pointed and chisel shaped, are
capable of 6 in (15 cm) penetration, and hollow tines are also available.
These are of chief use on golf courses with heathy matted turf as an
aid to water entry.

Large units giving from 8 to 9 in (20 to 23 cm) penetration are also
available. Both this model and the lighter one mentioned above can
either be obtained mounted on land wheels for tractor haulage or for
direct attachment to the hydraulic 3-point linkage of the tractor. This
system facilitates turning at the boundaries of the site.

CHAPTER TWENTY-FOUR

Artificial watering

It has already been pointed out that some 80 per cent of the weight of grass clippings removed from a lawn consists of water. Not only is soil moisture removed in this manner but there is a constant loss through transpiration by the grass leaves and by direct evaporation from the surface. Losses by evaporation are greater on a thin open turf than when there is a dense thick pile of grass to shade the surface soil.

In summer losses of moisture may in the aggregate be in excess of precipitation thus leading to drying out. Water then becomes the limiting factor to grass growth even though plant foods in the soil may be quite adequate. This often accounts for the poor response to fertilisers applied in the summer months.

Attention to the water needs of lawns and greens is therefore important, and is worthy of greater care than is usually accorded. There are some grasses, like the fescues, which as a result of their in-rolled leaves are remarkably resistant to drought and show a marked capacity for quick recovery, but other grasses are not so resistant and therefore their water needs must be satisfied more quickly. Thus, bent grass being less resistant than fescue requires artificial watering sooner if it is not to become very parched in dry seasons. Annual meadow-grass soon shows discolouration in dry weather.

Turf growing on lime-deficient acid soils is more susceptible to drought than turf on alkaline soils, while swards on thin sandy soils or under very intensively managed conditions, where root development is often poor, soon require artificial watering in the event of prolonged dry weather. Failure to satisfy this need is often a cause of weed invasion or weed increase.

Many theories exist as to what constitutes the best method and the right conditions for watering. Some people hold the view that watering should only be done early in the morning, others contend that watering should not be done until the evening, while a third group prefer it to be done throughout the day. Often it is said that the water used should not be cold but air-warm, and occasionally it is stated that the turf must always be warm when the water is applied. Ideally no doubt very cold water is less suitable than air-warm water, but it is certainly better than no water at all. Watering in the sun is not usually regarded as the best practice, although no harm appears to result provided the surface is not allowed to dry out and bake in the hot sun.

Most people worry so much about these details and similar ones that they fail to realise the importance of giving sufficient water. Frequently it is found that the water applied has merely penetrated about $\frac{1}{4}$ in (6·35 mm). Such half-hearted attention is apt to lead to the encouragement of moss and pearlwort and to the development of a much shortened root system. Watering, if it is to be done, must be done adequately, and as a rough guide, a minimum of at least 2 gal (9 l), but preferably 3 to 4 gal (13 to 18 l), should be applied to each sq yd (0·94 m²) whenever the operation is carried out. Unless applied slowly and given time to soak in, much water may be lost by run-off especially on ridges or sloping surfaces. The frequency of watering will depend, of course, upon the intensity of the drought and the water-retaining capacity of the soil, but it is not uncommon to find that watering is necessary two or three times a week. The aim should be to ensure saturation of the soil to a depth of several inches (cm). Inspection of the turf by removing a wedge with a knife is helpful in deciding whether or not sufficient water has been given. Often there are difficulties in the way of supplying sufficient water owing to inadequate natural supply or to curtailment of local water supplies. In dry weather, under these conditions, it is much preferable that a single thorough saturation be given rather than several very light sprinkles. Adequate watering is of far greater importance than any consideration of its temperature or the time or method of application.

Most of those responsible for turf upkeep delay artificial watering as long as possible in the fervent hope that rain will fall. The sod may therefore be much dried out before the first application. Under these circumstances it is always more difficult to get good penetration and it is always best to commence watering before the effects of drought have become obvious. Again, examination of the soil by cutting out a small section will give a guide as to the soil moisture and when watering should commence. High spots rather than hollows should be examined.

While poor penetration of artificial water may be due to allowing the soil to dry out, it may also be caused by a bad mechanical condition of the surface layer. In either event improved entry may be attained by pricking before the watering. This is best done by stabbing the surface with a sharp fork or by means of a spiked roller or some other form of spiking machine. Although 2 gal of water per sq yd (9 l per m^2) has been mentioned as a guide it will be wasted unless it reaches the grass roots.

From the above the following general guiding principles in watering may be enumerated:

1. Water before the effects of drought are obvious.
2. Assist penetration by pricking or spiking.
3. Water copiously.
4. Avoid watering in bright sunlight.

As regards the nature or quality of the water best suited for grass, most lawn owners have to take what they can get, but if there is any choice in the matter very hard water should be avoided. While no experimental data exist as to the relative merits of different qualities of water, practical experience indicates that hard water is apt to encourage weeds, like pearlwort, and earthworms. Water with a low degree of hardness (soft water) appears to be preferable.

The method of applying water to turf is in part governed by the source of supply. On small lawns the usual method is by means of a hose or small sprinkler. When using a hose a fine nozzle is necessary, otherwise top-dressings may be swilled away and the surface of the soil may be opened up. Adjustable hose nozzles may be obtained to ensure a finer spray. In deciding upon whether to use a sprinkler or a hose, attention must be directed to the nature of the terrain. On undulating ground or irregular banks, the hose is to be preferred. Where there are regular banks, however, and funds permit, spray lines can be used to deal with the area systematically. As a rule, sprinklers provide a finer spray than the hose jet and are much less expensive in labour since one man can attend to several or even leave them unattended for a time.

Before purchasing a sprinkler it is well to ascertain the pressure of water available since each sprinkler is designed for certain pressure limits. For mains supplies, an inquiry to the local water authorities will elicit the information, or the pressure may be tested by a gauge.

When supplies are delivered by a pump, the makers will give the information, but when the supply is by gravity from a cistern, the head may be calculated by allowing 1 lb per sq in pressure (6·89 kN/m²) for each 2 ft 4 in (71 cm) height above hydrant level. Thus a cistern 23 ft (7 m) above a tap will give a pressure of about 10 lb per sq in (68·87 kN/m²), while 46 ft (14·01 m) will give about 20 lb (137·74 kN/m²). These figures make no allowance, however, for pipe friction, which may cause considerable loss in a long run of small bore pipe or where there are many bends or obstructions. Pipe friction increases with greater speed of flow.

Sprinklers are designed by the manufacturers to give optimum efficiency when working at a certain pressure, and they may be classed as very low, below 12 lb (82·72 kN/m²); low from 12 to 20 lb (82·72 to 137·74 kN/m²); medium from 20 to 40 lb (137·74 to 275·48 kN/m²); and high, above 40 lb (275·48 kN/m²).

Apart from the consideration of pressure however, it is necessary to decide upon the amount of money available, and to ensure that the sprinkler will fulfill certain requirements. Thus, to be efficient, a sprinkler must be simple to work, it must cover the maximum area with even distribution, it must create a fine spray, and if it is a revolving type, must turn slowly to reduce wear and secure the maximum penetration. Further, a good sprinkler must be capable of being left untended, should be easily transportable, and should not cause pondage by leaking.

It is not possible to mention individually the wide range of rotary sprinklers available on the market to-day, but some idea of their capabilities may be derived from the following figures. A rotary sprinkler with wide arms will operate at as low a pressure as 6 lb (41·36 kN/m²), spraying a circle of 30 ft (9·14 m) diameter and delivering 130 gal (590 l) per hour. A similar sprinkler at 10 lb (68·87 kN/m²) pressure will water a circle 45 ft (13·71 m) and deliver rather more than double the above volume of water per hour. At 40 lb (275·48 kN/m²) pressure the same sprinkler will cover an 80 ft (24·38 m) diameter circle with 850 gal (3864 l) per hour; and at 100 lb (688·79 kN/m²) will water a circle of 120 ft (36 m) diameter, applying 1500 to 1800 gal (6818 to 8181 l) per hour.

The method of obtaining revolutions on the arms of the sprinkler is secured either by the back thrust of the water or by the impingement of the jet on a bobbing arm or on a small paddle geared on to the movable jet. These methods ensure the rotation of the spray.

Another type of sprinkler that has received some publicity operates after the manner of a gun. The water is delivered into a pressure cylinder partially filled with air and on reaching a certain pressure the water is released and thrown a considerable distance. At the same time the jet is given a slight turn. With this apparatus an area of about one acre can be watered without moving the 'gun'.

Most revolving sprinklers, when operating in still air, cover a circular area, which is a disadvantage on a rectangular or square area as the corners may be missed. At least two makes, fitted with oscillators, deliver a fan-shaped spray over an arc thus in theory covering a rectangular area—wind movement usually upsets this!

For rectangular areas spray lines are now commonly used, the jets being set to cover a width of 50 to 60 ft (15 to 18 m). These lines are made up in lengths, and there are two types, the fixed type in which the jets are inserted in such a way that a wide area is covered (usually the joints between the lengths are flexible so that the line can be arranged as desired), and the rigid type fitted with an oscillator which ensures that the jets shall be thrown backwards and forwards over a half-circle to cover a 60-ft (18-m) width. The cost of such spray lines depends upon the mounting and length, while lengths from 300 to 600 ft (90 to 180 m) can be arranged. Such lines are very largely adopted on tennis courts either on the ground or permanently fixed to the framework of the surrounding netting. They can be most useful on bowling greens. They have also been extensively used on racecourses but in many cases have been superseded by one or other of the self-travelling types now in production.

Another system of sprinkling provides sets of concealed jets below the ground, and these, when the water is turned on, pop up in a telescopic manner and spray the turf.

For those unable to utilise a mains water supply there are many types of portable or stationary pump on the market, and while they may be of little interest for the garden lawn they are being extensively adopted by sports and golf clubs when it is desired to provide an independent supply from a stream, pond, or well. In drawing from a pond or stream the slight risk of introducing weed seeds can largely be avoided by keeping the suction vent well below the surface either as a fixture or supported on a raft.

Although many golf clubs and large sports clubs have a running supply of mains water at convenient hydrants it is often the case that use of the water is banned by the local authority during the summer months when rainfall is low and evaporation high, i.e. at just the time it is most needed to ensure a sound and pleasing turf for the holiday season. This state of affairs has led many clubs, considering the installation of running water, to explore the possibilities of permanent pumping stations at nearby ponds or rivers or of artesian wells from which water can be delivered to the hydrants either direct under pressure or by gravity after being pumped to an elevated storage tank. Electrically driven centrifugal pumps have much in their favour for this type of work. The type of scheme to adopt naturally depends on local circumstances.

With a private plant not only is the recurring cost of the water avoided, but the supply may be used at will for watering, worming, application of fungicides or dissolved fertiliser dressings.

As regards piping, it is usual to employ a $\frac{3}{4}$ in (19 mm) hose, but a $\frac{1}{2}$ in (12 mm) is suitable for small supplies. Until recent years, braided rubber hose pipes have been used, and indeed are still available. Although highly efficient, rubber hose is heavy to handle. Hose of a Polythene 'Alkathene' and other plastic materials have to a large extent replaced rubber hose. Synthetic hose pipes are extremely resistant to the corrosive effects of fertilisers and soils, are much lighter than rubber and therefore easier to move about. The patent couplings now available are advised as they are instantaneous and save much trouble and inconvenience in dealing with separate lengths of pipe. Interchangeability of unions is, of course, most important.

CHAPTER TWENTY-FIVE

Earthworm inhibition and eradication

It is often a firm belief that the earthworm is a desirable, even essential inhabitant of lawns and greens. While no doubt its burrowing activities are valuable in stirring up the soil, providing aeration, improving the surface drainage and reducing consolidation, the habit of voiding the soil swallowed on to the surface as casts introduces a disadvantage that more than counterbalances any benefit. Even if it be conceded that earthworms are beneficial in opening up the soil, one must also concede the fact that present-day intensive management does not call for this help, since it can be provided much more thoroughly and uniformly by mechanical means. The soft squelchy and muddy surface found on turf in the autumn and winter seasons, followed by an uneven surface for mowing, can nearly always be attributed to the earthworm. Besides untrueing the surface of turf, and making it soft and sticky, the 'pan-caking' of the casts by walking upon them or rolling them down results in a thin open sward in which bent (*Agrostis*) is at a distinct dis-advantage as compared with the less desirable species like rye-grass.

Bit by bit information is accumulating about the habits and life histories of common earthworms. Their numbers are normally greater on moist loam soils and those rich in decomposing organic matter; they are much fewer and often absent under very acid conditions. It is said that breeding takes place mainly in spring and early autumn when high air temperature and humidity, as well as soil moisture, appear to favour activity near the surface. In dry and cold conditions the worms are found deeper in the soil and hence are difficult to expel artificially. Darwin estimated that the earthworm population of an acre (0·4 ha) of pasture consisted of 53,000 individuals weighing 356 lb (158·75 kg), and capable of moving to the surface 14·58 tons of soil per annum, in the form of casts. In one deworming experiment on infested turf at St Ives, an average yield of 306 worms per 6 sq yd (60 per m²) was obtained (20 estimations). The average weight of a single worm in the experiment was 0·7965 g, giving the total weight of worms per acre (0·4 ha) as 433 lb (196·4 kg). This experiment was done in spring, and when repeated in the autumn on an adjacent area only about one-third the above number of earthworms was extracted. Counts of casts on worm-ridden turf have given an average of 57 casts per sq yd (68 per m²) over 25 counts in a period of 18 months, with extremes of 22 and 100.

Many lawns show steady annual deterioration through failure to eradicate the earthworm, and the effect of their removal is at once shown in a finer, denser sward with a cleaner surface, and if the sward is used for games, in greater accuracy and uniformity. The elimination of worms from golf greens and fairways has done more towards making the game of golf enjoyable on heavy land in winter than any other factor.

It is usual to find that worm-ridden turf is also weed-ridden, since the bare places left by the casts are resting places for wind-borne seeds of weeds and coarse grasses. Also, worm casts often bring buried weed seeds to the surface.

As with turf weeds, earthworm inhibition and earthworm eradication must be treated as two separate aspects of the same problem. Before discussing earthworm eradication it is desirable to say something about the species found in turf and to indicate the way in which management has an effect upon earthworm invasion and activity.

Earthworm species

Investigations on the species, habits, relative proportions, and numbers of earthworms in soils below pastures have been carried out. It has been shown that there are 25 species and about 10 varieties or sub-species in Britain. Soil temperature and soil moisture have a marked effect on activity and cast production while the former history and soil texture markedly influence total numbers as well as relative numbers of the species present. It seems probable that two species only are responsible for cast formation in pastures, namely *Allolobophora nocturna* and *A. longa*. Work on the species and proportions of each in the turf experimental plots at St Ives Research Station has been done by Jefferson, who has identified the following:

Allolobophora calignosa f. *typica* Savigny.
A. calignosa Sav f. *trapezoides* Ant. Duges.
A. chlorotica Sav.
A. terrestris Sav f. *longa* Ude.
Octolasium cyaneum Sav.
O. lacteum Orley.
Lumbricus castaneus Sav.
L. rubellus Hoff.
L. terrestris Linn.
L. festivus Sav.
Eisenia rosea Sav f. *typica*
Eisenia venetia Sav f. *typica* and f. *hortensis*.
Dendrobaena subrubecunda Eisen.

The last three were found on infrequent occasions. The species *Allolobophora nocturna* has not been found at St Ives and it appears that casting is due entirely to *A. longa*, indeed this species would seem to be the chief enemy of the greenkeeper at any rate in the Midlands, north of England, and south of Scotland. It is found in a wide range of soils though it is most abundant on heavy loams. At St Ives it is abundant on plots having a pH greater than 5·5, mainly those that have received lime or lime-containing fertilisers. Below pH 5·5 the proportion of *A. longa* to other species falls off and the number of individuals is less. The species, however, is rarely dominant at St Ives, the distinction being held either by *A. calignosa* or one of two species of *Lumbricus—rubellus* or *festivus*. It is estimated that the population of earthworms in a plot that has received lime and a compound fertiliser since 1930 is in the order of from 360,000 to 400,000 to the acre (0·4 ha). The following is an average percentage of the earthworms removed, over a period of two years, from this plot:

	per cent
Allolobophora calignosa	48
A. terrestris longa	18
L.festivus	13
L. rubellus	9
L. terrestris	9
L. castaneus	1
Eisenia rosea	1
E. venetia	1

As the pH of this soil falls, the four species of *Lumbricus* take the place of *A. longa*. Some acid plots free from casts on the surface still have quite a high earthworm population.

Earthworm inhibition

Studies on the influence of management upon earthworm invasion and activity have indicated that mowing, top-dressing, fertiliser and sulphate of iron treatments all have an effect on the re-invasion of worm-free turf and upon activity. Thus mowing trials have shown that the height of cut influences worm invasion. On an area of worm-free turf where three different heights of mowing were maintained on separate strips for a number of seasons invasion was greatest on the longest mown plots and least on the shortest; for example, on the average there were 5 casts per sq yd (0·94 m²) where the grass was mown at $\frac{1}{8}$ in (3·17 mm) height, as against 12 for $\frac{1}{4}$ in (6·35 mm), and 15 for $\frac{3}{4}$ in (19·05 mm). In further mowing experiments it was found that on an area to which the cuttings were always returned earthworm casts amounted to an average of 15 per sq yd, while on the corresponding area from which the cuttings were always removed in the box, the average was 7 casts. In addition, the area to which the cuttings were returned was softer, moister, and contained slightly more organic matter, and presumably this condition favoured earthworm activity. It should be clearly pointed out that the number of casts formed can only be taken as a measure of activity and not necessarily the total number of earthworms present. Presumably, however, there is a direct relationship between number of casts and the population of cast-forming species.

Observations have indicated that heavy dressings of organic materials like rape or castor meal encourage earthworm activity, and that materials like peat have the opposite effect. Again, dressings containing lime favour invasion. Thus half the area of a weed-free bent lawn was treated once a year with sea sand containing 4·26 per cent of lime in the form of shell, while the other half of the area received sharp inland lime-free sand. After a period of four years, during which a total of approximately $5\frac{1}{2}$ oz (155·91 g) of calcium carbonate had been given as shell, per sq yd, it was found that the number of casts on this area was almost double that on the inland sand plots, average figures being 8 and 4·6 casts per sq yd respectively. Again, experimental plots that have received lime show the same phenomenon. For example, the plots receiving sulphate of ammonia periodically and no liming for a number of years had no casts, while plots receiving equivalent nitrogen in the form of nitro-chalk (48 per cent $CaCO_3$) the number of casts was 15·4 per sq yd; there was also an increase in weeds. Where plots had been receiving regular applications of sulphate of ammonia with sulphate of iron no casts were found, but plots similarly treated and receiving annual dressings of lime had over 30 worm casts per sq yd. When superphosphate was given with sulphate of ammonia the worm-free condition was maintained, while the addition of lime to the programme of treatment led to earthworm invasion represented by over 30 casts per sq yd. Nitrate of soda had similar effects.

Other experiments have shown that sulphate of iron used in conjunction with fertilisers that are not favourable to earthworm activity is beneficial in assisting control. Where, however, nitrogenous fertilisers favourable to earthworm activity were used in conjunction with sulphate of iron the result was to counteract the beneficial effects of the sulphate of iron

Ammonium salts with or without sulphate of iron have been found not only to prevent invasion but to reduce the numbers of casts on un-wormed turf. Thus counts have shown in one instance 2·7 casts per sq yd where sulphate of ammonia and sulphate of iron have been used, against 29·3 where the mixture had not been applied. Sulphate of iron alone also reduced activity on worm-ridden turf. For example 10 oz (283 g) of sulphate of iron in small amounts applied over four seasons reduced the range of worm casts counts from 20—40 per sq yd to 2—20, while an application of 13·5 oz (382·71 g) for the same period reduced the range of casts to 1—4 per sq yd. The variation is due to differences in the weather conditions between sample dates and the consequent fluctuations in activity. Some of the variation is due to averaging the figures for simplicity.

It may be concluded from the records given above that the kind of top-dressing, method of cutting (both in regard to height and the return of the cuttings), and the type of fertiliser treatment influences worm invasion and even worm reduction.

Methods of earthworm eradication

The principle involved in earthworm eradication is either to apply a liquid that will penetrate the soil and act as an expellent, or to apply a toxic material that will destroy the earthworms in the soil without necessarily bringing them to the surface. Liquid expellents may or may not also be killers. With liquid materials it is necessary to choose weather conditions that are warm and mild, when the earthworms are working near the surface and the expellent in solution reaches the earthworms by seepage and by flowing down the burrows. Generally, earthworm eradication is carried out in spring or autumn. There are a number of materials commonly used and a description of the methods follows.

Fig. 35. Earthworm invasion. *Left*: plot receiving regular dressing of nitro-chalk, invaded by earthworms. *Right*: plot receiving sulphate of ammonia at equivalent rate of nitrogen.

Mowrah Meal

This used to be the most widely used material, forming the basis of most proprietary worm killers. It is derived from the beans of an Indo-malay tree, known as *Bassia latifolia*, which are used as a source of oil. The residue after the extraction of the oil contains about 1 per cent of a sapo-glucoside known as mowrin, and it is this compound that confers worm-killing properties. The meal is applied in the dry form to the surface of the turf at from 6 to 8 oz per sq yd (200 to 270 g per m²) and is then copiously watered in. Frothing takes place and the mowrin is dissolved. At least 1 gal of water to the sq yd (4·5 l to m²) is necessary, but more should be given if possible. It is a common experience of practical greenkeepers and groundsmen that water applied under pressure is more effective than water applied, say, from a watering can. The earthworms rapidly come to the surface where most die.

Mowrah Meal unfortunately does not maintain the turf in worm-free condition for longer than 18 months at the outside, and in many cases for a very much shorter period than that. The material does not store well, and if allowed to become damp soon loses its properties. It should not be used for de-worming lawns where any of the solution or material is likely to reach fish ponds, as it is toxic to fish. Mowrah Meal contains about 3 per cent of Nitrogen.

The material is now difficult to obtain. In addition, the laborious method of application, involving the sweeping up and disposal of the dead worms, the very short control period and the introduction of better materials have resulted in Mowrah Meal losing favour as a worm control.

Among other materials that have been used in past years but are no longer used for various reasons are Tea Seed Meal, Perchloride of Mercury (Corrosive Sublimate); Copper Sulphate (Bluestone) and Potassium Permanganate.

Derris

This well known insecticide, although now losing its popularity, has been used extensively as a worm killer, but results obtained have been very variable. Thus a powder containing 0·5 per cent rotenone (the active principle) at 2 oz per sq yd (67 g per m²) has proved to be effective, killing the worms underground, but the period of control in some cases may be as low as three months.

Lead Arsenate

The use of lead arsenate for the control of soil pests is well established. It has a disadvantage that it is classed as a poison though it is almost insoluble in water. It is still popular, and used mainly on golf courses, but because of its poisonous qualities, not often used elsewhere. It has the advantage that it can be applied in the dry form and is therefore most useful where there is no supply of water.

The rate of application should be $1\frac{1}{2}$ to 2 oz per sq yd (50 to 70 g per m^2), the material being best applied at a time when the earthworms are near the surface and active. The material does not damage the grass, though at times a retardation of growth has been observed. At times the lead arsenate is slow to act, but at others quite marked results have been seen in as short a period as 10 or 11 days. Usually it requires a period of 2 to 3 months for any marked control to take place. The earthworms do not come to the surface and from 90 to 95 cent control, as judged by casts, is usual. Should any casts form on the treated turf they are always very small. The material is usually effective for 5 to 6 years, but cases are known where there has been immunity for upwards of ten years.

Lead arsenate powder is best applied either in neat form through a small lawn distributor or mixed with a bulking agent like coke breeze. It should be left for the rain to wash in. As it is a fine powder, it need hardly be said that it should not be applied in a wind. Lead arsenate is relatively harmless to poultry, but there have been cases in this country in which dead rabbits have been found in proximity to treated turf immediately after application. Although instances are known of lead arsenate being applied while sheep were grazing without harmful results, it is recommended that stock should be kept off until the material has been washed into the soil by rain. Several cases of poisoned sheep and cows have been reported. Stock should have no access to contaminated grass clippings. In several instances lead arsenate has failed to give results, particularly on alkaline soils, and so it is desirable at the outset to make trials on a relatively small scale.

It has been suggested, and there is some supporting evidence, that weeds are adversely affected by the use of lead arsenate. Though direct 'burn' of weeds has often been noticed no striking general control can be reported. The fact of earthworm eradication on a turf means that in all probability there is less chance of weed invasion, since it has been shown that the casts of earthworms often contain seeds of injurious weed species. Experiments at Cornell University have attempted to show that the use of lead arsenate prevented the germination of weed seeds, but the results were negative.

Colloidal Lead Arsenate
This liquid preparation of lead arsenate was first introduced for the purpose of controlling leaf-eating insects in orchards.

The makers recommend the use of colloidal lead arsenate at 1 pint to 2 gal of water per 20 sq yd, (0·56 l to 9·09 l to 16·72 m²), which is equivalent to 0·8 oz per sq yd, (26 g per m²) of powder lead arsenate. Carefully controlled comparative trials with colloidal lead arsenate and powder lead arsenate have been carried out at St Ives and it has been shown, so far as control is concerned, to be immaterial in what form the arsenical is applied provided the requisite quantity of lead arsenate reaches the soil. Using the recommended rate of the colloidal the quantity of lead arsenate applied is but slightly more than that given in a $\frac{3}{4}$-oz (21·26-g) dressing of the powder. Such light dressings of powder have not given control for long periods, although some temporary relief has usually been enjoyed. The trials referred to above failed to support the supposition that the fine particle size of the colloidal is of any advantage or leads to any improved control of earthworm activity. In order that the equivalent of a $1\frac{1}{2}$-oz (42·51-g) rate of powder lead arsenate should be given in the colloidal form it is necessary to apply 1·87 pints to 20 sq yd (1 l to 16·7 m²).

Calcium arsenate
Considerable interest has been shown in commercial calcium arsenate as an earthworm eradicant in turf, since the arsenic content is higher than that of lead arsenate and the cost lower. Unfortunately calcium arsenate is relatively unstable and on decomposition yields soluble arsenic compounds which are toxic to plants.

Trials, using material consisting predominantly of basic calcium arsenate, have given good control of earthworms, a suitable rate being 1 to $1\frac{1}{2}$ oz per sq yd, (32 to 48 g per m²). Unfortunately, the detrimental effects which followed were sometimes severe and persistent, so that a general recommendation cannot be made for use on fine turf.

Chlordane

This is a very effective worm-killer, introduced to the British market about 1961. The original products contained 75 per cent emulsifiable concentrate, but this has now been reduced to a 25 per cent emulsifiable concentrate under Ministry of Agriculture regulations. It is also available as a 5 per cent or 20 per cent granular formulation. Suitable rates of application supply 12 to 16 lb (5·43 to 7·25 kg) of actual chlordane per acre (0·4 ha), e.g. 4 pints (2·27 l) of emulsifiable concentrate or 6 to 8 lb of 20 per cent granules per 500 sq yd (2·71 to 3·62 kg per 418 m²).

The granular material can be spread by hand (wearing gloves) or with a mechanical distributor after bulking with a carrier. The emulsifiable concentrate should be applied by sprayer or watering can after diluting with water—40 gal or more per acre (181·83 l per 0·4 ha). Chlordane is a toxic chemical and should be handled with great care taking every precaution as indicated on the container. Many people indeed, are reluctant to use this very efficient worm-killer, a persistent organo-chlorine substance, because of its effect on birds which may eat affected worms and insects.

Although showery weather in the spring and autumn are the best times of application, the timing of the operation is not as crucial as with other less effective worm-killers. The majority of worms are killed below the surface and a reasonably long period of control, in excess of 12 months may be anticipated. Several trade products are available and prices are variable.

Carbaryl

Worm-killers based on this chemical have proved to be effective, and are far less toxic to bird and animal life than Chlordane. However, its persistency is somewhat less than that of Chlordane. Because of its limited penetration into the soil, it is likely that any of the deeper living, beneficial and non-casting earthworm species will not be affected. The chemical rapidly breaks down in the soil, avoiding the possibility of a build up to toxic levels.

Best results can be expected when the material is applied during suitable warm and moist weather conditions in spring or autumn, on closely-mown turf. Light watering or rain after application will help to make the treatment satisfactory. In ideal circumstances, control can not be expected for more than one season.

CHAPTER TWENTY-SIX

Insect pests of turf

Insect pests of turf are fortunately few, but with one of them, the leather jacket, the damage to turf may be very severe unless its depredations are prevented at an early stage. Most of this chapter will therefore be devoted to the leather jacket, its life history and eradication, but a number of other harmful insects will be referred to later.

Leather jackets

Nearly everyone must have heard of this grub but only a few realise that it is the larval or grub stage of the long-legged fly known as the crane-fly, or daddy-longlegs. The grubs of all crane-flies are at present grouped together and called leather jackets. No morphological differences are known between the grubs of the various species, but even if they were known they are obviously so minute as to be only distinguishable by specialists.

Damage

The grub may cause damage in all parts of the country, and to food crops as well as to turf. Most instances of turf damage are reported from areas on the sea coast, but there are records of attacks at inland stations also. Perhaps golf courses suffer more than any turf sward, and because of the areas involved, control is proportionately more difficult. Bowling greens and sports grounds generally may suffer, and in epidemics during the last few years much serious damage has been

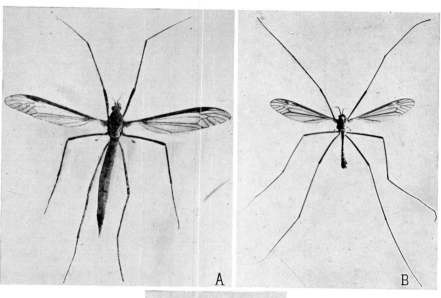

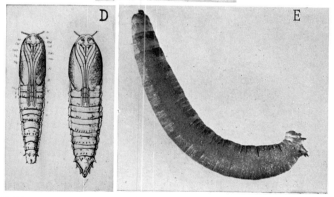

Fig. 36. Life history of the crane fly (*Tibula* sp.)
   (a) Female, 1:3:1.
   (b) Male (natural size).
   (c) Eggs 3:1.
   (d) Pupae: (left) male & (right) female, 1:3:1 (by courtesy of Dr Kurt Selka).
   (e) Full-grown grub or leather jacket, 2:1.

done to turf swards up and down the country. The grubs feed just below the surface of the ground, devouring roots and basal parts of the stems. As many as 1,000 grubs to the sq yd (0·94 m²) have been obtained, and attacked turf is generally located first by bird activity, and later, especially if drought intervenes, by the dying or serious browning of the overground parts of the sward. In severe attacks large tufts of damaged turf are loose and can be pulled out by the hands. In mild muggy conditions surface feeding may take place, while in cold conditions the grubs are said to move deeper into the soil.

Life history
The life history of the leather jacket has been worked out in greatest detail for the common species known as *Tipula paludosa*. The female fly of this and other species is easily distinguishable from the male by the fatter body and the presence at the end of the abdomen of a pointed ovipositor consisting of two rigid blades between which the eggs are extruded by spasmodic movements of the body; they may even be shot out with some force. They are usually laid by the female as she rests amongst the herbage, though at other times the ovipositor is bored into the soil with a twisting movement and the eggs deposited below the surface. The adults are on the wing from the beginning of August until the end of September and on the average live about 10 days. The eggs are less than 1 mm in length, are black with a metallic lustre and counts have shown that the average possible number with *T. paludosa* lies between 250 and 350, with extreme figures of 48 to 487. In from 11 to 15 days the eggs hatch, the peak of hatching being about the second week in September, though it may vary with the season and district. The grubs at this stage are very minute, delicate, and susceptible to drought. Weather conditions in late August and September have therefore an important bearing on the occurrence of epidemics. Mild wet weather is very favourable to them.

By October the grubs are hardier, steadily increase in size, and become more voracious. They feed all through the winter on decaying vegetable matter and living roots until they reach the stage of the familiar legless grey grub. The full size of a well-fed extended grub is $1\frac{1}{4}$ to $1\frac{1}{2}$ in (31 to 37 mm) long. The grub when fully fed becomes passive in the soil, before the pupal stage, which lasts from 2 to 3 weeks, during which metamorphosis to the adult occurs. Under the right conditions the pupa struggles to the surface, the back of the brown skin splits and the mature insect emerges into the light and dries its wings. The eggs are fully formed in the females and shortly after emergence fertilisation takes place and laying commences, the whole process of propagation occupying but a few hours. The crowds of adults often seen in late summer consist in the main of spent adults which are carried hither and thither until destroyed by the elements.

Species
Examination of records shows that at least eight species of crane-fly have been found causing damage to turf or crops of various kinds and a list of them is given below:

> *Pales flavescens* Linn.
> *P. maculata* Meig.
> *P. flavipalpis* Meig.
> *Tipula paludosa* Meig.
> *T. oleracea* Linn.
> *T. lateralis* Meig.
> *T. vernalis* Meig.
> *T. variipennis* Meig.

Sampling experiments have indicated that *T. paludosa* and *T. oleracea* are the most widespread, while of these two *T. paludosa* largely predominates. There is a possibility that *P. maculata* is commoner than breeding-out experiments have shown, and *T. vernalis* has at times been observed in turf. Differences in shape and markings of the eggs of three *Tipulæ*, namely *paludosa*, *oleracea*, and *vernalis*, have been found while it seems that *oleracea* lays on the average a greater number of eggs than *paludosa*.

Methods of control
There are several difficulties in the way of accurately studying methods of control, not the least of these being the habit of migration. Further, infestation of turf is never uniform, and areas may be found that are intensively invaded whereas near-by parts may only be lightly attacked. For example, the outer edges of golf greens are often much more heavily attacked than the more central parts. Many of the erroneous reports published about the control of grubs in turf may be attributed to the failure to realise these differences in numbers, which may lead to a belief that a certain treatment has been more effective than another, whereas the difference is entirely due to a difference in original infestation.

Natural methods of control all play a part in mitigating epidemics. For example, birds eat the adults as well as the grubs. Observations have shown that the grubs are often parasitised by a small fly, *Bucentes geniculata*, the larva of which lives on the tissues of the grub. To what extent this fly controls the pest is not known. Two generations of the fly occur in one season. In some experiments the number of grubs on control plots dropped from 250 per sampling unit to 65 between January 8 and March 3. This may be attributed either to the action of hard frost, birds, cannibalism, or possibly migration.

The observation that adult flies are attracted to light has often prompted the use of light traps. The bulk of adults emerge from the soil by late morning and most of the eggs are laid before midnight. Specimens caught in light traps have been examined and it has been found that only about 5 per cent of the eggs have not been laid by midnight, that is to say 95 per cent have already been deposited before the fly was caught in the trap. In light-trap experiments 62 per cent of the crane-flies caught were *Tipula paludosa*, while only 3 per cent were *T. oleracea*, and it is interesting that in the latter species, the trapped females contained a large number of eggs, perhaps only 5 per cent having been laid. Trapping would therefore appear to be of little use with the commonest species, *T. paludosa*, though it may be helpful with the less frequent *T. oleracea*. Whatever the control treatment adopted in turf it must be of such a nature that it is harmless to the grass but effective in either bringing the grubs to the surface or destroying them below. Also, turf that is in good heart will recover rapidly after eradication, just as vigorous turf will be less seriously harmed in the event of an epidemic.

One method of control that has received some publicity is to soak the turf and cover overnight with tarpaulins or rubber mats. The grubs are collected underneath the following morning. The method is not suitable for large areas, and, anyhow, no information exists as to the percentage of grubs removed.

A Paris green and bran mixture has been found effective in agricultural practice, and is standard recommendation, but the method is open to the objection that it must only be used in mild conditions when the grubs are likely to come to the surface to feed, while a second difficulty is the poisonous nature of the Paris green. Naphthalene is sometimes recommended for the treatment of turf containing grubs, but at a rate of application effective in reducing the pest, damage to the turf results. On arable land it is, however, useful. Ammonia solutions have also been tried on turf, and one quart of '880 ammonia' in 50 gal (227 l) of water applied to 50 sq yd (41 m^2) is quite effective in bringing the grubs to the surface.

Ortho-dichlorobenzene, when emulsified (64 per cent) and mixed with a proportion of Jeyes fluid, gives remarkably good results as an expellent. I gal (4·5 l) of the concentrated emulsion is diluted with 400 gal (1818 l) of water and applied at the rate of 1 gal per sq yd

(4·5 l per 0·83 m²). The grubs come to the surface, where they lie comatose and must then be swept up. Provided the soil is moist and the application of the liquid uniform, no harm is caused to the grass.

Since the advent of DDT and BHC it is seldom used except as a testing fluid to find out if grubs are present in the turf.

Lead arsenate (PbHAsO$_4$), DDT and BHC have all been investigated for the control of leather jackets at various centres. In the case of lead arsenate no significant difference was found between the $\frac{1}{2}$ oz, 1 oz, and 2 oz dressings of the powder (16, 32 and 64 g). The $\frac{1}{2}$ oz (16 g) is recommended for practical purposes since cash outlay must be considered. The arsenate may be used direct, or after bulking with a carrier being applied either by hand or by means of a distributor. As regards longevity of the treatment, the indications are that it is better to apply $\frac{1}{2}$ oz (16 g) powder each season rather than rely on the 1 oz and 2 oz (32 and 64 g) dressings remaining effective for more than one year. Where there is any danger from using lead arsenate, such as in gardens or on lands to which stock may have access, lead arsenate should not be used.

Experiments with DDT and BHC against leather jackets have proved the value of these new insecticides for rapid control and they are now extensively used in practice.

DDT is the name given to a chemical compound called *Dichloro-Diphenyl-Trichloroethane*. Although first synthesised in 1874 its insecticidal properties were not discovered until 1936 in Switzerland, but it received a great deal of publicity for the part it played in dealing with insect pests associated with war-time activities. War-time secrecy delayed publication of the official story of DDT until August 1944. DDT is a white crystalline compound with a faint pleasant smell but the pure substance is not met with outside the laboratory. Since it is a powerful insecticide it is used in formulations containing fairly low percentages of the chemical.

In some experiments, an infestation of 212 grubs per sq yd (0·94 m²) was reduced after three weeks to 4 per sq yd where $\frac{1}{2}$ oz (16 g) of 5 per cent dust had been used, and reduced to nil with $1\frac{1}{2}$ oz (48 g). As a practical recommendation 5 per cent dust may be utilised at $\frac{1}{2}$ oz (16 g) per sq yd, and in practice excellent results have been obtained. Further work using DDT emulsions showed that a rate equivalent to 1 gal of 5 per cent emulsion in 400 gal of water per 800 sq yd (4·5 l in 1818 l per 668 m²) of turf gave adequate control, and even lower rates gave some results.

Turning now to BHC. This is a British discovery and the initials refer to Benzine Hexachloride. Commercial benzine hexachloride contains a number of chemical isomers of which the gamma-isomer (gammexane) is the active one. Benzine hexachloride, or more correctly, the gamma-isomer of it is also a powerful insecticide and is usually sold in preparations containing comparatively small proportions of actual chemical. A dust containing 5 per cent benzine hexachloride of which 13 per cent was gamma-isomer, used at $\frac{1}{2}$ oz per sq yd (16 g/m²) reduced an infestation of 212 grubs per sq yd to 27 per sq yd after 3 weeks. Three months after treatment, tests showed no grubs to be present where $\frac{1}{2}$, $\frac{3}{4}$ and 1 oz per sq yd (16, 24 and 32 g/m²) had been used. At $\frac{1}{4}$ oz (8 g/m²) only 6 grubs were found. In practice it has become usual to apply a $3\frac{1}{2}$ per cent dust at 1 oz per sq yd (32 g/m²).

DDT and BHC are persistent organochlorine insecticides and are reputed to have caused considerable damage to many species of birds. Under the Pesticide Safety Precautions Scheme, these chemicals must not be applied to permanent or temporary pastures for grazing or silage or hay. Although these materials have proved very effective in controlling leather jackets, their use is likely to be limited and subject to rigid control.

Formulations containing Chlordane are available as insecticides, and treated areas are kept free of leather jackets and other turf pests for about 12 months.

Insecticides containing Carbaryl are likely to be used to control such pests as leather jackets, chafer grubs, bibio grubs and cutworms.

Cockchafer grubs

In some districts, particularly on light land that is well wooded, epidemics of chafer grubs occur. They do extensive damage by devouring roots of grasses and much secondary damage is caused by birds in their search for grubs. The commonest chafer found in turf in this country appears to be the Garden Chafer (*Phyllopertha horticola* L.). The adult beetles are found in June and so are sometimes called 'June beetles', and there is one generation per annum.

It should be realised that the grubs retreat deeper into the soil during winter, so that any control materials used should only be applied in late summer, early autumn or spring, when the grubs are near the surface and likely to be devouring the grass roots.

The large cockchafer (*Melolontha melolontha* L.) is at times found in turf. It has a 4 to 5 years' life cycle.

Dung beetle grubs

The grubs of *Aphodius* spp., rather like small chafers in appearance, are sometimes found in turf in the spring. They cause little harm to the turf, but bird action is serious.

Fly larvæ

The greyish brown larvæ or grubs of the two-winged fly (*Dilophus febrilis* L.) or Fever Fly and of the St Mark's Fly (*Bibio johannis* L.) are sometimes found in turf during the spring or autumn in clusters or nests $\frac{3}{4}$ in to 1 in (19 to 25 mm) below the surface. Superficially the grubs resemble small leather jackets for which they are often mistaken, but closer examination shows that unlike leather jackets they have well-developed shining brown heads. The fever fly grubs feed principally on decaying organic matter and are therefore not so harmful as leather jackets, the damage consisting mainly of thin loose patches round the nests or clusters. The life history, briefly, of *Dilophus*, is egg laying in May, with the grubs pupating about the end of August, and the adult flies emerging after about one month. The progeny of these flies over-winter as larvæ and emerge as adults the following spring to continue the cycle. Control as for leather jackets.

Ants

At times lawns, especially on sandy soils, are disfigured by ant hills, which also make mowing difficult. A successful method of control is to inject carbon disulphide into the nests. Chlordane as well as BHC dusts have also given good results.

Other species

The Dor beetle and the Lunar dung beetle are sometimes found in turf but apart from the inconvenience caused by throwing up small mounds of soil do no harm to the grass.

Occasionally in sea marsh turf the beetle *Bledius tricornis* Herbst. is found. It tunnels into the silty earth and throws up small casts. It does not appear to persist in turf once it has been transferred to inland situations.

Severe damage from 'cutworms' has occurred from time to time in some European countries. The caterpillar is the larval stage of certain night-flying moths. Eggs are laid in the late summer and the young grubs feed in the autumn, hibernate at the onset of cold weather, then start feeding on roots and basal parts of shoots the following spring. DDT, BHC and Chlordane have given good results.

CHAPTER TWENTY-SEVEN

Fungal diseases of turf

The steady rise in the standard of turf requirement in recent years coincides with improved knowledge of turf culture, improved materials and better implements. Improved standards have involved the adoption of very intensive methods of upkeep, and there is consequently a greater tendency for fungal diseases to assert themselves. Fungal diseases of intensively managed turf are not new, though there is little doubt that the artificial conditions under which grass often exists have increased the severity of fungal attack. At the same time, the modern golfer, bowler, and even lawn owner is more fastidious and critical, and there is a demand for turf free from all blemishes. The very fact that greens and fine lawns generally have improved makes small areas of discoloured grass much more noticeable than they would be on a less perfect sward. A discoloured area on a turf is not necessarily indicative of fungal disease, as wear and tear, damage from water-logging, or irregular application of fertiliser may well be responsible, but it often happens that discolouration has originated through fungal attack. Changes in the physiological conditions in which grass is growing, such as an alteration in the state of the soil, in the type of fertiliser used, in water-retaining capacity, and in air humidity and temperature, all affect the internal economy of the grass and may create conditions predisposing the plants to attack by disease organisms. Plants in which vitality has been lowered by combination of such factors or plants which are 'overfed' are more susceptible to attack, but many disease organisms are able to attack healthy plants.

Greater attention has been drawn to a number of fungal diseases of turf in this country, either because they have become more widespread or because more notice is taken of them in view of the deeper interest now displayed in turf culture. When a disease breaks out, immediate effective control is vital, which in turn requires quick identification of the problem. It is therefore proposed to describe the main diseases encountered in turf management.

Diseases of seedlings and newly-sown turf

Depending on the time and type of infection, failure of grass seed establishment due to fungal activity may be classified into two types 'pre-emergence' and 'post-emergence' damping off.

Pre-emergence damping off or 'seed rot' is typified by failure of grass seeds to braird. Several species of fungi are responsible; members of the genera *Pythium, Fusarium* and *Helminthosporium* are most commonly recovered from rotted seed. When sowing it is always wise to use healthy clean seed and to sow on a well-drained, firm, fine seed bed under suitable growing conditions. Seed dressings based on Captan 75 per cent at 1 oz per 28 lb (28 g per 12 kg) or Thiram at $1\frac{1}{2}$ oz per 28 lb (42 g per 12 kg) are particularly beneficial to the smaller seeded grass species which are most commonly the victims of pre-emergence blight.

Post-emergence damping off occurs after brairding. Patches of attacked seedlings assume a yellow or bronzed appearance, eventually collapsing or toppling just at or above the ground surface. Fungi of the genera *Fusarium* and to a lesser extent *Pythium* and *Helminthosporium* are the species most frequently encountered, but under very wet conditions *Agrostis* spp. are prone to attack by *Cladochytrium cæspitis*. Species of *Olpidium* may attack the roots of seedlings or appear a second year after seeding, causing affected plants to wither and 'burn' over patches of varying size. Should an attack develop, Cheshunt compound at $\frac{1}{2}$ oz in 1 gal water to 1 sq yd (16 g/4·5 l to 0·94 m²) normally prevents further spread of the disease, and application of ammonium phosphate at $\frac{1}{4}$ to $\frac{1}{2}$ oz per sq yd (8 to 16 g/m²) has been effective in some cases.

Diseases of established turf

Fusarium Patch disease

This is the commonest and most widespread disease of turf in this country. It is caused by the fungus *Fusarium nivale* (Fr.) Ces. and is found on all classes of intensively managed turf. The fungus has been

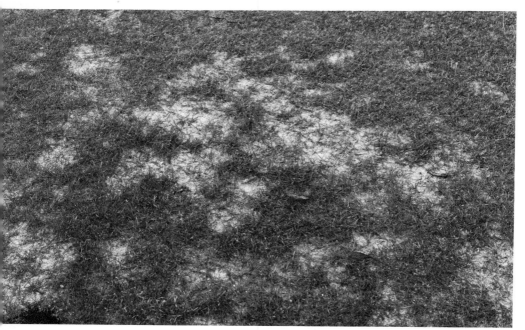

Fig. 37. Fusarium patch disease.

known on the continent of Europe for nearly a century where it occurs
as a parasite on cereals, but as a disease on turf it was first noted in
this country in the late 1920's. Attacks by the disease can occur at
any time throughout the year when weather conditions are suitable,
but most commonly disease patches are found in the months of
September and October, or during mild periods in winter. The first
symptoms are the appearance of small brown or yellow patches about
1 in (2·5 cm) in diameter; these patches may increase in size by
regular lobular extensions until they reach perhaps 1 ft (30 cm) in
diameter. If there are many patches on an infected turf area they may
coalesce. Under mild moist conditions a fine pink or white cotton-like
growth of fungal mycelium appears on the surface of the patch.
Although there are a greater number of attacks in spring and early
summer the disease makes most headway when the vigour of the grass
is low, as in the autumn and winter months. Earlier in the year when
growth is more vigorous the grass is usually capable of keeping up with
the fungal attack. Annual meadow-grass, certain strains of browntop,
creeping bent and red fescue are susceptible while perennial rye-grass
seems generally to be resistant to the disease. The fungus over-winters
as dark brown aggregates of mycelium embedded in dead plant
tissues. When suitable weather conditions appear this mycelium starts

growth and eventually spreads, attacking grass blades and crowns, the patches of diseased grass increasing in size. Under suitable conditions masses of sickle-shaped spores are produced in spore balls on older killed tissues. These spores are dispersed by means of the wind and on feet, implements and sports gear. It was shown by Bennett that the continental strain of *Fusarium nivale* and the British one behave somewhat differently. The disease caused by the strain *F. nivale* found on the Continent is known as 'Snow Mould', a term which is also applied to the disease in America. Bennett proposed the name of Fusarium Patch Disease' for the British form and the name should be generally adopted. Although the disease in this country sometimes follows a thaw of snow it is by no means exclusively associated with it, although it has been shown that the British strain is capable of growing under a snow cover. The organism is capable of growing over a wide temperature range of between 1·1 and 29·4°C, with an optimum temperature of around 20°C. The soil *p*H has little influence on the disease.

The organism apparently requires abundant moisture to grow actively on grass, but bad attacks can be related to such factors as:

(a) weakening of grass following intensive management of the turf.
(b) an excess of nitrogenous fertiliser, usually due to excessive dressings during the late summer.
(c) the presence of thatch.

Any treatment which tends to reduce surface moisture will tend to reduce the likelihood of attack. Aeration, switching in the morning to disperse dew and the removal of screening trees or shrubs which impede the free air flow over the surface should be undertaken.

In terms of chemical controls, it is really desirable to think in terms of a preventative rather than curative programme. For prevention, it is necessary to start applying fungicide in the autumn and repeat as required during conditions that favour fungal infection.

The choice of chemicals available has been greatly increased with the development of the first systemic fungicides, two of which, Benomyl and Thiabenzadol have proved to be highly successful against many turf diseases especially fusarium patch. Being systemic they remain within the grass and therefore form an ideal basis for a preventative control programme. Possible treatments are:

(a) Mercurials.
(i) Mercurous Chloride (Calomel); 3 oz per 100 sq yd (85 g per 93·6 m²) applied as a coarse spray in 25/30 gal of water (113/136 l).

(ii) Mercurous/Mercuric Chloride mixture; here 1 oz (32 g) is replaced by Mercuric Chloride and applied as above. Better results will be obtained if a wetter is added but since a wide variety of mercury based fungicides are readily available in the prepared form, these are more convenient to use and should be applied as per manufacturer's instructions.

(b) PCNB (Quintozene); this will give good control of the disease, but better results will be obtained if the wettable powder form is used, applying 6 oz per 100 sq yd (170 g per 93·6 m^2) in 2/3 gal of water (9/13 l). Frequency of treatment for both Mercury and Quintozene being at about 3 to 4 week intervals.

(c) Systemic Fungicides.
 (i) Benomyl (commercially available as Benlate); usually applied at 4/6 oz per 100 sq yd (113/170 g per 93·6 m^2) at a high volume rate.
 (ii) Thiabenzadol (commercially available as Tecto Systemic Turf Fungicide). Usually applied at 2 oz per 100 sq yd (56 g per 93·6 m^2) at high volume.

The systemic fungicides differ radically from conventional turf fungicides in their application, since they are absorbed through the root system and require high water rates at application to ensure penetration into the soil.

Corticium disease
This disease is found commonly in all parts of the country. Fescues are apparently most susceptible but bents, annual meadow-grass, rye-grass, creeping soft-grass, and some other species are also attacked. It is generally noticed as a general pink tinge imparted to the herbage and by the appearance of pink or red 'needles' which are found on the bleached leaves. The disease has often been described by such names as gelatinous red mould, autumn rust, leaf rust, and red thread. They may lead to confusion and should be avoided.

The fungus is found attached as a pinkish layer adhering to stems and leaves of grasses. It spreads between the grass blades binding them together and under humid conditions is quite gelatinous. Spores are produced on the surface of the layer adhering to the plant tissues. In addition the fungus produces pink coral or needle-like outgrowths from near the tips of the dying grass leaves. These consist of the aggregates of mycelium, at first gelatinous but later becoming dry and brittle. When in this condition they are easily detached from the leaves

Fig. 38. Corticium disease of fine turf.

and spread by wind or on feet or implements, setting up new infection centres. The needles are capable when dry of existing for at least two years and being able to produce disease again.

The disease may occur at any time in the growing season but it is most commonly found in late summer. The fungus which was first noted in the middle of the last century was given the name of *Isaria fuciforme* and is often still referred to in older works on turf management of a general nature by that name. It is now correctly termed *Corticium fuciforme* (Berk.) Wakef.

Although the bleached patches of grass caused by this disease are disfiguring, the plants are generally not killed off and recover when conditions for growth of the fungus are no longer suitable. Bennett who has also studied this fungus has found that the optimum temperature for growth is 21°C, a common summer temperature, while the indications are that a *p*H of 4·8 to 5·2 is the optimum. The disease although found on well-managed turf is more usual when the sward is low in vigour and particularly when deficient in nitrogen, and often a nitrogen dressing will effect some improvement in response to the disease under these conditions. Since the disease is far less serious than Fusarium, a curative rather than preventative approach should be adopted. Chemical treatments as put forward for fusarium are recommended with the exception of mercurous chloride (Calomel), but providing the application of a nitrogenous fertiliser is permissible, the results obtained by the dual approach will be better than the fungicidal treatment alone.

Ophiobolus disease of turf

This disease is widespread on grasses, but fortunately it is not common in Great Britain, although in recent years the number of outbreaks have increased. In the autumn of 1951 it was noticed that samples of sports turf from many parts of Great Britain were infected with the fungus O. graminis. During 1952 the fungus was recovered from turf sent from as far apart as Orkney and Southern Ireland, and the disease was found to be much more common than had been suspected. The general symptoms of the disease may be seen throughout the year but are most noticeable during summer and autumn. Small bleached and sometimes bronzed patches of turf a few inches across are the first noticeable macroscopic symptoms. The patches gradually increase in size over several years, the plants in the centre dying out, their place being taken by weed species. These invading species vary according to soil type, reaction, and sward composition. Round the edge of the patch the diseased grass appears as a bleached ring and as it has little root hold it may be peeled off in a skin. If individual diseased plants are examined, but especially late in the year, say from September until about April the next year, their bases will be found to be dis-coloured and the fruiting bodies of the fungus will be seen as black specks (approximately 0·5 mm in diameter) under the lower leaf sheaths. The stolons and rhizomes will also appear discoloured. The disease has so far been noted only on Agrostis tenuis, A. stolonifera, and Poa annua. The fungus Ophiobolus graminis has a variety avenæ which causes black foot-rot, take-all, and whiteheads of oats and other members of the Graminæ. Strains of this fungus are responsible for the disease in sports turf, which often occurs after an acid Agrostis turf has been limed. It seems to be favoured by wet conditions. The fungus is soil-borne. Conventional control measures, including the new systemics, have little or no effect, and since in its early stages it can easily be confused with fusarium patch, those managing turf in high pH areas should be wary, especially in wet conditions. Samples of the diseased grass should be expertly examined under the microscope, and if Ophiobolus is confirmed, treatment using Phenylmercury Acetate (containing 2·5 per cent mercury) should be applied at the rate of 2 oz of fungicide per 40 sq yd in 4/6 gal of water (56 g per 33 m^2 in 18/27 l). Treatment should be repeated at 10 day intervals in con-junction if possible, with treatments of sulphate of ammonia. Recently

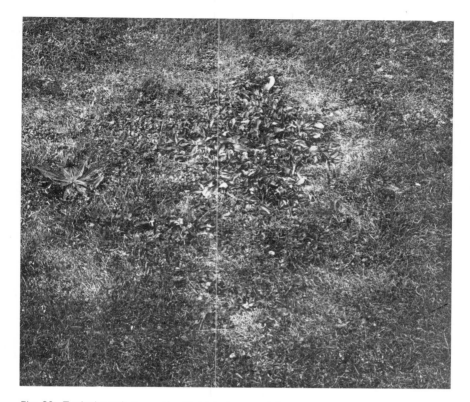

Fig. 39. Typical patch caused by *Ophiobolus graminis* var. *avenae*.

Chlordane has been found effective as a preventative material, where again, in conjunction with the use of sulphate of ammonia, control superior to that of fungicides has been obtained. Treatment with Chlordane consists of periodic sprayings using 16 oz (Chlordane 25 per cent) per 100 sq yd in a minimum of 10 gal of water (453 g per 93·6 m² in 45 l).

Dollar Spot

Bennett first found this disease in Great Britain in 1933 and since then the causal organism, *Sclerotinia homeocarpa* Bennett, has been found on turf from many parts of Britain. For all practical purposes the disease is confined to *F. rubra* L. ssp. *rubra* and is particularly damaging to sea marsh turf, which suffers rapid deterioration as the fescue is killed out. In Britain Dollar Spot may be observed at any season of the year, but it is likely to be most frequent during the late summer and early autumn. The spots are from 1 to 2 in (25 to 50 mm) in diameter and approximately circular, though in well-established infections they may coalesce to form irregular patches. Like Corticium disease (with which early Dollar Spot symptoms are easily confused), Dollar Spot is more severe where the plant vigour is low and light dressings of sulphate of ammonia will effect some improvement. Outbreaks of the disease can be controlled by any of the measures suggested for fusarium patch, although again, chemical treatment in conjunction with dressings of sulphate of ammonia produces better results than the fungicide alone.

Brown Patch disease

Although the fungus responsible (*Rhizoctonia solani*) has been isolated from turf in this country it does not appear to be the cause of disease. It is, however, a serious problem in the United States.

Fairy rings

Fairy rings are the manifestation on the turf surface of the activities of certain soil inhabiting fungi mostly belonging to the *Basidiomycetes* (Cap fungi). These fungi grow in the soil from a central point in ever-widening circles, the mycelium of the fungus ramifying in the soil between the roots of the turf plants. One or more rings of lush green grass are generally found at some period of the year at the periphery of the ring.

Fairy rings may be classified into three main types according to the number and position of the stimulated zones of grass. In the first grade there are two rings of stimulated grass between which is a bare zone which generally shows up during the dry period of the year. On this bare zone little grass is found. There may, however, be a cover of moss. It is probable that the reason for this bare zone is that there is so much mycelium in the soil that the grasses have been 'droughted out'. Rings of grade 1 severity in this country are generally caused by *Marasmius oreades* Fr. and they are the most difficult to deal with.

In rings of the second grade of severity there is only one ring of dark green grass round the edge of which are found fructifications of the causal fungus at its normal time of fruiting. Rings of this type are commonly caused by species of *Lycoperdon* (Puff ball) and *Psalliota* (Mushroom). There is much less mycelium in the soil with rings of this type.

Rings of the third grade of severity generally do not have a stimulated zone of grass but only a ring of fruiting bodies of the fungus. Many species of fungi grow in rings.

Fairy rings of the first grade of severity are the most difficult to

Fig. 40(a). Fairy ring in park land turf.
     (b). Lawn: close-up of fairy ring.

control because of the impervious nature of the bare zone of soil. Many people dig out the infected turf and soil, replacing with new. It is sometimes found difficult to ensure that all infected soil is in fact removed.

A number of materials have been tried for chemical control but of these 40 per cent formalin, originally suggested in New Zealand, is the only one toxic yet able to penetrate infected soil. It is, of course, toxic to grass. The following technique has been devised for *Marasmius* rings:

A. Mix well together:

> 10 gal (45 l) water
> 6 pints (3·140 l) of 40 per cent formaldehyde (formalin)
> $\frac{1}{2}$ pint (0·28 l) non-ionic wetting agent, e.g. Teepol, Lissapol NDB, etc.

This solution is enough for 10 sq yd (9·36 m²).

B. Proceed as follows:

1. Determine the extent of the inner and outer green rings (if both are present). Mark off 1 ft (30 cm) inside and outside these zones.
2. Lift the turf from the marked area and discard—it is infected.
3. Fork round periphery of lifted parts, breaking up soil 9 in (23 cm) deep. Continue until whole is dug as fine as possible.
4. Prepare the solution and put in a wash tub or barrel nearby. Use to sterilise tools.
5. Apply solution, using a can. Soak the soil.
6. Seal up for 7 to 10 days using polythene sheet, tarred paper or sacks, the idea being to retain the fumes.
7. Remove covering and stir soil with a fork. Leave exposed about 2 weeks.
8. After the formaldehyde has dispersed make up levels, prepare a seed bed and sow. Alternatively the area may be turfed.
9. The process is best done in late spring and summer when the mycelium is most active.

As an alternative to formalin, Corrosive Sublimate (Mercuric Chloride) at the rate of 2 oz per 22 gal of water may be used (56 g per 99 l).

The formalin method of treatment may also be used with rings of the second grade of severity, i.e. those generally caused by *Lycoperdon* spp., and *Psalliota* spp., the mycelium of which is much less extensive in the soil.

For rings of the third grade of severity, to suppress the production of fruiting bodies a solution of 2 oz (56 g) magnesium sulphate (Epsom salts) in 1 gal water to 1 sq yd (4·5 l to 0·94 m²) holds out prospects of success. This solution may also be tried in the control of *Coprinus* spp. whose fruiting body is termed the Shaggy cap.

Slime moulds

Occasionally the plasmodia of 'Slime Moulds' (Myxomycetes) are found covering the turf, particularly in damp situations. Two of the commonest are *Didymium crustaceum*, and *Mucilago spongiosa*. Little is known about 'slime moulds' in turf but they generally do not cause much damage and disappear as the turf dries out. Attention should be paid to improving surface drainage. The use of an organic mercurial applied in solution by means of a suitable sprayer is recommended if the area is large, the treatment being repeated if necessary.

Other growths

It is convenient here to include a number of non-fungal growths found in turf. A very common growth in neglected lawns is the lichen *Peltigera canina* L., found as brown overlapping leafy structures. Control is best effected by general improvement of the fertility, i.e. application of a compound fertiliser. Liming may be required but the lichen is sometimes found on calcareous soils. It is favoured by damp shaded conditions especially where there is a northerly aspect.

On water-logged turf or turf that is inclined to retain moisture on the surface through sealing up by heavy rolling, gelatinous growths of a blue-green alga (*Collema* spp.) may occur. Little is known about their control, but watering with dilute sulphate of iron has been practised with some degree of success. Aeration should be carried out.

CHAPTER TWENTY-EIGHT

Eradication of vermin

The damage caused to turf by the action of rabbits, moles, field mice, and certain birds is sometimes serious, so that it is desirable that methods of control should be considered here.

Moles

Apart from the habit of throwing up mounds of earth, the surface may be upset through the collapse of the burrows. Very often in making shallow surface burrows the mole will push up a ridge of soil, so doing a lot of harm, especially on newly-sown ground. Normally they are only found in turf where there is a plentiful supply of earthworms.

The methods of exterminating moles may be grouped under three headings, namely trapping, poisoning by baits, and gassing. Trapping involves the finding of a well-used tunnel or run, and then carefully setting in that run one of the two types of trap in common use—the pincer or scissor trap or the 'Duffus'. While this is best done by a professional mole catcher, 'amateurs' should be encouraged in their attempts to control these pests.

Poisoning should only be carried out by the professional. The most widely advocated method of destroying moles is by means of earthworms dipped in strychnine solution, and then dropped into the runs for the moles to eat. However, the sale or supply of strychnine is prohibited under the present poison regulations, except to those who have obtained a written authority from the Ministry of Agriculture. It follows that professionals are the only people that can have strychnine in their possession for this purpose, and these men can be found in most districts willing to undertake the work of eradication on a contract basis.

Two methods of gassing may be mentioned, the first being by means of various cyanogenetic compounds, and the other by means of exhaust gas. Various proprietary dusts are on the market, and can be blown into the runs by a blower. Exhaust gases from internal combustion engines have been successfully used, though it presupposes accessibility. When either method of gassing is used, the exits to the mole runs should be sealed, usually with earth, so that the complete system of the mole run is saturated with gas.

Rabbits

The fecundity of the rabbit is so well known that it need not be stressed here. If rabbits are numerous they may cause much inconvenience through scratching and reducing the productivity of the turf, though in their defence it must be said that in their grazing they select principally the clovers and rye-grasses, leaving the finer and less palatable grasses relatively unharmed.

The introduction of the disease myxomatosis caused a widespread reduction in rabbits throughout the country. There are signs of revival, however, in various places due, no doubt, to breeding from animals having a resistance to the disease.

Gin traps, prior to their prohibition in 1958, used to be one of the ways that rabbits were kept under control. Apart from snaring, netting and shooting, gassing affords a method easy of operation where warrens exist, and it is recommended as being the most humane and efficient. The dusts used for the purpose, generally hydrocyanic acid gas in the form of powdered cyanide compounds, produce the gas when brought into contact with damp air. Death to the rabbit is said to be rapid and painless.

The dusts are projected into the burrows by means of hand or powered blowers, and any holes in the warren from which the gas can be seen to be escaping should be filled in, and of course, the main entrances should also be blocked after the operation has been completed. Exhaust gases from car or tractor can also be used, a hose being employed to convey the fumes from the exhaust to the burrow.

A more economical method for the treatment of small infestations is called 'spooning'. 1 oz (28 g) of powder is put in the burrow about 12 in (30 cm) from the mouth, the hole then being closed firmly with turf. A concentration of gas thus built up will last for about 24 hours.

Rats and field mice

These pests can be a great nuisance in tool sheds and store places. Not only can they do a great amount of damage, but they can be a source of rat- or mouse-borne disease. In particular, over 40 per cent of the rats in England and Wales are carriers of Weil's Disease. This disease, which has been responsible for some deaths, is water-borne, and is particularly dangerous in places where rats have urinated.

Most poisons recommended to control rats and mice are baits containing anti-coagulants like warfarin. Anti-coagulants prevent blood from clotting, and when animals eat baits containing these materials, they die, mainly as a result of internal bleeding.

Other anti-coagulants are Coumatetralyl and Chlorophacinone. Ready-to-use baits based on all three materials are readily available. Future infestations should be discouraged by clearing away from both inside and outside buildings any rubbish that can afford harbourage and shelter to these pests. Clear out piles of sacking and old nets, hang up bags of grass seed from the roof of the shed, or keep it in a tin container. Above all, clear away any food droppings.

Anti-coagulants are poisonous, to other mammals and humans, as well as to rats and mice. Safety precautions must therefore be taken to make sure that the baits set can only be reached by the pests for which they are intended.

Birds

The two species of birds that pay most attention to turf are the starling and the rook. In some districts pheasants cause damage. The starling, in searching for grubs like leather jackets, punctures the turf with its beak, and as it is beneficial in reducing grubs it should not be harmed. The rook with its larger beak and habit of using its claws often tears up large areas of turf in search of food, usually cockchafer grubs, fever fly grubs, and dung beetle larvæ, but the grubs of leather jackets are the main cause of the search. The usual methods of shooting, scarecrows, and hanging up a dead bird, may be tried, but often the simplest method is to eradicate the soil pests to which the birds are attacted.

Sometimes new-sown soil is disturbed by sparrows dusting in the loose surface. On small areas this can be prevented by arranging across the area a few black cotton threads supported on short sticks.

CHAPTER TWENTY-NINE

Turf growing under trees and in difficult situations

In the course of this book many general directions for treatment have been given, but it is impossible to lay down instructions for all eventualities and conditions. Certain special cases are dealt with below, but where unusual circumstances occur it is again stressed that technical advice should be taken.

Turf under trees

A lawn ornamented with trees upon which the sward is continuous below the branches and extending up to the bole or trunk, is most attractive. It is difficult to accomplish this in practice because of the poverty, shade, dryness in summer, and the repeated dripping from rain water collected on the branches during wet weather. The latter is a serious problem in industrial areas or on the edge of towns where the rain is charged with varying amounts of chlorides, sulphates, mineral acids, and suspended matter. The shade factor itself is important, since if deep it deprives the grass of much of the necessary light; to take an example, maintenance of a good sward under the dense foliage of a beech tree is wellnigh impossible. The first operation in endeavouring to create or improve turf below trees is judiciously to lop them, yet carefully preserving their shape.

It is always desirable on lawns under trees to leave the grass rather longer than in the open, and periodically to sweep it clear of leaves, conifer needles, branches, twigs, and other débris. Moss is often common under trees and should be kept down by occasional raking, and renovation with seed may be necessary from time to time. Conditions of poverty must be avoided by occasional light fertiliser dressings, and light liming may be needed. The water requirement of the tree and the umbrella effect of the branches may result in serious surface-moisture deficiency for the grass and so occasional artificial watering may be required if the turf is to survive. In some instances it is necessary to renew the turf almost annually beneath trees, and re-turfing is better on the whole than re-seeding. Certain grass species are much more tolerant of shade conditions than others, and amongst these are notably rough-stalked meadow-grass and wood meadow-grass. They should therefore be included in seeds mixtures for these conditions, in conjunction of course with the finer fescues and bents.

Lawns in towns and cities

The attempt is often made to produce grass swards in the centre of cities, and while tolerable results may be obtained during the summer, the shade of buildings during the winter is often so continuous owing to the angle of the sun that the grass gradually deteriorates. Apart from the deep shade from buildings, however, atmospheric pollution is usually severe, and although high acidity created in the soil may be corrected by liming no way is known of preventing the harmful atmosphere affecting the grass through the leaves—the assimilating organs of the plant. Where grass has to be grown in the centre of cities it is usually necessary to renovate it annually since winter kill is so severe. Late autumn sowings should, of course, be avoided.

The effects of shadow from buildings, e.g. spectator's stands, on sports turf used in winter usually shows as a thinner turf, more muddiness (causing bad soil structure) and at times greater weediness.

Moorland soils

Under conditions of very high soil acidity the establishment of grass from seed may be inhibited, and although this problem may not occur often on lawns, it is nevertheless quite frequent on golf courses, since they are often constructed on land that is more or less agriculturally derelict. Experiments have shown that light liming is sufficient to establish the common bents and fescues even when this is not sufficient to satisfy the full lime-requirement of the soil. Wavy Hair-grass (*Aira flexuosa*), which is naturally tolerant of acid soils, will establish without this assistance. The use of phosphate on such soils is also important. There is often a tendency for heather to encroach subsequently into established turf. This may be checked by very occasional liming and by fertiliser treatment to encourage a denser turf.

Sandy soils

The establishment of grasses on sandy soils, derived from sand dunes or alluvial deposits, requires great care, since moisture is often deficient. Late summer sowings normally prove more satisfactory than those in spring which may have to face drought conditions in the young stage. In the preparation of a seed bed it is necessary to pay particular attention to the incorporation of organic matter and to use seeds mixtures containing high percentages of fescue. Sodding on sandy soils is successful provided it is carried out in the earlier part of the winter and bone-meal dressings below the sods assist root development. Sandy soils are often acid soils (unless very close to the sea) and this factor should be borne in mind in relation to liming when establishing new grass from seed.

Heavy clay soils

Perhaps the most difficult for both lawn and sports field such soils retain water in wet weather and become very hard in dry. They usually carry heavy growth in spring and summer, easily churn up when played on in wet weather and they are not easy when it comes to making seed beds. They can soon become over-compacted when handled by heavy equipment.

It is important to maintain a good cover of grass since once bare progressive decline of the sward can be rapid. Surface dressings of sand and fine grit dilute the clay while repeated spiking assists water entry. The drainage system must be good, indeed there is much to be said for laying a clinker-ash bed below the top-soil. Any form of heavy rolling is most harmful to the soil structure.

Verges and slopes

Verges and slopes should receive similar treatment to the rest of the area. The difficulty on slopes very often is that they dry out in the summer weather, especially when facing south, and fail to recover before moss invasion commences. They also become poverty stricken, so that fertiliser treatment is necessary. The failure of water to penetrate on banks can be largely overcome by hollow tine forking. In some instances clay and stones are left near the surface, so making maintenance difficult. The best improvement is then brought about by re-laying and incorporating better soil. Slopes are difficult to maintain when steep. They should therefore be as 'gentle' as possible.

Narrow 9-in to 1-ft (23- to 30-cm) verges give an air of poverty and they are difficult to manage. A more pleasing effect can be obtained if the verge is at least 2 ft (60 cm) and preferably 3 ft (90 cm) broad. It should be carefully levelled and always mown with a roller mower. Creeping bent should not be used for verge making.

The renovation of neglected lawns

Much has already been said about the general treatment of lawns, but it may be helpful to bring together here all the points concerning the improvement of neglected turf. In dealing with the subject it is rather difficult to find a starting point, because the steps to be taken depend so much upon the symptoms and upon the individual case. For example, the condition of the turf may be due to having made a bad start, to lack of attention, failure to realise the amount of work necessary to produce good turf, and to spasmodic efforts of upkeep. Signs of a wrong start may be sought in insufficient soil, sub-soil near the surface, and water-logging—which may be shown by the nature of the weeds, by the presence of the wrong types of grasses for producing a permanent sward and, on playing fields, by areas of mud. Even if a good start has been made it may be followed by neglect resulting in weed and moss invasion, worm activity, disease, and invasion by leather jackets. Then the site may have been abandoned for some time with the result that the sward may have developed into a tangled mass of unkempt grass.

Where a bad start has been made and the turf is water-logged it is often best to lift and re-lay after giving attention to the surface soil. If, however, the soil is good while water-logging is bad, the drains may be faulty or inadequate and need attention; but where the condition is not very bad surface tubular forking may be sufficient to effect an adequate improvement. At any rate, in wet conditions tubular forking could be tried first before embarking on the major operation of re-laying or draining.

The presence of wrong grasses like perennial rye-grass may also be cause for re-sowing, but very often much improvement can be brought about by renovating the surface with seeds of better grasses and later keeping the turf constantly mown and dressed, thus gradually destroying the coarser growths.

On a neglected lawn or sports field where the grass has grown long, the first procedure should be to mow it down, using perhaps a rotary mower, and then to allow the sward to recover. It may then be possible to gauge whether there is sufficient bent or fescue grass present to make a permanent turf possible. Some little time may be allowed to elapse in order to obtain this information, and if bent and fescue are present in sufficient quantity the turf can most likely be brought into condition by general treatment with fertiliser or by weed-killing mixtures. If some cocksfoot is found it can be depended on to die out as a result of regular mowing and treatment. On the other hand, the mowing may reveal coarse grasses like rye-grass and Yorkshire fog, as well as weeds; in such an event a new start is probably the best. It is often cheaper in the long run to take the 'plunge', skin off the old turf, cultivate, fallow, and re-sow with fine seeds. Or it may be more convenient to dig in or plough in the old turf.

In lawns where weeds have become strongly established, a suitable selective herbicide should be used. Where they are used, a nitrogenous dressing should precede the treatment. Some renovation with seeds may also be wise, but care should be taken that the herbicide used does not affect the germination of the seed. If the turf is reasonably free from weeds, though thin and sparse, it will probably respond to a general fertiliser, followed by a dressing of sulphate of ammonia and careful attention to mowing.

Neglected turf often becomes worm-ridden and here eradication of the pest is the primary necessity. Another sign of neglect is moss—often more a sign of poverty than bad drainage or high acidity. Light raking and dressings of sulphate of iron and mixed fertilizer should be tried first of all.

Renovation with seed has already been mentioned. When it is to be carried out it should be preceded by mowing; the surface should then be vigorously scarified with rakes—or on large areas with harrows or mechanical scarifiers—until the seed bed is formed. The condition of the turf at this point will look hopeless, but it is surprising how rapidly it recovers. If the lawn is poverty stricken, treatment with a compound fertiliser should precede the sowing. The seed should then be scattered on the surface and worked in by matting or brushing. Light composting may be done on small areas but in all cases light rolling should follow.

In these circumstances it is difficult to obtain a really good seed bed in comparison with one made by full cultivation, so that very often the establishment rate of the grass is poor.

Where space permits, a turf nursery is a great stand-by. Patches containing Yorkshire fog or pernicious weeds may then be cut out and new turf inserted. Hole cutters up to 10 in (25 cm) in diameter may be had for this purpose. Needless to say the nursery should match as closely as possible the turf on which it is to be used, and in laying small turves in this manner they should be placed level or slightly below the general surface. The level can always be made up by top-dressing later.

Fungal diseases of turf are often caused by wrong treatment rather than neglect, although failure to deal with an attack sometimes leads to almost complete loss of the turf. It is therefore best after diagnosing the presence of disease to apply a fungicide. The same remarks may be applied to leather jackets, which if neglected and present in sufficient number may cause very serious harm to any lawn or sports turf.

In conclusion, it may be said that attempts are often made to resuscitate turf by various processes of renovation, when the quickest and cheapest way would be to start again. If mosses, rye-grass, and resistant weeds are present in abundance this alternative should be favourably considered. A fresh start provides a golden opportunity for thorough cultivation, with perhaps catch cropping, as well as for soil amelioration using organic matter, with gritty materials in addition when the soil is heavy.

CHAPTER THIRTY-ONE

Some 'Don'ts' in lawn upkeep—a summary

Most of the common mistakes made by lawn owners in establishing or managing their turf have already been mentioned in their appropriate context, but it may perhaps be of assistance if such failures be summarised in this chapter.

The secret of establishing a good lawn, or in fact any turf sward for games, is to make a good start; the preparation should not be hurried or skimped because this will most certainly lead to increased maintenance costs in the future. When operations are being planned it is important to look ahead and to bear in mind that a turf sward is permanent and that the period of construction offers the only opportunity for materially altering the physical nature of the soil.

The work of sodding should be completed by January or at latest February. It is true that good results are sometimes attained by turfing later than this, but the risks of drought damage become greater the longer the work is deferred. On sandy soils earlier turfing is better. Further, it is well not to use sods of uneven thickness, not to beat the sods into position, and not to roll heavily. On a well-prepared sod-bed, using good turves of even thickness, the latter operations are not necessary.

Except in warmer districts, sowing a lawn in the latter part of the season is best done no later than the end of August if good establishment is to be obtained. Sowing in spring should not be done before buried weed seeds have had an opportunity of germinating. Sowing should never be done on a bad seed bed or on one containing ungerminated weed seeds. Neglect of the seed bed is often a cause of future difficulties, and sowing clean seed on dirty land or bad seed on well-prepared land are both wasteful. Sowing should be done uniformly on a dry surface, and the seed should not be raked in too deeply. Sowing on heavy wet land should not be attempted until some pre-treatment has been carried out with sand and organic material. Cheap seeds mixtures for fine lawns should be avoided: they usually contain rye-grass. For the finest lawns rye-grass mixtures are quite unsuitable. Good quality blendings may, however, be used for second- or third-rate results. It should be remembered that grass seeds can be bought by name like the seed of any other plant. Seeds mixtures with many species have been found unnecessary, therefore for most purposes it is best to buy simple mixtures containing species or strains designed to meet the special requirements of fine turf.

Many lawn owners are mistaken in fertilising their turf excessively so that a soft lush growth, susceptible to disease, results: There is sometimes a tendency to listen to agricultural advice and to scatter raw dung on the turf. This is usually harmful, and it is better to allow the manure to decompose first in a compost heap with soil. Late March and early April are usually early enough for spring treatments. The last fertiliser dressing of the growing season should not be given later than the end of August or early September, though bone meal or compounds in which it is the main ingredient may be given later. It is perhaps unnecessary to point out that fertilising in winter is both harmful and wasteful, yet at times this mistake is made. When manures are purchased some attention should be given to the value of the material as plant food, always realising that small quantities of materials are proportionately more expensive to buy. Faulty distribution of the fertiliser on the lawn may be the cause of uneven colour or perhaps scorching of the grass. With a little patience and ingenuity uniform spreading may be achieved by stringing off the turf and by bulking with a carrier if a distributor is not available.

When top-dressing with sands or charcoal, smothering of the grass must be avoided, or it is likely to be checked and disease may then appear. If there is danger of this it is better to make the application in two half dressings; such dressings are best given before growth finishes in the autumn or just after it starts in spring. Sands containing clay particles should be avoided, as also sands of the moulding type, since both tend to bind in the turf and produce a compact layer. Sands containing lime should be avoided unless there is no alternative or unless there is some special reason for using them.

It must be remembered that mowing the lawn at long intervals is undesirable. It should be done regularly in accordance with the growth of the grass. Spasmodic cutting is harmful to the grass and deprives the soil more heavily of plant foods. Mowing two or three times a week is to be preferred, provided that the blade is not too low.

In the winter the grass should not be allowed to grow long or raggy, and occasional topping in open weather is desirable. There are points both for and against the return of the clippings. On the whole it is wise not to return them consistently, but only when they can be of service as a mulch in dry weather. The best results are got by regular switching before mowing and by mowing in different directions. Shaving the grass short in winter and early spring is harmful and the blade must be set higher than in the main growing season. With newly-sown turf, intensive mowing is harmful and topping is all that is required until the sward is well established, and in this connexion particularly a blunt or badly-set machine should not be used since it will 'drag' the tender seedlings.

Most intensively managed lawns must be watered but the top should not be sprinkled lightly in the belief that frequent light waterings are the best. An occasional thorough soaking is preferable, and it is easy to examine turf by taking out a plug to see how far the moisture has penetrated. Routine pricking is often omitted, but this is a mistake, because it is an aid to water penetration. Dry areas in summer benefit from local hand pricking. Slow application with a spray consisting of small drops is best, and uniform application should be aimed at so that the turf benefits evenly throughout the sward. One way of aiding penetration is to apply a portion of the water, then to return after an interval and apply the rest. Watering should commence before the soil is showing serious signs of drought.

Worming is an operation in which failure to get results has often been due to the choice of wrong weather conditions. A cold atmosphere or dry soil are unsuitable; mild muggy conditions should always be chosen. If it is not possible to de-worm, switching or brush harrowing as a means of scattering the casts should not be neglected.

A frequent result of neglect is weed invasion, and it is best to carry out eradication by a gradual process rather than a sudden one. Lawn sand and similar dressings referred to in the chapter on eradication should not be applied during drought, and must be carefully used on very matted turf since this is apt to suffer badly and to recover slowly. On the other hand, lawn sand mixtures should not be used during wet weather or their scorching action on the weeds will be lost, and the material may simply 'feed' the weeds. The optimum should be dry conditions with a moist soil. When eradicating weeds many lawn owners expect a magical recovery of the remaining grass. Very often it is essential to renovate the area with seed. The grass surviving from weed-killing work may, for instance, be only a shy creeper or even a tussock-former incapable of spreading over the bare ground. Occasional dressings of general fertiliser supplying phosphate and potash should be given, if weed-killing work is being carried out systematically.

The selective weed-killers should not be used in drought nor during or immediately prior to rain. Good growing weather is necessary, i.e. warm atmospheric conditions and plenty of moisture in the soil. Close adherence to the recommended rates is very important, and on no account should the spray or dust be allowed to drift on to other plants in the garden or neighbouring gardens.

Rolling is usually abused. An occasional rolling may be necessary, but the modern roller mower does a good deal of compressing. Worm casts should not be rolled out. This is harmful to the turf. Many lawn owners fail to appreciate that they can get better results by top-dressing to produce an even surface than by rolling. Rolling when the grass is thin or the surface very wet is harmful, and for most practical purposes on lawns a 2- or 3-cwt (100 or 150 kg) roller occasionally used will meet the purpose.

Neglect of aeration is one of the commonest faults on lawns and turf used for games, though there has been much enlightenment in recent years. Over-compression can be relieved by forking or spiking, which not only assists surface drainage and root formation but air entry and better use of fertilisers. Routine use of spiking machines on lawns is much to be commended.

The lawn mower is a vital implement in lawn upkeep, and must not be neglected; after use it should be cleaned and dried. Periodical greasing and setting of the blade is necessary, but one must not expect the perfect finish produced by an expensive fine cutting machine from one costing a fraction of the money.

It is impossible to make rules for all classes of turf and all conditions. Each lawn owner, greenkeeper, or groundsman must study his own turf. Where in doubt or where conditions are abnormal there should be no hesitation or loss of prestige in seeking and acting upon independent advice. Many examples could be quoted in which the reasonable person 'thinks' he knows, adopts a certain line of treatment, and having done so asks afterwards whether he has made the right decision! Quite often later history proves his decision to have been wrong.

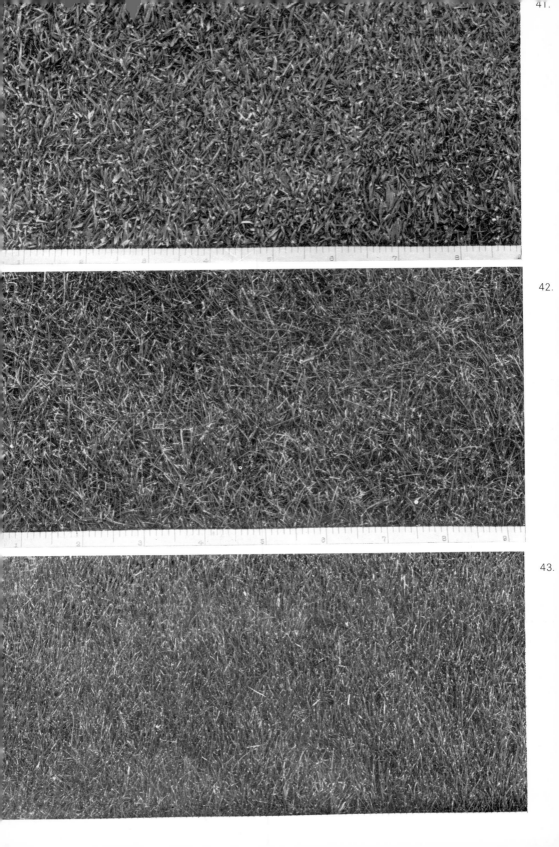

41.

42.

43.

45.

Established turf
Fig. 41. Browntop.
Fig. 42. Chewing's fescue.
Fig. 43. Fine-leaved fescue.
Fig. 44. Annual meadow-grass.
Fig. 45. Perennial rye-grass.

A diary for the year

No hard-and-fast time-table of operations in the upkeep of lawns can be made. It will be obvious that it is impossible in a general account because of the variations in local climate and season, individuality of the turf, the altitude and the nature of the soil. The diary given must therefore be taken as a general guide or indication as to the approximate time at which operations should be done, and variations will be necessary to meet individual cases. It applies in particular to lawns but can readily be adapted to turf used for various games.

January

This is often a bad month as regards weather, and in wet and snowy conditions outdoor work may be impossible, so that preparation of composts, ready for the season, should continue. Constructional work may probably be in hand and re-turfing should be finished off during the month, while during hard frosty weather the opportunity should be taken to complete carting work. Wet periods provide an excellent chance to study the correct working of the drainage system. Mowing is unlikely to be necessary, so the machines can be overhauled. When turf is used for games like golf, care should be taken that it is not damaged by play immediately after a thaw.

February

The bad weather may continue, but in damp, mild periods a start may be made with de-worming, or if it cannot be done, brush harrowing on large areas and switching on small areas may be carried out in dry conditions to scatter the casts. It is a good plan to compost lawns in this month—if it has not already been done. Any land that is in course of preparation for spring sowing should be well cultivated this month, and mossy turf may be dressed with sulphate of iron in preparation for later treatment.

March

Often in March there are signs of growth that may be misleading, but on no account should the turf be keenly mown. If desired, topping may be done with the blade set high, since cold weather often intervenes and newly-mown grass is susceptible to wind damage. After frost has lifted the turf, rolling on a dry surface may be carried out once or twice. Light sanding can be useful, and towards the end of the month, the weather being open, the first dressing of spring fertiliser may be applied. In northern parts or higher altitudes, it is better to defer this until the early days of April. De-worming can take place in suitable climatic conditions. Land for autumn sowing should be dug before the end of this month.

April

The frequency of mowing is usually increased in accordance with weather conditions, which may or may not be conducive to growth. Renovation of existing turf with seed should be carried out, and if leather jackets are present, eradication is advisable before damage becomes serious. The opportunity of doing this may occur earlier. Towards the end of the month a further light dressing of compound spring fertiliser or a dressing of sulphate of ammonia may be given, and at this time of year, a light attack of fusarium patch disease may occur. Switching before mowing and preventative spraying is advisable. With newly-laid turf, additional composting should be carried out.

May

Except in warm districts, where sowing may be done in April, the seeding of new turf should be carried out this month. Before sowing there should be a fallowing period in which dormant weed seeds have the opportunity to germinate, seedlings being destroyed by successive hoeings. When the grass seedlings are up they should not be over-mown. In May and June annual meadow-grass seeds profusely, and if it is desired to check it, drag brushing to raise the panicles should precede mowing. From now on mowing will occupy an increasing amount of time and it may be made more intensive. There will be a tendency for other operations like hand picking of weeds and weed-killing to be crowded out, but they should be continued where possible in the intervals. This and the succeeding month usually provide ideal conditions for obtaining maximum control with the selective weed-killers but drought should be avoided.

June

Mowing is in full swing this month, and as dry weather often intervenes care should be taken to raise the blade and allow the cuttings to return as a mulch. Light composting is beneficial and artificial watering preceded by spiking may be necessary. It is too late to eradicate leather jackets. Fallowing of land for late summer sowing should continue this month and the next.

July and August

Light fertiliser treatment with sulphate of ammonia is advisable and careful regulation of the mowing. There are signs of growth falling off in these months and of the encroachment of weeds like pearlwort. On the first sign of pearlwort it should be removed bodily or dressed out. The first batch of crane-flies may be emerging from the turf towards the end of August, and opportunities may occur for switching these as they emerge, so killing large numbers. If artificial watering is necessary, pricking should precede it. Final cultivation of land to be sown should be finished by the third week of August. The last fertiliser dressing of the season should be completed on established turf about the end of August. Selective weed-killers may be used, but growing conditions are not always so suitable.

September

Seeding of new areas is best completed before the end of August but in milder climates it may continue into the early part of September. The new sward should be watched carefully for damping off, and if any signs appear spraying should be done. Preliminary worming work may commence unless the soil is too dry, at any rate the worm-killer may be secured and any worming tackle got ready. Top-dressing with sand towards the end of the month is advisable, and hand forking and spiking may commence. The amount of mowing should be reduced, the blade being raised. Weed control with selective weed-killers is best completed for the season during this month.

October

Towards the end of September and in October, fusarium patch may become serious, and if so spraying should continue at intervals. Worming, hand forking, and spiking are all seasonable, while constructional work should commence. Composting of the turf at this time of the year is desirable, and of course much time will be taken up in sweeping up leaves where trees surround the lawn.

November and December

During these months testing for the presence of leather jackets, if suspected, should be carried out. A decision may then be made as to whether full control measures are required. The grubs are usually from $\frac{3}{8}$ to $\frac{1}{2}$ in (0·95 to 1·25 cm) long at this time. If earthworms are present as well, then Chlordane may be used, but it must be remembered that as frosts occur, worms and leather jackets retreat deeper into the soil. Constructional work will now be at its height, and on light soils, re-turfing should be completed. The weather in these months may interrupt operations, and the preparation of compost can be started. If applications of lime are to be given, these months are suitable, while bone meal may also be applied.

PART FOUR

Turf for sport and other purposes

CHAPTER THIRTY-THREE

Golf course management

The management of turf to meet the requirements of the game of golf is a subject worthy of much wider treatment than is possible in one chapter of a book dealing with general lawn and turf upkeep. It is impossible, therefore, to do more than bring together the salient features and the broad lines of treatment that should be adopted in practice. Not the least difficulty in treating the subject is the large area of land involved. On the same course the soil may in one part be light-sandy and on another extremely heavy; there are almost certain to be variations in aspect and altitude. Further, for the purpose of the game the separate portions of the course, namely, greens, fairways, and tees, demand different grades of treatment. Then there are the natural differences between courses, as well as differences created in their evolution through passage of time or in construction. Some courses are built on ambitious lines while others are simpler or have been evolved from small beginnings. All these factors together make the subject a wide one, and it may well be imagined, therefore, that no set course or programme of upkeep can possibly be laid down, much less can the attempt be made in one chapter to deal adequately with all aspects. All one can hope to do is to indicate the many problems of management and the basic principles involved. Many of these have already received detailed description in considering the upkeep of fine lawns, and the chapters dealing with seeds, fertilisers, diseases, and pests should be freely consulted.

Upkeep of putting greens on golf courses is the most intensive form of turf culture, and this alone introduces special problems. As distinct from other games golf is played all the year round, the others being either summer or winter sports, although on many congested grounds the same ground is used. This alone introduces special difficulties, for example, continuous wear and tear, often of an insidious nature, the difficulties of maintaining a good putting surface in the winter, and the difficulties of finding a period when drastic renovation or re-construction can be done without undue interference with players. All work on golf greens must be done by stealth, and the expert greenkeeper is a past master in treating his turf with the minimum inconvenience to the players, who, if they are of first-class calibre, will object to even trifling inconvenience. Surmounting of these difficulties has evolved a type of greenkeeper who is resourceful and capable of dealing with almost any eventuality; who is a keen observer, artful yet artistic, and though seldom appreciated to the full by those he serves, is worthy of our respect.

In establishing a new course it is first necessary to consider the proposed site as to whether it provides suitable natural features on which to lay out the holes. The services of a golf architect are best enlisted since he will be able to judge the potentialities of the land and to make the most of them in laying out the holes with gentle undulations which will bring out a variety of shots, so providing interesting playing conditions. Ample space to avoid cramping and danger is essential and the artistry of landscape construction must always be considered. Natural attractions like gently undulating land ornamented with heather, gorse, broom, or other plants make the best golfing country. The best turf for golf is undoubtedly found on heathlands, old parklands, and seaside links where the finer-leaved types of grass like the bents and fescues are dominant. On moorland courses moor mat-grass and wavy hair-grass also occur while on seaside links red fescue is often a dominant grass. On many seaside courses there is a tendency for moorland conditions to develop with an increase of bent and grass species found on peaty soils. Unfortunately many courses are laid on land which gives no help to the architect, so necessitating a good deal of landscape work.

Course design is more art than science, and is a subject upon which there are many conflicting opinions. It is beyond the scope of this account to deal with golf architecture, but some of the points upon which there is general agreement are worthy of inclusion here.

The present-day fashion in architecture is 'strategy', and the setting of a series of conundrums so that a player has to think out the best shot to reach the hole. The game should provide both mental as well as physical exercise. Fairway bunkers should be designed to govern the play of the hole and should penalize the scratch player's shot that has not been quite good enough. There must always be alternative routes to the green for short and long handicap players. The lay-out should encourage the player to incur a risk in the hope of securing a definite advantage, and the reward, if he is successful, should be proportionate to this risk. As to greens, these should be orientated properly and guarded with bunkers to catch the shot not played skilfully enough.

Every advantage should be taken of the natural features of the land, and the lay-out should be such that if possible no two consecutive holes are played with or against the same wind, and each hole should have distinct characteristics.

In constructing a course the artistic sense must have full play, and in making artificial features like mounds, hillocks, and hollows, they should be fashioned as though the natural process of wind and rain erosion had been at work. Good natural scenery with undulations enables the architect to present new views at each hole.

The general course length should not be below 6,000 yd (5,460 m) nor longer than about 6,500 yd (5,915 m), but there is to-day a tendency to extend still further. Preferably there should be three loops of six holes radiating from the clubhouse, or if the land does not permit this then two loops, so giving two starting points. The 'up and down' or grid-iron system of lay-out is dull and should be avoided, but of course the lay-out is very dependent upon the shape of the selected land and the funds available. Unfortunately land is often secured for golf course purposes without first of all exploring its ultimate possibilities for a well-designed course.

The cost of constructing a course is very variable and no exact figure can be given, but it is clear that new courses are likely to be few and far between bearing in mind present-day costs. Some increase in the number of Municipal courses is to be expected while the popularity of miniature or pitch and putt courses is spreading. There is much to be said for these since they can often occupy a piece of land quite unsuited to other games and they provide much healthful recreation. An 18-hole miniature course requires from 4 to 6 acres (1·6 to 2·4 ha).

Many well-conceived golf course schemes have been spoilt at the outset by faulty construction, by providing inadequate top-soil and by spending too little on cultivation and pre-treatment before sowing. Very often inadequate drainage and bad bunker construction lead to increased upkeep costs as well as much inconvenience to players for many years. In laying out and constructing a course it should be borne in mind that the course has subsequently to be maintained, therefore big undulations on a green surface, for example, should be avoided, and an adequacy of top-soil always provided. While large undulations are no doubt spectacular they lead to many upkeep problems, such as skinning of the turf by the mowing machines, shortage of space for the pin, and the mowing of large areas that are unnecessary and do not 'earn their keep'. On heavy land new greens should be adequately drained, while on lighter soils provision of water for coping with drought is now considered an essential. The chapters on drainage and watering should be consulted.

The method of sowing and pre-treating land should follow the lines laid down earlier in this book and thorough cultivation of the soil is essential. For putting greens there can be little doubt in the mind of anyone who has carefully studied the subject that a stand of bent, or of bent and fescue combined, gives the best all-round results. In practice, however, most greens contain a mingling of annual meadow-grass among the bent and fescue shoots, and one of the problems of golf-green upkeep is to keep this annual meadow-grass in subjection whilst favouring the bents and fescues. Many beautiful fescue and bent turf greens, particularly on seaside courses, have been lost through the adoption of treatments more favourable to annual meadow-grass than the fescue and bent. The fescue and bent greens are more closely associated with the lighter and poorer soils, but on heavy land greens consisting of almost a pure stand of annual meadow-grass are more frequently found.

To be a good golf green it is necessary that the surface should be true—and the golfer will excuse many blemishes provided he is able to putt accurately. Uniformity in colour and speed of the turf are important, and the grass should be capable of holding the ball on the line of the putt. The surface must be sufficiently well managed to resist wear and tear for twelve months of the year, and it should be reasonably resistant to dry weather. A good green should never be absolutely flat; undulations must be provided and sufficient space must be left for placing changes of the pin. Long, gentle undulations are best in which, with a flat space of at least one yard around, the position where the hole will be placed. The greens may be tilted to the left or the right, so necessitating greater skill in judging strength of stroke and direction. The surface of the green must be visible from the point at which the stroke to the green is played.

The difficulties of playing for twelve months of the year have already been mentioned, and in view of this great care is necessary with the greens in the winter months, especially during frost, when damage is likely to be severe. Clubs that are fortunate in having good approaches to the greens sometimes close, or temporarily close, the putting surface for a resting period, and this is beneficial especially during frost—though rarely received with equanimity by the golfer.

During the growing season mowing occupies the bulk of the time of the groundstaff. Here, uniformity through the eighteen greens is necessary. A variety of precision mowers are available for this operation. Many greens, however, are cut much too closely, and better results would be obtained by raising the blade slightly and cutting just as frequently. Boxing of cuttings, rolling and aerating have already been discussed under the upkeep of fine lawns, and reference should be made to the appropriate chapters. Much benefit has been derived from hollow tine forking in many cases.

Top-dressing is a subject to which special reference may usefully be made. It has already been stated that a true surface is essential, and today this condition is produced by top-dressings with composts, sand, peat, and mixtures of such materials for the purpose of filling the depressions, rather than by heavy rolling to compress the lumps. The preparation of compost heaps, and suitable apparatus for preparing the dressings have already received notice in earlier chapters. Composting has largely become a standard operation.

Weed problems on golf greens as well as fairways are often serious, and reference should be made to the appropriate chapter. Perhaps the most persistent and difficult weed on putting greens is pearlwort, after which may be placed mouse-ear chickweed, clover, and yarrow.

The approaches to golf greens are often neglected. Their purpose is to merge the fairways into the greens and to provide a run up to the putting green. They should be maintained in condition somewhere in between the putting green and the fairways. Mowing should be done more frequently and more keenly than fairways, and fertilising, worm-killing, and weed-killing must of course be more intensive. A good approach is a stand-by when the green requires renovation or resting or when there is frost, and for this latter purpose alone the production of good approaches is well worth while.

Perhaps no portion of the golf course receives less treatment than the tees, yet these areas are the very ones that receive the severest wear and tear. Neglect of the tees is usual, and although it may be argued that provided the surface is level and not sticky, bare ground would be satisfactory, yet nothing is more objectionable than a tee that has been cut to pieces by clubs or worn by constant traffic. Most tees conform to the conventional rectangular shape, thus nullifying much of the artistry and natural setting built into the course elsewhere. Tees nearly always require some re-turfing where the course is intensively used, and at short holes often require annual re-sodding. In many cases, especially at short holes, they are much too small for the amount of use. The life of the sward may be much prolonged by ensuring adequate drainage, by removing earthworms, and by occasional applications of fertiliser and top-dressing. The request is often made for a special species of grass capable of withstanding wear and tear on a short-hole tee. It is doubtful whether any species of grass is tough enough to withstand the severe punishment meted out, and the problem is essentially one of paying greater attention to upkeep by re-seeding, by resting, and by having an area sufficiently adequate to enable play to be distributed, so giving the surface a fair chance for recuperation.

Most clubs neglect their fairways, though in recent years there has been a greater realisation of the fact that constant wear and tear and regular mowing result in depreciation. Within reason the closer the 'lie' on fairways, the better will be the golf. Much improvement can be effected on fairways by spiking or harrowing and applying a general fertiliser. Above all, de-worming effects outstanding improvement and many excellent fairways have been created out of a muddy sticky surface by the removal of this pest. On some heavy land courses winter conditions have been improved by the use of ground sulphur but it is well to take advice before embarking on such a course of treatment because under the wrong soil conditions much damage may result. The general lines of treatment accorded to fairways depend entirely upon the nature of the grass, the soil, and whether weed-killing is involved. The programme adopted must therefore take into account the special conditions found, and to spread the cost a rotational system may be followed. Many instances are known, however, where fairways have been wrongly treated, with the result that worm and weed infestation has become greater rather than less. In treating large areas, where considerable sums of money may be involved, it is always best to obtain the advice of those who have made a special study of the problem.

The remaining turf areas on a golf course constitute the 'rough', and to-day the tendency is to mow the grass at intervals thus keeping it within reasonable bounds. This is understandable because an overgrown tussocky rough leads to much inconvenience and delay through search for lost balls. Many clubs have been compelled to add to their cutting machinery in order to cope with this additional burden. Unfortunately, to mow in this manner leads to a certain monotony of play, but by judicious planting of gorse, broom, and heather, great improvements can be effected to the artistic appearance of the course. Certain grasses are also useful, namely, sea-lyme grass and marram on seaside links, and *Brachypodium* and tufted hair-grass on inland situations.

These plants help to break up the ground, and with flowering shrubs much beauty may be added. Merging of the rough into the fairways and other parts in play should always be the aim.

Grazing of sheep on courses is often a vexed question. No doubt sheep help to reduce weed invasion, but the objectionable fouling of the land and the damage to bunkers usually results in more being spent in up-keep than brought in by rental. No first-class course now supports sheep if they can be dispensed with, but unfortunately some clubs only occupy the land on condition that grazing be carried out, whilst in other instances common rights prevent the exclusion of ponies and other stock.

Every course should have its turf nursery ready for re-constructional work or patching damaged greens. It may be worked down from the natural turf or prepared from seed upon a cultivated area.

It is interesting to reflect that the best courses found to-day are laid on sand dunes, moors, heathland, and commons, that is mainly upon the poorer types of soils which are less suitable for agricultural purposes and support the finer types of grass. Unfortunately, through lack of alternative sites, many courses have been laid on land that could be more usefully employed for crop production, and it is felt that in the future more consideration should be devoted to the utilisation of waste land which could not be brought into crop-bearing condition without a tremendous expense. These poor lands support the right types of grasses for turf, require the minimum of fertiliser treatment and, above all, need minimum attention from the mower. There must be many areas of poor land of this type that would make excellent courses, and to which access can now more readily be attained since the introduction of easier and cheaper transport.

An eloquent appeal has been made by Sir R. George Stapledon, in his book entitled *The Land, Now and To-morrow*, for the provision of more golf courses. It may be held that the number available at the present time is ample to meet the demand, but the author argues that golf is the best way of enjoying beautiful scenery and obtaining healthful exercise while still participating in a game without being unpleasantly crowded. He states that playing a game makes at least some demand on persons' originality and personality, and he pleads for a greater number of what he calls 'primitive' courses, that is courses that have cost a fraction of the usual amount to construct, where there will be no luxurious club-house, where the fairways will be broad rather than of good texture, and where the greens will be small and the hazards few and of a natural type. Stapledon claims that if primitive golf at low expense could be adopted by the masses of people it would form the best antidote to the hurry of modern life, the best cure for the mass psychology of modern town-life, and a step towards the right use of leisure. For such primitive courses to come into existence would necessitate golf developing into a rage as did the cinema and dog-racing some years ago and he firmly believes that there is a need for greatly extended facilities for primitive golf.

One of the first necessities in maintaining a golf course, however, must be a first-class greenkeeper resourceful in the management of his course and able to adapt his programme to suit weather or golfing events. He must be conversant with new ideas and ever prepared to learn from others or by his own past mistakes. He must also be willing to co-operate with the club secretary and chairman of the green committee in general maintenance work and in making minor constructional improvements to the course. Upon the greenkeeper rests the onus of preserving continuity of treatment and management. He should keep written records for his own benefit and those that come after him. He should be responsible to one person, and one only, from whom he should receive his orders and instructions.

Improvements in lay-out are the prerogative of the golf-course architect who has studied his subject and has a flair for the job. In practice one often finds that as soon as the mowing season is over the ground staff on a golf course are ordered to construct a new green, to fill in a bunker or make a new one, to remove a mound, or to carry out some such non-essential piece of work. This is the bugbear of green-keeping, since a well-qualified man will always have plenty of winter work in hand in preparation for the coming growing season. Another difficulty in maintaining courses is the tendency to experiment, and many good courses have been seriously damaged by ignorant application of some far-fetched idea. The present system of managing golf courses involves the election annually of a green committee. While this may at times have advantages, it is usually deterimental to the course, since there is nearly always lack of continuity of policy through the changing personnel, and the members are generally business men who forget that grass is a growing plant and that it is subject to the vagaries of season and climate.

CHAPTER THIRTY-FOUR

Upkeep of turf for bowls, lawn tennis, and croquet

Most of what has been written in the earlier chapters may be applied to the upkeep of fine turf for the games of bowls, lawn tennis, and croquet, though some variation and allowances must be made in accordance with the requirements of the particular game concerned and the standard of excellence desired. While management is just as intensive as on putting greens, there is the difference that absence of winter play provides a resting period when repairs can be effected.

Bowling greens

The subject of bowling-green upkeep is one that can only receive broad treatment in these pages, but the ever-increasing popularity of the game and the establishment of many new greens (principally welfare and municipal) has brought so many more people into touch with bowling-green upkeep that a general account of management and some of the difficulties may be found helpful. The bowler is perhaps the keenest and most critical user of fine turf, and as many problems in the later life of a green are related to a bad beginning it is advisable to start by a consideration of the building of a new green.

Construction
The majority of greens are made from seed, while on occasion, some are turfed. This complete turnabout in the procedure of a few years ago is directly attributable to the increasing difficulties of obtaining suitable supplies of turf and to the improved cultivars of seed available.

If autumn sowing can be carried out, the green having been constructed in the summer months, play may be possible with careful management for the second half of the season, although preference should be given to a full growing season without play. It is vitally important to use only suitable seed and to prepare the site in such a way that it will ensure a permanent sward. Where sowing is carried out, successful results have been obtained using browntop in combination with Chewing's fescue. Sowing solves the difficulty of finding good turf and the establishment cost is less, though the start of play may be longer delayed than if the green were turfed.

A turfed green can be constructed during the winter months, and with ideal conditions ready for light play about June, but again, preference should be given to a full growing season without play.

It is customary to use sea marsh turf for new flat greens whenever funds permit. Information is given in a previous chapter. The turf is somewhat variable, especially as regards relative proportions of the two grasses, and often creeping bent is dominant to the complete exclusion of the fescue. Careful watch should be kept for turves containing *Glyceria maritima* (*Puccinnellia maritima* (Huds) Parl.), a species unsuitable for fine turf formation.

The 'soil' in which sea marsh turf grows is in reality a fine sandy clay deposited by high tides over the surface. When this layer is compressed by rolling and treading on a green it becomes compact and so leads to difficulties in upkeep. It is true to say, though rarely appreciated by those who stress the value of the grass species present, that it is the ability of sea marsh turf to roll out into a keen flat firm surface that has largely earned the turf its reputation among bowlers.

In choosing the site for a green, it is necessary to avoid heavily-wooded areas, and to select land with gradual contours, as it is best to dig out the formation level of the green on the solid. The flatter the site the lower will be the cost. If on the slope, the 'fill and draw' method must be adopted and an adequate period left for settlement of the 'fill'. Where a green is constructed near trees, the shade factor will cause difficulty in upkeep. A green must above all be convenient of access, and it should be adjacent to an available water supply.

The game of bowls takes two forms;

(*a*) the universal 'Rink Game' played on flat greens, and

(*b*) the 'Crown Green' game, peculiar mainly to Yorkshire and Lancashire, played on greens having an approximately central crown of 6 to 12 in (15 to 30 cm).

A crown green is normally about 40 yd by 45 yd (36 m by 41 m), but regulation size is 45 yd (41 m) square. Flat greens are usually 42 yd (38 m) square. Rinks for competitive play should have a width of 19 ft (5·7 m). They should be turned periodically to minimize wear and tear at the ends.

The English Bowling Association through their laws concerning the conduct of the rink game, give specific details of the size of the green, the width and depth of the ditches, the slopes and heights of the banks surrounding the green, and some items are as follows:

1. *Green and ditch:* the green should form a square of not less than 40 yd (36 m) and not more than 44 yd (40 m) a side, and shall be surrounded by a ditch, which shall not be less than 8 in (20 cm) nor more than 15 in (38 cm) wide, and it shall be not less than 2 in (5 cm) nor more than 8 in (20 cm) below the level of the green.
2. *Banks:* the banks shall not be less than 9 in (23 cm) above the level of the green, preferably upright, or alternatively at an angle of not more than 35° from the perpendicular. No steps likely to interfere with play shall be cut in the banks.
3. *Division of the green:* the green shall be divided into spaces called rinks, each 19 ft (5·7 m) wide. For domestic play, the green may be divided into rinks not less than 14 ft (4·2 m) nor more than 19 ft (5·7 m) wide.

The recommendations for the construction of a bowling green include excavations and a piped drainage system, laid around and throughout the excavated area. A layer of broken stone to a depth of 4 to 6 in (10 to 15 cm), well packed and levelled can then be laid over the area, topped by a layer of finer broken stone. On top of this is superimposed a layer of light soil of about 4 to 6 in (10 to 15 cm), on which the prepared seed or turf bed is made.

This form of artificial construction is often adopted for Cumberland or sea marsh turf, and while it may produce a green quickly, there are invariably upkeep difficulties. In many instances in the tiled drain system, branch drains have been laid as close as 6 ft (1·8 m) apart. This has often resulted in 'over-draining' of the green. Intervals of 21 to 33 ft (6 to 10 m) are more sensible and economical.

On flat greens turfing is done in the diagonal direction but on crown greens laying should begin at the centre and proceed radially in concentric rings. The laying must be carried out carefully so as to ensure uniformity of surface. After the turves are laid they should be rolled and given a dressing of sharp clean sand.

When a green is to be sown, the preparations are the same except that over the fine stone layer, at least a 6 in (15 cm) stratum of light soil is needed—9 in (23 cm) is better. The majority of crown greens made from inland turf are laid upon soil overlying broken stone, and these greens cause much less difficulty in upkeep than sea marsh turf.

Upkeep

As the construction of flat greens is more or less standard it might be expected that all greens could be maintained on a common plan, but experience shows that greens differ markedly and that the variations in the programme of treatment are considerable. The skeleton treatment usually applied to a bowling green involves autumn and spring fertiliser treatment, forking, and sanding, while hand picking of weeds and careful management of play are necessary to get the best results. A common autumn treatment involves tubular forking followed by a dressing of bone meal and granulated peat followed by 5 to 6 tons of sharp clean sand and in the spring a dressing of general fertiliser. One or two inter-seasonal dressings of sulphate of ammonia, spread with a bulky carrier, or given in solution, are usually required also.

Tubular forking is particularly valuable on turf of the sea marsh type because the layer of silt in this turf becomes very compact and fails to encourage root development. It also bakes hard in summer. Perforation by tubular forking leads to a marked improvement in growth and in root development. Sea marsh turf readily 'caps' on the surface so that pricking, mechanical raking and harrowing are necessary. The operation of forking a flat bowling green should start in one corner and proceed diagonally.

It may safely be said that all sea marsh turf suffers sooner or later from invasion by annual meadow-grass, and often it would be true to say that the sea marsh turf has merely acted as a temporary sward until this volunteer grass becomes well established. Evidence points to *Poa annua* being favoured by the heavy use of mixed fertilisers though in some instances the tendency is for creeping bent to increase first of all at the expense of the fescue, since it can spread rapidly with its vigorous runners. Meadow-grass invasion may largely be checked by maintaining the green with a minimum of fertiliser and by regular brushing at flowering time, combined with boxing off the clippings.

The problem of preventing invasion of annual meadow-grass, or of eradicating it once it has entered a green, is one of great difficulty, but experiments have indicated that it may be possible to spray greens with a dilute solution of poison of such a strength as to kill the *Poa annua* selectively while leaving the fine grasses, bent and fescue, only temporarily harmed. Such treatment would, of course, involve a period in which the green was thin and of poor colour, and it cannot be attempted without expert advice and a botanical analysis to ascertain whether there is an adequacy of bent and fescue eventually to take the place of the *Poa* destroyed.

Common weeds encountered in sea marsh turf are sea milkwort, sea plantain, starweed, and sea pink or thrift. Perhaps the sea pink is the commonest of these species, but they can all be controlled by selective weed-killers. Scurvy grass (*Cochlearia*) is also found at times in this type of turf. Some poorer grades of sea marsh turf contain clover, which is little in evidence until regular mowing begins or when dressings of phosphate may favour its rapid spread. Weeds that invade the turf and may prove serious are pearlwort and chickweed, but these are easily controlled by selective weed-killers. *Glyceria* introduced in sea marsh turf dies out under mown conditions, and may thus cause bare places.

It should be appreciated that a bowling green must provide a dead true, keen surface, capable of withstanding intensive play. The run of the woods must not be deadened by heavy growth and the green must be of such a nature that it drains rapidly after heavy rain. Freedom from weeds, disease, and other blemishes is essential, and a tidy well-managed green should be ideal. Some heavy rolling in the spring may be necessary (4- to $4\frac{1}{2}$-cwt (200 to 225 kg) roller) to establish the surface, but there is a tendency on bowling greens to overdo this operation. Usually throughout the season the compressing action of a good 10-bladed roller mower is sufficient, supported perhaps occasionally by a light elm or iron roller 3 to 4 ft (0·91 to 1·20 m) wide. A roller, specially designed for bowling greens, is available; a simple device permits it to be used as a light or heavy roller at will.

Other operations necessary in the maintenance of a good green are regular surface spiking or pricking, drag brushing before mowing, and seasonal rolling, for which an elm roller of about 100 lb (45 kg) is usual. A hole cutter for patching and a mat for working in top-dressing are both necessary, while some clubs possess small mechanical distributors for applying dressings though it is doubtful whether these are desirable or necessary for such a relatively small area as a bowling green. As fertilisers are given bulked with carrier hand broadcasting should suffice. In dry summers watering is usually necessary and should commence before the turf is dried out. Very few bowling clubs take the trouble to provide themselves with a small turf nursery made from sods like those used on the green. This is very important because often at the end of the season patches have to be put in, especially at the ends of the rinks or in the corners of crown greens. Further, few clubs maintain a small compost heap, but while heavy composting is not necessary, a small quantity is useful in distributing dressing or adding to sand or peat to make a composite material. If no room exists for such a heap then 'made-up' top-dressings have to be used.

The management of the play on a green must be carefully studied by the man in charge, who in the case of flat greens must arrange that the rinks be turned at right angles periodically and that the wear is distributed evenly by occasionally missing out one rink so as to bring the wear at the rink ends on to a new position. Moving the rink marker even a matter of 2 ft (60 cm) each day before the start of play, can play a large part in the even distribution of wear. Excessive wear on the edges of the greens favours the invasion of annual meadow-grass and loss of the finer grass. The general method of pest and weed control, and the principles underlying intensive management, are as described in Part Three which should be consulted.

Lawn tennis courts

The general lines of upkeep on tennis courts should follow those laid down for the maintenance of a good lawn. It is essential, however, that trueness, firmness, and uniformity should be secured in order to give a good and accurate bound to the ball. The turf must also be sufficiently durable to withstand reasonable wear and tear, and to this end it is important that the herbage should not be so succulent as that required on, for example, a golf green.

In laying out a new tennis court the best orientation will be found to be NNW to SSE, though north and south will do. Good light is just as important as a good surface, and a suitable background of shrubs or trees is desirable. In laying out the site, adequate room must be provided, with plenty of run back and side run. A run back of 20 to 21 ft (6 to 6·3 m) and 12 to 14 ft (3·6 to 4·2 m) at each side of the court is the ideal. Careful levelling of the site is most important but a slight cross fall is not detrimental since it helps water run off. If excavation is done, an adequate period for settling should be allowed, though this will be less if the soil has been built up layer by layer and each one carefully consolidated.

A system of drainage is necessary on all but the lightest soils, and if the level area has been cut from a bank, a drain should be inserted at the foot. As well as a drainage system, amelioration of the top soil should be considered. At the least a layer of 6 in (15 cm), and preferably 9 in (23 cm) of good soil should be aimed for, and as pointed out in the general section on the construction of lawns, amelioration with organic matter or gritty materials is important. Whatever is done, very careful levelling is essential.

In constructing courts there is the usual problem as to whether to seed or sod, and decision is usually determined by whether or not supplies of good turf can be obtained at reasonable cost. More and more lawn tennis courts are being put down to seed and the chapters about sowing seed and the purchase of suitable mixtures should be consulted. When the court is established, it must receive regular and careful mowing, and in management the aim should be to produce a hard true surface—rather like a cricket wicket. In attaining this ideal the soil may often become over-consolidated, but this condition can be relieved nowadays at the end of the playing season by systematic use of spiking machines or once in, say, three years by tubular forking.

Earthworms often upset the surface of lawn tennis courts seriously, and their eradication is therefore imperative. Weed-killing should also be carried out, especially if there is any tendency for plantains to spread on the hard surface in which it is able to thrive. Clover should be dealt with rigorously, by raking, by applying dressings high in nitrogen, and by the use of selective weed-killers.

Most club courts and many private tennis courts suffer severe wear and tear, chiefly on the base lines, by the end of the season. As play usually continues until nearly the end of September, it is then too late to obtain a satisfactory establishment of seed able to withstand winter and the shocks of spring play. If there are a number of courts it is usually possible to close at least one by the end of August so that renovation by seeding can then be done successfully. By and large, however, it is customary to repair the base lines by re-turfing. In doing this, many clubs import turf from a field or another site, but find that it fails to match and does not give good conditions for the following season. A better plan, therefore, is to utilise turf from the surrounds or from between the courts, the scars being then re-turfed with new sods or sown the following spring. The part that receives the maximum wear is a strip along the base line for a distance of about 11 ft (3·3 m) either side of the centre line of the court. Outside this, wear and tear is rarely serious. Sometimes where there is sufficient room, it is possible to make a left or right shift of the courts by some 20 or 22 ft (6 or 6·6 m), thus enabling the re-turfed area to have a season of reduced wear and tear, while the maximum play takes place on an area that has been longer established. After a second season, return to the original positions can take place. Sometimes where courts are placed end to end, an end shift is possible, placing the base line in the second year about the position of the service line of the first year. Naturally the practicability of such a device depends entirely upon the space available, and unfortunately many single or groups of courts are so hemmed in that there is no room to adopt this suggestion. As already stated, the general lines of manuring, spiking, and top-dressing should closely follow those laid down for general lawns, though care must be taken not to use heavy quantities of sand, which are apt to give a crumbly surface unable to last the season.

It is not within the scope of this account to deal with hard courts, except to say that difficulty may be experienced in controlling moss. For this a common treatment is an application of a 5 per cent solution of caustic soda, but there are many other weed-killing materials that will achieve this purpose, e.g. sodium chlorate, borax and a mixture of these.

Croquet lawns

For croquet lawns a fine, keen, fast turf, but not necessarily hard, is required, and the surface should approximate in quality to the finest type of golf green. The general lines of treatment to adopt are similar to those for golf greens, always bearing in mind the advantage that croquet lawns have in not being required during the winter months, at which time systematic forking, harrowing, and general renovation can be carried out without the disadvantage of interrupting play. The absence of undulations eliminates many of the difficulties of mowing, dressing, and watering so often experienced on undulating golf greens.

CHAPTER THIRTY-FIVE

Management of football, hockey, and cricket grounds

Hockey pitches

In order to keep the ball on the ground and permit good stick work, a keen firm, true surface must be available for this game, and it is therefore necessary that the pitch should be well drained and reasonably level. Ridge and furrow land must be re-laid and regular mowing is important to provide ideal conditions. Many old-established grounds are laid on matted bent-fescue turf, which, when well mown, rolled and spiked, gives an excellent dry surface during the winter months.

Rolling being occasionally necessary it is usual to find that the surface of hockey pitches has a tendency to retain moisture and for pan to form at a depth of 2 to 3 in (5 to 7·6 cm), so preventing seepage, and giving a wet spongy surface, although at several inches depth the soil might be reasonably dry. Great improvement can be effected in these circumstances by systematic spiking with one of the machines on the market for the purpose. The spikes should penetrate about 4 in (10 cm), and on very wet places, hand forking will also be necessary. When making a new ground on heavy land, land drains and soil amelioration should provide conditions so that if ponding takes place, it may readily be relieved by forking to allow the water through. Worm activity in hockey pitches often causes a slippery surface, with the ball constantly picking up mud. De-worming is the first step to improvement in such circumstances, and generous sanding will assist surface drainage.

The area between the 25 yd (22 m) line and the goal, especially inside the striking circle, as well as the central bullying area, receives the maximum wear. When play finishes these parts must be renovated with seed after thorough raking to prepare a seed bed. A dressing of fertiliser should be given to assist establishment. It is better not to attempt turfing since dry weather may result in serious cracking. Many grounds are sown with rye-grass, which does not give that fine-textured turf necessary for the best playing conditions, but if rye-grass is already present then leafy strains of this species should be included in the mixture for renovating the striking area. Otherwise non-rye-grass mixtures are best for general use on first-class grounds.

Many schools and colleges use their hockey fields during the early part of the season for rugby or association football. This makes the provision of a good hockey surface difficult, but there may be no alternative, though it is unfortunate that the heavier games should not be played after the hockey season instead of before.

Occasional fertiliser treatment and regular mowing, followed by routine rolling in the growing season, will keep the surface in good condition. Many grounds are mown with heavy motor machines, but better results would be obtained by mowing with the triple type of machine thus enabling rolling to be better controlled.

Association and Rugby Football pitches

The long playing season of more than two-thirds of the year, including preliminary practising periods, coupled with the fact that these games may be played in very wet conditions or following frost, results in very heavy wear and tear.

On professional association football grounds the wear is so great that there is little left at the end of the winter but a mere triangular patch of grass in each corner. Intensive renovation each spring is therefore necessary on such grounds, but the difficulty is that play does not cease until the end of April, and as practising begins in August, only May, June and July are left in which to effect recovery. Under these conditions rye-grass should form the main ingredients of the seeds mixture because it is the grass species able to establish itself most rapidly in the time available. In order to gain some time, seed is often scattered on to the pitch before the end of the season, and thus trodden in. It is true that a percentage of this becomes established and starts growth before the major operation of renovation begins, but far better results are obtained by shallow forking to put the seed slightly below the playing surface. While most clubs are prepared to renovate their pitches at the end of the season, they often do so in a very haphazard manner, and the seed bed thus produced is so poor that establishment and growth of the grass is feeble. A good seed bed must be produced, in many instances with a soil that has lost its structure.

Spiked and smooth chain harrows, tilther rakes, sacrifiers and machines designed specifically to tilth and re-seed the ground in one operation can provide the soil conditions necessary for successful renovation.

During the winter months, occasional rolling becomes necessary, and the surface often becomes wet and greasy through the puddling action of the feet. Under such conditions the moisture is retained on the surface even though the ground may be well drained. Regular routine spiking and heavy sanding will do much to prolong the life of the pitch and give better winter conditions.

The pitch should be levelled as soon as possible after play, and it should be remembered that rolling can not level a pitch. Chain harrows, scarifiers or brushes can provide a level without undue compaction. This must be done to guard against a sudden fall in temperature causing freezing in the uneven state, thus possibly jeopardising the next game. When rolling is done, it should be done as lightly as possible, consistent with the provision of a good surface, and if possible carried out only when surface conditions are favourable.

Weeds of football grounds are easily controlled by the use of selective weed-killers. Care however, must be exercised in the use of these materials when renovation has been carried out and the sward is not mature.

A compound fertiliser should be given each spring to assist establishment of the turf, and during the summer months the grass should be kept mown, though not too keenly. On a general sports ground, football pitches often form part of the outfield of cricket pitches, and so are mown as a regular maintenance feature.

The introduction of spiking and slitting into ground upkeep programmes, is one of the most striking developments of recent years, and many clubs can testify to the prolonged life of the pitch and better playing conditions that result.

Normally, less attention is devoted to grounds for rugby than that for association football. Renovation with seed at the end of the season may be necessary, but a much longer growth of grass may be left to resist wear and tear of the playing season. The longer growth will also help to ward off frost in the depth of winter. During these winter months when frost appears likely, many clubs use a straw covering, which involves a not inconsiderable expenditure on labour and purchase of straw.

The use of electric soil heating wires have been evaluated, and as a result of practical recommendations, systems have been installed at a few league football grounds, using insulated wires and mains voltage. The underground wires in some instances have led to a restriction of deep spiking. A system of soil warming using plastic pipes and hot air has been introduced in recent years, and has proven its worth under practical conditions. Perforated pipes are run under the ground, and air, warmed by a small heating plant, is fed into them. The warm air passes through the perforations in the pipe, and rising to the surface, warms the soil and melts the snow and ice. The system has automatic settings, and when set correctly, will start to operate if the temperature drops below the accepted level.

Cricket grounds

The upkeep of cricket grounds is a subject upon which many diverse views exist, and probably no two groundsmen will agree as to the best way of preparing and maintaining a pitch. The two distinct types of turf on cricket grounds are the square, which must be able to withstand wear and tear and give a true playing surface, and the outfield which must be well mown and occasionally rolled to give a fast surface. Outfields are often the site for winter games pitches, and if it can be arranged that hockey rather than association or rugby football is played adjacent to the square, then the outfield, because of the rolling involved in preparing good hockey pitches, will prove to be quite suitable in the summer following.

The square is the 'holy of holies' to the groundsman, who often lavishes nearly all his personal care and attention on it. Here, raking, close mowing and rolling produce a result that is a mere apology for a turf. Indeed, maintenance of a first-class pitch is more a question of careful top-dressing and of discreet use of the roller than of turf upkeep.

Among the attributes of a good cricket square are that it should be of adequate size, and that except for the top three inches, the soil should be of a free draining nature. The top three inches should be of a heavy clay nature, so that it can be rolled out into a smooth firm surface to provide the pitch. In clay soils, it will be necessary to provide satisfactory drainage, while on light soils it will be necessary to incorporate a heavy soil.

Annual top-dressings of a clay loam soil, 6 to 10 lb per sq yd (3 to 5 kg per m^2), carefully spread and luted in, will help to preserve the surface for good pitches. This is the policy adopted by the majority of groundsmen today, and with adequate preparation will provide a pitch with bowler and batsman competing on equal terms. No soft compost material should ever be used, and any tendency for a fibrous mat to form should be rigorously prevented. No light soil or sand should be used as top-dressing, as this type of material would cause pitches to crumble.

Marling of pitches is an operation that is sometimes resorted to in the absence of a proper programme of top dressing. It should be carried out in the late autumn, and an annual dressing of from 1 to 2 lb of marl per sq yd (0·50 to 1·00 kg per m²) would be applied, and worked well into the surface by brushes and allowed to weather down.

A compound fertiliser is beneficial about the end of September. In view of the heavy rolling and the compact nature of the soil, and sometimes marl on the pitch spiking, with chisel tines preferably, should be carried out in the autumn before top-dressing. Scarification should be carried out on the whole square, with the main 'clearing out' operation being done in the autumn. De-worming may also be necessary, if the worm population interferes with the preparation of pitches.

The final preparation of a pitch for play begins about a week before it is needed, and involves mowing, raking, further mowing and further raking to thin out and remove the top growth. Rolling, and further rolling will be needed to consolidate the pitch, and if the weather is dry, watering of the pitch will be necessary during this period. It is an accepted feature of pitch preparation though, that water should not be applied to the pitch in the three or four days preceding the match. It should be noted however, that any watering needed, should be done so that the water penetrates to a depth of about 3 in (7·6 cm).

A curious relic of groundsmanship of a past era is that of 'doping' a pitch. A week or ten days before a pitch was needed, a mixture of 60 to 80 lb (27 to 36 kg) of cow dung was made with 14 lb (6·3 kg) of marl, and 40 gal (180 l) of water. After standing for three or four days, it was sieved and applied to the surface of the pitch after watering. When this odious mixture was nearly dry, it was rolled out to a 'shirt front'. Needless to say, what with the shortage of cow dung and the improvement in the techniques of groundsmanship, this performance is quite properly discontinued.

A compound fertiliser is sometimes applied to the square in early April, although some groundsmen hold back this dressing. In many instances, if the autumn work has been carried out properly, there is no need of fertilisers in early spring. It is wise to dress a pitch as soon as possible after use so as to encourage recovery, and so permit use at a later date. During the season, all worn patches caused by the bowlers, batsmen and other players should be promptly renovated with seed or turf. Before renovation, the pitch can be opened up with slitting tines, and where necessary given a good watering. Though the widest and deepest of the worn patches are best patched with turf, this must be kept well-watered to resist the effects of drought. Heel marks and other such damage on the pitch can be eased up with a knife, then pressed back into place with the foot. Any soil introduced to the pitch in the renovation process should be of a heavy nature.

The aim of a groundsman should be to produce a pitch that in the first place is true and has a fair bounce. In past years the marling of pitches led to pitches favourable to the batsman and heartbreaking to the bowler. The ideal pitch would be one that allows both batsmen and bowlers to make the best use of their techniques, the batsman exercising all his resources to circumvent an attack consisting of accurate length and controlled spin.

The ideal preparation of a county wicket should aim to give a pitch sufficiently durable to withstand two full day's play; it should give the bowler a chance on the third day; it should not be dangerous as far as personal injury is concerned; and it should give life to the ball.

Some attention must always be paid to the practice wickets, which should receive the same treatment as that of the main pitch.

The outfield should be mown short, kept free of weeds and worms, and to be of such a surface that will enable a well-struck ball to travel evenly and quickly to the boundary. A well-drained outfield is important, and ideally there should be a slope of not more than 1 in 85 from the square in every direction.

Sports grounds used all the year round

At most schools and colleges, and on many club grounds, the fields are in use almost continuously all the year round—cricket in summer, football and hockey in winter. School grounds do receive some rest in the Christmas, Easter, and Summer vacations, but this is made up for by the very heavy use during term time, when each ground may have to carry several games a week. Where hockey or football grounds are transformed to cricket outfields for summer use, rapid renovation at the end of the winter season is necessary, all places that are worn being sown with seed and dressed with fertiliser. For this purpose an application of sulphate of ammonia with carrier produces rapid response. Before sowing takes place, however, uneven places must be well raked and harrowed, and even some soil added, the aim being to produce as good a seed bed as possible with a truer surface. At the end of the cricket season a general compound fertiliser should be given in order to establish the grass before winter play begins. Systematic spiking is also helpful at this point, and much can be done to improve conditions by de-worming and by attention to drainage.

The amount of wear and tear on hockey and football pitches can often be reduced materially by shifting the goals from time to time. On school grounds there is often room to do this.

In some districts lacrosse is the popular winter game, played on fields set aside for the purpose or upon cricket outfields. The nature of the game does not involve so much cutting up of the ground as in hockey or football, and provided the turf is well drained it soon recovers at the end of the playing season. A certain amount of wear and tear takes place where the play is concentrated, and if considered necessary or desirable, renovation and fertiliser treatment may be given.

CHAPTER THIRTY-SIX

Upkeep of polo grounds, racecourses, dog tracks, and other turf areas

Polo grounds

It is essential that polo grounds should be laid in the direction of north to south in order to avoid playing into the setting sun which is not only dangerous but a disadvantage to the team playing towards it. Ideally the ground should slope gently on the line of the diagonal and this facilitates drainage. The rules of the Hurlingham Club Polo Committee require that a ground shall not exceed 300 yd (274 m) in length and 200 yd (182 m) in width if unboarded, but if boarded the width shall not exceed 160 yd (146 m). There must be a safety zone within about 30 yd (27 m) of the goal line and within 10 yd (9 m) of the boards. From this it will be seen that a full sized unboarded polo ground requires a turf area 360 yd long by 200 yd wide (329 by 201 m), while if boarded the area necessary is 360 yd long by 180 yd wide (329 by 164 m). Ideally also a polo ground should be laid on a medium loam soil, because in wet conditions a clay soil is too slippery while in dry weather it becomes too hard. On the other hand, very sandy soils are dusty and may also become rather hard in dry seasons.

If the skill of players and the speed of ponies is to be exercised to the full a true and level surface is a necessity. Moreover, the turf should be tough and able to resist the hoof action, providing at the same time a sure foothold for the ponies. Any tendency for the turf to tear up in long strips must be avoided. The fact that polo is a spring and early summer game, played for 6 or 8 weeks, makes it unnecessary that the ground should be laid upon a cinder foundation. The latter part of the growing season is available for recuperation.

The eradication of weeds on polo grounds must receive attention because, even if the ground be level, its trueness may be destroyed by weeds preventing true running and causing a slippery surface. With broad-leaved plantains, for example, the ball may jump from 3 to 6 in (7·6 to 15 cm) off the ground and if it is rolling slowly it may be turned off several inches. Large patches of clover form a slippery surface for the ponies, which may fall heavily when attempting to turn. Daisies are also best eradicated, because they will cause a polo ball to jump and diverge from the line when it is running slowly. Similarly dandelion, yarrow, and buttercup are best eradicated before they have opportunity to increase.

Perhaps the most important aspect of the maintenance of polo grounds is the mowing, and no more than 1 to $1\frac{1}{2}$ in (2·5 to 3·7 cm) of growth must ever be allowed. Keen mowing with gang mowers is essential. The grass must be kept short because a long growth provides heavy play and is tiring to the players. Even after the end of the playing season it is desirable to keep the ground topped, and in the winter months, if the weather has been open, an occasional run over with the mowers will be needed.

In conjunction with mowing, systematic rolling is necessary, using a wide agricultural roller. If earthworm casts are numerous, rolling causes a slippery sealed surface, and therefore their eradication is essential if the best results are to be obtained. They also cause an uneven surface and gang spiking machines will provide the aeration and relieve the compression caused by rolling.

It is useful to apply a compound fertiliser in the early spring and again when play ceases after the season. After the end of the playing season too, renovation with seed may be required, harrowing the seed in and lightly top-dressing with soil. The provision of turf nurseries for patching badly-damaged portions, especially in front of goal is worth while. From these general points, it should be possible to elaborate a system of management to suit most grounds.

Racecourses

The ideal turf for horse racing and training is that found on heaths and downs, where the mat-forming grasses, the bents and fescues, often aided by mat-grass and wavy hair-grass, have developed over a period of many years a thick springy layer of fibre. The sites for the older race-courses were undoubtedly chosen deliberately because of the nature of this turf, though no doubt accessibility was an auxiliary factor. The excellent springy turf found at Ascot, Newmarket, Doncaster, and on the downland racecourses, to mention a few instances, is of this matted type. The reason for its popularity for horse racing and training is that the springiness acts as a shock-absorbing layer between the hoof and the underlying soil. This type of turf drains well and there is little fear of harming the horses; even those with doubtful legs can be kept exercised in dry weather. A course constructed on a medium soil is best because a very dry soil is apt to be dusty and a clay soil provides such hard going in dry periods that there is a greater chance of the horses' legs being damaged. In wet conditions clay soils are apt to be treacherous.

It is unfortunately a fact that on old-established racecourses, much of the springy mat of fibre has been lost, either through wrong use of fertiliser or applications of lime, or both, and no doubt this loss has been assisted by the punching and tearing action of the hooves, which tend to destroy such mat. On present-day courses it has therefore become the custom to leave a long growth of grass in order to give a shock absorbing cushion instead of that formerly provided by the fibre below the surface. One problem in connection with racecourse upkeep is the retention of matted turf or its recovery where lost. Dressings of granulated peat are valuable in aiding mat formation. The grass should not be allowed to grow too long, as this might result in a loss of density in the turf. Good results are obtained by regular mowing with gang mowers set to cut a height of about 2 in (5 cm), later allowing the grass to grow a little longer immediately before a meeting. By this means a much denser turf is obtained with more shoots per unit area, and balance between the finer-leaved grasses and the coarser-leaved species is distributed in favour of the former. On light sandy soils peat may be used as a top dressing, and on heavy soils sanding is beneficial. On hurdle and steeplechase courses a rather longer and more tufted turf is desirable. A proportion of cocksfoot may be used, but the grass should not be sown on courses used for flat racing since a more uniform and shorter mown turf is required.

The question of watering racecourses has to be considered, and early methods involved the application of water from a system of perforated pipes arranged round the rails. Unfortunately this may easily leave unwatered a strip of turf immediately adjoining the rails, thus giving harder going than on the part receiving the bulk of the water. Better results can be obtained by using pop-ups or the self-travelling types. These are used in preference to other types because they give good uniformity of application with minimum attention. In addition, spiking or slitting should be adopted to facilitate the entry of such water and to open up the soil wherever it has the tendency to be poached through the pounding action of the hooves.

Between races it is necessary that torn up turf shall be replaced by stamping down. This means a good deal of casual labour must be available. After a race meeting further attention to torn turf is needed and hoof-marks should be filled with sandy soil and seeded. Between race meetings regular mowing with occasional rolling must be done to prepare the surface. An uneven surface becomes dangerous in dry weather. When the soil is moist, rolling is therefore important. Light spring fertiliser treatment, and even a light dressing of a nitrogenous fertiliser a few weeks before a race meeting will give good results.

Moles and rabbits must be ruthlessly destroyed otherwise the soft ground caused by their runs or burrows may easily bring a horse down.

Even going is the essential pre-requisite for a successful racetrack.

Dog tracks

A uniform hard-wearing turf is required. It should be regularly mown at about $\frac{3}{8}$ in (9 mm) height and kept free of weed. Wear and tear at the bends is considerable and periodic re-turfing here is nearly always necessary. A turf nursery is desirable.

The turf should not be too soft but on the other hand hardness is harmful to the dogs' feet. For winter racing it is important to protect the turf from frost and several methods are used, e.g. covering with peat and sweeping off before a race meeting, covering with straw and, thirdly, a process of stuffing straw into the ground and, as it were, thatching the surface. Soil warming methods, of electric wires under the surface or that of using hot air through plastic pipes, would appear to offer alternatives to the above.

Turf on made-up land

In the neighbourhood of many towns, sports grounds have been laid out upon land made up of tippings of household and other refuse. Unless tipping is carefully controlled however, the results are poor, but on 'controlled tippings', excellent swards may be produced. Notable examples of controlled tippings in relation to the provision of playing fields have occurred (and are still occurring) in many areas where steeply sloping or broken land unsuitable for building, has been secured and converted into valuable recreation fields.

Before tipping commences any useful top spit is removed to one side, the refuse being then tipped in layers 6 ft (1·8 m) deep and in strips 36 ft (11 m) wide, with banks at an angle of 40 degrees. Vehicles deposit the refuse on the upper level just clear of the front bank of each 36 ft (11 m) strip and so each layer gets well consolidated by the repeated passage of vehicles. Great care is necessary to bury soft materials at the lower levels, to flatten tins and bottles, and to bury paper, the surface being finally finished with ashes and gulley or road sweepings followed by the top-soil. On deep sites the building up continues in 6 ft (1·8 m) layers and this method of compression permits little spontaneous combustion, though the exposed ends of banks have been known to smoulder and to sink considerably.

Topping of the sites with at least 6 in (15 cm) of soil or preferably more is necessary, after which seeding may follow. If turfing is to be done a little less soil is permissible but seed has been sown on only 2 in (5 cm) of soil, with resultant failure. With good preparation, excellent turf can be formed, and in one instance where a cricket out-field was sown with a mixture of fine fescues and bents, the sward was as good, if not better, than many found on natural land.

At times, fields produced on controlled tips suffer in late summer and autumn from the occurrence of the toadstools of the Shaggy-cap fungus (*Coprinus comatus*). The caps of this fungus cause eruptions and upset the surface, and, worse still, as they ripen they change to an inky black mass that is most objectionable. The phenomenon is worst on newly-made fields and gets less as the tip matures.

Play grounds

Most municipalities now provide play grounds for children, and these are usually in two areas, one exclusively for the use of infants up to 5 years, and the other for children of 5 to 6 up to 11 years. Unfortunately on many grounds near the centre of cities an attempt is made to produce turf, but the intensity of use makes the result most unsightly. Here it is much better to treat the surface with shale or tarmac rather than attempt to produce grass. In areas that are not so near to the centre of cities a turf made from mixtures containing rye-grass is best, and regular renovation must be carried out. Many play grounds are seriously neglected, with the result that bare places appear, particularly in the neighbourhood of apparatus such as slides, swings, and so on. Being placed in permanent positions the wear immediately around the apparatus is considerable and therefore steps should be taken from time to time to prepare a seed bed and renovate or, better, make a permanent hard surface. The turf on play grounds should not be allowed to become unduly long, or the sward is unpleasantly wet for playing, and some degree of drainage is necessary to ensure that the maximum use is made with the minimum of wear and tear. An occasional general fertiliser will do much to counteract the damage to the grass.

Cemetery turf

Cemetery grass has perhaps the least work of any turf sward and is probably the most neglected. Often it is weed-infested. In many cemeteries rotary mowers are used to control growth. While ornamental lawns present little trouble from the mowing angle, this is not so in cemeteries, mainly old ones, where mounds on graves are permitted and where kerbs are numerous. The tidy and orderly management of the grass in cemeteries would be facilitated if the 'lawn cemetery system' were more widely adopted and the older burying grounds gradually converted. While there are machines available that will cut up to the coping edges of the monuments, thus enabling the work to be accomplished more rapidly than by hand, the job is still not easy nor is it quick. Keen mowing is not necessary, but it should be carried out regularly, and as this will lead eventually to some difficulty with weeds, occasional treatment to control daisies or plantains on heavily-trodden paths is necessary. Every cemetery should be provided with a turf nursery from which sods may be obtained for patching paths or turfing graves.

Playing fields

It is perhaps appropriate in concluding this chapter to refer to the work of the National Playing Fields Association. The Association was founded in 1925 and incorporated by Royal Charter in 1932. It relies entirely on voluntary contributions for its existence. Its main function is to encourage the provision of playing fields and children's play grounds. Persistent propaganda has undoubtedly brought the need for more playing facilities to the notice of Government Departments, Local Authorities, and the public generally with the heartening result that the nation as a whole has tended to become more playing-field-minded.

Advice on the general, legal, and technical aspects of playing field provision is obtainable from the Association through its affiliated County Branches. Applications for grant aid are considered, if eligible, under the current grants policy.

The desirability of obtaining sound advice before carrying out constructional work, draining, seeding, and fertilising, or when considering subsequent maintenance, is stressed if full value is to be obtained for money spent.

The NPFA recommends that for adequate public playing facilities a minimum of 6 acres (2.4 ha) of publicly-owned and permanently-preserved playing space per thousand of the population is essential. This standard is exclusive of any privately-owned sports facilities, woodlands, commons, pleasure grounds, ornamental gardens, full-length golf courses, or other open spaces where the playing of games by the general public is neither encouraged nor permitted.

CHAPTER THIRTY-SEVEN

Establishment and upkeep of airfields

Although large aircraft runways are now the basis of all major airfields, there are still all-grass fields in use for light aircraft. Also there are large grass areas on most airfields lying between the runways and the various taxi tracks.

Ideally the land should have a light to medium loam soil with a gentle fall and provision for the disposal of drainage water. If the soil is too sandy, it will not resist the rush of air from the air-screws and treatment with heavier soil becomes necessary. On the other hand, very heavy soil usually results in drainage problems and a soft muddy surface.

Landing grounds are usually made from pasture or arable land though at times heath or parkland turf has been used. There is no specified minimum size for an aerodrome, and indeed some grass strips are extremely small, and although some of these small grounds have received little or no preparation, this often proves to be the exception.

It is very seldom that the area needed for an aerodrome requires no constructional work, and broadly it can be reckoned that any work required will depend on the amount of traffic and type of aircraft in-volved, thus more work will be needed at a busy airport with facilities for taking off and landing of passenger and freight aircraft, than on that needed for a light aeroplane club. In preparing a new ground, extensive levelling may be required, involving the transport of large quantities of earth. Slopes up to 1 in 80 are permissible but steeper gradients require reduction. After ploughing, small undulations of 8 to 9 in (20 to 23 cm) can be smoothed out by mechanical grading machines but in doing this, exposure of the sub-soil must be avoided. Where it comes to the surface it must be dug out and top-spit applied. Sometimes levelling can be done by merely adding soil to depressions, leaving the higher portions untouched.

The drainage of airfields is of paramount importance, and many of them suffer very severely in wet weather from water-logging or even ponding on the surface. Special attention must always be devoted to ensuring adequate drainage of heavy land. If the soil is porous an elementary scheme of drains is all that is necessary. Very often on old pastures there are ditches and hedgerows, and after the hedges and trees have been dragged out it is possible to use the ditches as the skeleton of an adequate drainage system, to which laterals may be taken. Thorough drainage is most important in the neighbourhood of the buildings and tarmac apron, because wear and tear is concentrated here. Old pastures taken over for a landing ground may be very much pitted and broken by the feet of stock and often the use of a roller weighing 13 to 15 tons will effect sufficient improvement, but sometimes peg or even pitch-pole harrowing may be necessary to prepare the surface.

Cultivation is best carried out by tractor ploughing, followed by harrowing, flat rolling and Cambridge rolling to prepare the seed bed. In carrying out ploughing it is advantageous to break the sub-soil, but whatever is done the aim should be a truly level surface. Before sowing it is important that the land should be treated with a pre-seeding fertiliser of an inorganic nature, and organic matter should be worked in, unless verbal enquiry indicates the soil to be in 'good heart'. When there is doubt advice should be sought.

Before discussing suitable grass species, it may be best to say something about the requirements of an airfield sward. Trueness has been mentioned, but the turf must also be sufficiently strong to resist the constant traffic of lorries and cars and the friction from pneumatic-tyred landing wheels to which brakes are being applied. Smoothness without jarring means a surface uniformly firm, free from hard and soft spots, and with a cushion of grass. The sward must not be too long, because if it gets out of hand, it becomes tussocky and consequently uneven. On the other hand, a fine sparse growth provides a surface that is non-resilient and jars the plane on landing. Although it may be of secondary importance, the turf should be pleasing in appearance and of good colour. It should also be drought resistant.

Grasses capable of forming a thick cushion are required. On lighter land non-rye-grass mixtures are best, and should contain cultivars of bent and the fescues as well as smooth-stalked meadow-grass. For heavier soils, rye-grass mixtures should be used with a background of bent, fescue, and rough- or smooth-stalked meadow-grass. Again, choice should be made of recently introduced or well-tried cultivars. In both types of mixture it may prove advantageous to include some 10 per cent by weight of yarrow seed, though its main value is on light soils for binding it by means of its tough underground rhizomes. Yarrow has the disadvantage of losing leaf in winter but as a rapid coloniser it is valuable. The possibilities of creeping bent, which would presumably be helpful in colonising bare areas, do not appear to have been explored. The *Cynodons*, which are creeping in habit, have been extensively used for planting airfield swards in tropical countries.

Clover is best omitted from the seeds mixture because it provides a slippery surface when wet and dies back in the winter months. No doubt it has valuable recuperative powers and contributes some nitrogen, but the aim should be to produce a ground that does not require the recuperative action of such a plant as clover.

As regards maintenance, one important matter is the constant renovation and treatment of worn or bare places. If these are not treated they develop into deeper depressions eventually causing serious upset to the surface. Large scars should have soil added and be renovated with seed while on heavy soils sand should be incorporated.

By now, the value of regular spiking has been realised and wide gang spiking machines are extensively used to help to counteract the compressing action that is necessary in producing a true surface, as well as opening the soil to allow surface moisture to penetrate. The sward must be kept regularly mown, and is usually carried out with multiple unit gang mowers, drawn by tractor. A nine unit outfit, cutting a 20 ft 6 in (6·25 m) swath, working at a speed of 7 m.p.h. (11 km/hr), is able to cut 12 acres (4·85 ha) an hour.

Occasional fertiliser treatment of airfield turf is essential, especially on the central portion, if the sward is to be kept in vigorous condition and provide a good cushion for landing. The possibilities of using granulated peat for assisting the cushioning effect do not appear to have been investigated.

Licensing of aerodromes for public use is the prerogative of the Civil Aviation Authority. Aerodromes not in public use require the approval of the planning authority for their siting in consultation with the Civil Aviation Authority, but need not be actually licensed or tested for the standards of the grass surface.

PART FIVE

Turf upkeep in other countries

CHAPTER THIRTY-EIGHT

Turf upkeep in some other countries

Introduction

A brief outline of the developments in the scientific study of turf upkeep in other countries has already appeared in the introduction to this book. It will be remembered that the first recorded experimental work with lawn grasses began about 1885 in Connecticut, USA, to be followed in 1890 by the laying down of turf plots in Rhode Island. Following this the United States Green Section was formed in 1924 and the establishment in Great Britain of the Board of Greenkeeping Research (now The Sports Turf Research Institute) took place in 1929. Other countries were not slow to take up the investigation of turf problems, and New Zealand set up a Board of Greenkeeping Research (now the Institute for Turf Culture) in 1932, and various states in Australia are now conducting experiments and collating information. In South Africa the pioneer work was done by the late Dr C. M. Murray, whose activities, going back to 1904, provided the stimulus that led to the investigational work now in progress on a wider scale at the South African Turf Research Station, Witwatersrand.

Published information based on the results of scientific investigations into turf growing in other countries is singularly scanty, except in the United States, where most state colleges have issued bulletins on turf production in their own districts. In addition, the bulletins of the Green Section and of such state colleges of agriculture as have conducted specialised experiments provide a mine of information about turf culture in the USA. It is desirable, however, for the sake of overseas readers, to include in this section some general information on turf problems in other countries, based either upon available literature or upon information acquired by direct inquiry.

In studying the reports of experiments on turf grasses one cannot help feeling that other countries are not labouring under the influence of traditional methods as we are in the home country, there is less reluctance to try new methods of upkeep, to experiment with new species and strains of grasses, and to devise better ways of controlling turf pests. It is further apparent that much of the scientific work in progress is mainly devoted to finer turf such as is suitable for golf and bowling greens. Nevertheless the majority of it is applicable to ornamental lawns and sports grounds in general.

The most potent factor in growing grass for turf is the climate, especially the factors of rainfall and temperature. To a lesser extent the soil and topography determine the species of grass available, but the climate is of primary importance. The incidence of insect and fungal pests and the general difficulties encountered in intensive management of grass in turf swards are largely determined by climatic factors. We are fortunate in Great Britain in having a temperate climate with the rainfall fairly uniformly spread throughout the year, and these factors have made this country pre-eminently suited to growing grass. In other countries much wider extremes of temperature are encountered and the conditions are more variable throughout.

The influence of climate, mainly temperature, is clearly seen in the distribution of the bents and fescues on the one hand, and the Bermuda grasses (*Cynodon* spp.) on the other. Thus, approximately between latitude 35°N and 35°S *Cynodon* is the major turf species, while north and south of this belt bent and fescue provide satisfactory turf. The bent of the temperature zones is analogous in its habit of growth, soil requirement, and leaf-forming propensity to the *Cynodon* of tropical and sub-tropical countries.

The significance of *Cynodon* in turf production is so important that it may be well to give here the common names by which it is known in the different countries. Thus, in the United States the common name is Bermuda grass, in South Africa, Kweek, in Egypt, Neguil, in India, Doob, in Malay, Serangoon, and in Australia, Couch. *Cynodon*, like *Agrostis*, is very variable morphologically and physiologically, and is a summer grower able to tolerate heat. Normally it fails to resist cold, though some strains are able to tolerate slight frost. In summer it needs less water than *Agrostis* and it thrives best on heavy soils, making a dense turf.

Fig. 46. A plant of Bermuda grass (*Cynodon dactylon*) as used in tropical countries for lawn formation.

As far as golf turf in tropical countries is concerned *Cynodon* unfortunately thrives best during the off-season, while in the cooler playing season the colour and density is apt to be poor so that over-sowing may then be needed.

New Zealand

It is perhaps appropriate that first place be given to the consideration of turf production in New Zealand since the climate in that country approximates broadly to conditions in Great Britain.

The climate in New Zealand is temperate over large areas, but in North Island summer droughts are common. Under these conditions sowing is best done in autumn, about the third week of March, just before the break up of the drought and before the winter commences. On the other hand, over large areas of South Island summer rainfall is well distributed and in these parts spring sowing is advisable. In the drier parts of South Island, however, autumn sowing is preferable but some three weeks earlier than in North Island.

Turf maintenance procedures are very similar to those practised in Great Britain, particularly in respect to fertiliser treatments. Again, in line with results as found in this country, browntop and Chewing's fescue can be relied upon under average conditions to produce a dense turf. The proportions used are usually 4 parts browntop to 6 parts Chewing's fescue.

The majority of weeds encountered are the same as those found in Great Britain, though there are various species peculiar to New Zealand. Among these are Onehunga weed (*Soliva sessilis*), pennyroyal (*Mentha pulgium*), hairy pennywort (*Hydrocotyle moschata*), small soldier's button (*Cotula australis*), waxweed or shiny pennywort (*Hydrocotyle americana*) and Westport weed (*Cotula dioica*)*. All can be controlled by the use of selective herbicides.

Some of these plants are, however, used for making 'weed' bowling greens mainly in parts of South Island. Waxweed, hairy pennywort and creeping button weed are mostly used but another plant kidney weed or Mercury bay weed (*Dichondra repens*) has also been planted in some instances in the drier parts of North Island.

New Zealand, like all countries, has its share of soil pests, and as regards earthworms, they are dealt with on the same lines as in Great Britain. In some districts the grass grub (*Odontria zealandica*) is a serious pest of turf and is rather similar in habit to the garden chafer of Great Britain. The adult is on the wing in late October, November, and December, and sometimes into January. It flies at dusk, the female burrowing into the turf to lay her eggs. The grubs live on the turf and by April and May maximum damage results. In colder weather the grubs remain quiescent until August when in the warmer weather they become active again. Pupation takes place in September and October. Control can be achieved by using the methods as in Great Britain, that is by using lead arsenate at $\frac{3}{4}$ oz per sq yd (24 g per m²), or by using Chlordane, DDT or BHC.

In certain parts of the country subterranean grass caterpillars (*Porina* spp.) are common; they live underground, emerging on to the surface at night to feed. Control may be effective by watering the surface with a suspension of lead arsenate, 3 lb to 50 gal (1·3 kg to 227 l) to which a spreader has been added. This coats the leaves with a fine film of the arsenate, so resulting in the caterpillars being poisoned. Poison baits made from bran and lead arsenate or Paris green have also proved successful, but both DDT and BHC are effective.

Wherever lawn management is on an intensive scale the sward is

* Both this species and *Cotula squalida* have been found invading lawns in Great Britain.

apt to suffer from fungal diseases, and turf in New Zealand is no exception. Three species have been isolated from diseased turf and described, namely *Sclerotinia trifoliorum* Erikss., *Rhizoctonia solani* Kuhns, and *Corticium fuciforme* (Berk.) Wakef. The symptoms of the disease caused by the first-named fungus are circular patches, 6 to 8 in (15 to 20 cm) in diameter, in which the turf first turns yellow, then brown and finally dies. The attack takes place in irregular areas. The second species causes the disease known as Large Brown Patch—a prevalent turf disease in the United States. It appears first as small circular brown areas 2 to 3 in (5 to 7·6 cm) in diameter, which gradually increase in size. The third species, *C. fuciforme*, causing the complaint sometimes known in New Zealand as 'Red thread' disease, appears as light brown patches with the red coral-like fructifications of the fungus. The remedial measures recommended in New Zealand for all these species are the same as those advised for turf diseases found in Great Britain.

The general principles of lawn upkeep as far as mowing, top-dressing, fertiliser treatment and general management are concerned follow those adopted in Great Britain, already described in the earlier part of this book.

Australia

The species of grass used for turf formation are *Cynodon dactylon*, known among Australians as Couch or Indian couch, and Queensland blue couch (*Digitaria didactyla*), both summer grasses and a poor colour in winter; and browntop and creeping bent—winter grasses of good colour in the cold season. In addition Carpet grass (*Axonopus compressus*), Kikuyu grass (*Pennisetum clandestinum*), and Germiston grass (*Cynodon transvaalensis*), have been introduced into various parts. The first two are only of use in providing coarser turf.

In Queensland greens are made almost exclusively of blue couch (*Digitaria*), but couch (*Cynodon*) is preferable for inland districts as it is more drought resistant. Winter-growing grasses such as browntop or annual meadow-grass should be introduced for use in the winter months. It is problematical as to whether the introduction of bent into the Brisbane area and Coastal belt instead of blue couch is worth while, on account of the extra labour necessary for upkeep, though trials in highland districts are advised. Latitude 35°S forms the approximate border-line between economic growing of bent turf to the south and couch turf to the north. At Fremantle, Adelaide, and Sydney, couch thrives better in summer than bent while in Melbourne bent does better than couch.

In Sydney the tendency is to replace couch turf with sowings of bent (*Agrostis*) because of its better winter qualities, provided that adequate water and a moisture-retaining soil can be prepared. A compromise may be effected by thoroughly scarifying the couch greens in autumn and sowing upon their surface 3 to 4 lb of browntop (*A. tenuis*) per 1,000 sq ft (1·5 to 2·0 kg per 100 m²). The requirement in Australia is for a one-grass green, giving a perfectly uniform surface as far as colour and texture are concerned. The high summer temperatures and the need for heavy watering constitute the determining factors in deciding the species of use. Cooler conditions permit greater use of bent. Unless couch greens are well managed and regularly top-dressed 'nap' formation may become serious. Bent greens may also develop 'nap'. Pricking and tubular forking to counteract 'dry patch' and to facilitate water movement are important operations.

Many of the weeds common to turf in Great Britain are also encountered in Australia, for example, cat's-ear, dandelion, and white clover. Among the grasses, annual meadow-grass (*Poa annua*), or as it is known there, annual winter-grass, is frequent. *Paspalum dilatatum* (known in Australia as Crab grass) is a common weed, and hand weeding is usual. Leguminous weeds are creeping tick clover (*Desmodium triflorum*), and suckling clover (*Trifolium dubium*). *Soliva sessilis*, a South American plant, common in New Zealand under the name of Onehunga weed, is known in Australia as JoJo or Bindii. Among weed species encountered are Capeweed (*Cryptostemma calendulacea*), and the South American plant known as Whitlow Weed (*Paronychia brasiliana*). Lawn sands or selective herbicides give good control.

The main soil pests are earthworms and the Tasmanian grass grub or web worm, which eats the foliage in patches. In addition, there is the white curl grub larva of the black beetle (*Pentodon australis*), which devours the grass roots and is active between December and April. Earthworms can be controlled on the same lines as in Great Britain, by the use of Chlordane or Carbaryl, while the grubs can be attacked and controlled by the use of DDT and BHC. Chlordane will also give good control.

Mole crickets, and a number of other soil insects cause damage at times. The Scarab beetle (*Aphodius tasmaniae*) has been found in South Australian lawns. The use of insecticides as above will control the ravages of these pests.

Among the fungal diseases, brown patch and dollar spot have been identified, and various strains of blue couch and bent are susceptible.

The fungicides as used in Great Britain are an effective means of control.

Malaysia

Malaysia is situated in the wet tropical zone, the climate being charac-terised by high humidity, heavy rainfall and reasonably uniform temp-eratures. Seasonal variations in the rainfall pattern are caused by periodical changes in wind direction. The climate is responsible for the rapid weathering of rocks, the formation of the soil and soil types agreeing closely with the various geological formations.

With few exceptions, Malaysian soils are deficient in NPK. Lateritic outcrops and semi-impervious lateritic/clay pans are not uncommon, and drainage in coastal-alluviam soils is often restricted to a certain extent.

Generally speaking, Malaysian soils are acidic in character, the pH usually varies between 4·5 and 5·5, the alumino-silicate complex can have high fixative powers on P_2O_5 availability, and in some isolated instances can assume toxic concentrations.

Under European conditions, soils of this type would normally require heavy dressings of lime, however in practice it has been found that heavy dressings of lime are ineffectual and it is preferable from every point of view to apply light dressings of lime.

There has been a very marked improvement in the production of grassed surfaces and ground maintenance in Malaysia in the past ten years, and although local varieties are used to a great extent, introduced varieties have increased the scope and range of grasses that are available.

The choice of grass for turf formation in Malaysia varies considerably and depends on the soil, climate, latitude and local conditions. The main species used are as follows;

Axonopus compressus (Carpet Grass; Rumpit pait); a shallow rooted perennial grass with short stolons. A native of South and Central America and the West Indies, it was first seen in Singapore in 1903, subsequently being established at the Government Experimental Centre at Serdang in 1921.

Carpet grass thrives in fairly moist situations in both the highlands and lowlands, and is now used extensively for sports fields, polo grounds, and as a grass cover on airfields and housing areas.

Although it is normally propagated vegetatively, with the advent of improved seeding machinery and suitable stabilising emulsions, excel-lent results have been obtained by seeding and over-spraying with plastic and resinous materials. Carpet grass responds well to nitrogenous and phosphatic fertilisers. Close mowing should be avoided, and clippings should be allowed to lie on the surface.

Cynodon dactylon (Bermuda Grass; Ramput minyak); with its wide range of varieties it is in all probability one of the most important species of grass for turf production in the tropics. This long-lived perennial with its spreading habit of growth is very adaptable to a wide range of soils and climatic conditions. Although it thrives in fairly heavy soils in the USA, it prefers light, well-drained sandy soils in Malaysia. *Cynodon* is not at home in the climatic conditions pertaining in Central and Southern Malaysia. Growth is relatively weak, and as it is not strong enough to resist the invasion of weeds and strong-growing grasses, its use is limited to small areas of fine turf such as tennis courts and golf greens, where a high standard of maintenance can be practised. In reasonably dry, well-drained areas of North Malaysia, *Cynodon* does well and is often used for both fine turf production and erosion control on banks and slopes. It responds to regular and fairly frequent nitrogenous dressings, provided the phosphate supply is maintained.

Digitaria didactyla (Australian Blue Couch; Serangoon); a fairly compact, narrow-leaved type of grass with slender runner. It does not form an undesirable mat on the surface, but it needs a well-drained soil and unrestricted drainage. Although it thrives at fairly high altitudes, growth in the lowlands is relatively weak, the grass lacking vigour, and constant maintenance is essential to control invasions by strong native grasses and weeds. It responds to regular and frequent nitrogenous dressings, and is used extensively for greens and tennis courts. It is propagated vegetatively.

Zoysia spp. (Manila Grass; Siglap); a dwarf species of grass native to Japan, Korea and the Pacific. It is not uncommon in Malaysia, and of the three types in the peninsula, *Zoysia matrella* is more extensively used for turf production than *Zoysia japonica* and *Zoysia tenufolia*.

Zoysia matrella; grey green in colour, has stout stiff runners and stiff leaves with sharp points. It can form a dense, springy turf on sandy soils and is often used in coastal areas as it is not adversely affected to any extent by salt spray.

It is drought resistant, hardy, but rather slow to establish. As it forms a stiff springy surface turf, its use is usually limited to erosion control on banks, and grass cover for sports fields and lawns. As seed is very scarce, *Z. matrella* is propagated vegetatively. Provided the phosphate and potash supply is maintained, only sufficient nitrogen should be supplied to maintain the grass in good condition.

Zoysia japonica; a relatively coarse grass with a broad leaf, usually propagated vegetatively, and although it is used occasionally for lawns in dry, sandy areas, establishment on wet areas should be avoided as growth tends to be rampant very quickly in these conditions. So long as the phosphate and potash supply is maintained, only sufficient nitrogen should be applied to keep the grass in good condition.

Zoysia tenufolia; generally known as Korean Velvet Grass, it is used for small lawns that are not subject to hard wear. This grass, which forms a dense very low turf with an attractive appearance, tends to die back if close mowing is carried out. As with other *Zoysias*, *tenufolia* is propagated vegetatively.

Paspalum conjugatum (Sour Grass; Ramput pahit); a very coarse aggressive, perennial grass, native of tropical America, which thrives in moist and shady conditions. It is widespread through the peninsula. In Malaysia, its use as a grass cover is limited to shady areas where it is often found mixed with *Axonopus compressus*, and as it produces an abundance of leaf, regular and frequent cutting is essential as it tends to smother other grasses. It can be propagated by seed or vegetatively, and applications of fertiliser should be reduced to a minimum, as otherwise a very coarse, rank growth is produced.

Chrysopogon aciculata (Love Grass; Temuchut); a fairly short, perennial grass, common in South East Asia and widespread in Malaysia, where it is used occasionally as a grass cover for lawns and sports fields on poor, sandy soils. It is an extremely hardy, drought-resistant grass, producing stiff flower stalks with husked awns which adhere to any objects they touch. Frequent mowing is necessary and the use of this grass is limited to areas where the soil is too poor or dry for other varieties to survive. It responds to fertilisation and top-dressing, and can be propagated by seed or vegetatively.

The general principles involved in the preparation of greens and sports grounds under Malaysian conditions, conform to those found in the United Kingdom. Careful preparation, adequate fall and an adequate drainage system is essential if a good grass cover is to be maintained for any length of time. In light soils, the question of artificial drainage may not arise, but on heavy lateric/clay soils it may be necessary to undertake

sub-soiling operations, provide an efficient drainage system and/or a layer of hard core covered with good quality top-soil to a depth of 6 to 10 in (15 to 25 cm).

As regards fertiliser treatment, it has been found that regular and frequent dressings of sulphate of ammonia or compound fertilisers with a high nitrogen content are desirable to encourage leaf growth, provided that the phosphate supply is maintained. On large areas of grass that do not have to be maintained to a high standard, clippings can be allowed to lie on the surface after mowing, and a good standard can be maintained by the annual application of rock phosphate, at the rate of approximately 1 to 2 oz per sq yd (30 to 60 g per m²). On sandy or poor quartzite soils that may be deficient in potash, it may be necessary to include or raise the potash content of fertiliser applications.

Caterpillars, sucking insects and grubs of various types which can cause serious damage can be controlled by applications of lead arsenate, DDT, Chlordane, BHC dust or Parathion. Although it is difficult to completely eradicate termites, a measure of control can be obtained by the application of paradichlorbenzene, hydrogen cyanide, carbon disulphide, lead arsenate or Chlordane. Fungal diseases can be controlled by the use of mercury, thiram or cadmium based fungicides.

Egypt

The climatic conditions in Egypt are such as to demand constant watering or irrigation. The previous attempts to grow bent and fescue grass failed through the high temperatures experienced, and attention is now being concentrated upon the production of grass from strains of *Cynodon* known in Egypt as Neguil. As in other tropical climates it is very variable, and a suitable strain must be utilised. The turf is produced vegetatively by planting the runners in rows 6 in (15 cm) apart, and it is used on polo grounds, golf greens, bowling greens, croquet lawns, racecourses, and cricket grounds.

Until recent years golf greens in Egypt were composed of sand, but latterly the better understanding of grass production has led to the substitution by *Cynodon* turf for many sand greens. The native type of *Cynodon*, or Beladi neguil, is now giving way in many places to improved imported strains of *Cynodon* from Uganda and still farther south. The native strains can be retained for golf fairways. The imported strain not only stands the heat of the Egyptian climate but a few degrees of frost. Constant watering is necessary. Experiments have shown that routine dressings of Nile mud and sulphate of ammonia, supported by occasional phosphatic dressings, form the ideal treatment.

A common pest in greens in Egypt is the mole cricket. Lead arsenate, at 1 oz per sq yd (32 g per m²), Chlordane, DDT or BHC are effective controlling agents.

India

A great deal of the turf produced in India, is often by means of a native strain of *Cynodon* called, in India, Doob. The grass is grown vegetatively on prepared soil, and grows rapidly, producing a continuous turf in a few months. The native strains of doob are able to withstand the intense heat and the rainy periods. Doob requires a liberal supply of easily assimilated nitrogen, and regular dressings of sulphate of ammonia, supported by applications of sand, can lead to a dense fine turf, relatively free from weeds. Regular treatment with sulphate of ammonia can hasten the conversion of a mixed sward to a pure sward of *Cynodon*, and the regular use of sulphate of ammonia for lawn purposes in India is advised for routine use. The rate may be $1\frac{3}{4}$ lb of sulphate of ammonia per 100 sq yd (800 g per m^2). The sand used must be sharp and clean, and the occasional use of a roller is recommended. The best response with the sulphate of ammonia is obtained in the cold weather at the beginning of November, when its action is more rapid than in the rainy period. Minimum amounts of phosphate should be used, as heavy amounts tend to strengthen rival grasses to the detriment of the sward.

South Africa

The scientific study of turf culture in South Africa really dates from 1904 when Dr C. M. Murray first became interested in the establishment of grass greens at the Royal Cape Golf Club.

South Africa has a great diversity of climatic and topographic conditions. For instance there are golf greens and bowling greens at all altitudes from sea level to 6,000 ft (1854 m), and under rainfall conditions of less than 5 in (12·5 cm) a year up to 60 in (152 cm) in certain localities. Further, there are parts of the country where rainfall is confined almost entirely to the summer months, with a long cold dry winter, while in the Cape Town districts there is a winter rainfall and a long hot dry summer. Between these two extremes is a part of the country where the rainfall is more or less distributed over the whole year. This wide range of climatic conditions makes turf culture in South Africa a complex problem. It is gratifying to find, however, that in spite of the complexities the area known as the Reef conforms, as far as sports purposes are concerned, to the ideal recreational requirements laid down by Stapledon in his book *The Land, Now and To-morrow*, where he advocates 10 acres (4·94 ha) of turf per 1,000 inhabitants.

Turf upkeep in South Africa is further complicated by wide diversity of soil types, many having a low phosphate content, whilst low organic matter content often means that a soil readily becomes hard and dry.

Much of the work in South Africa has been concerned with the selection and propagation of strains of grass suitable for fine turf production and capable of withstanding the extremes of temperature so often encountered. One of the best-known strains of *Cynodon* was selected by Dr Murray and used for planting the Royal Cape Golf Course; it is now known as 'Royal Cape' and specimens of it have been sent to almost all parts of the world for comparison with native strains.

Another type, now usually known as Florida grass, was isolated about 1908 near Johannesburg, whilst Bradley grass, which was isolated before 1910, is gaining favour. Other strains are Elgin upright, Douglas, Umgeni, Campbell, Elliot, Magennis, and many others named after the finders, or the places at which they were found. Among other grasses to be found in South Africa are the *Digitaria* species, giving their best colour in the hot season; Kikuyu Grass (*Pennisetum clandestinum*) often used for rugby pitches; and *Paspalum*. The vegetative method of propagation is normal for lawns and greens in South Africa.

Insect damage to turf is in some parts severe, and is often caused by two kinds of termite. One type attacks old leaf sheaths and stalks of grass in situ, and the other a forager that cuts the grass stems and leaves, carrying them underground to their nests. Another pest is the mole cricket, and the larvae of the cockchafer beetle causes harm on some golf courses. Active larvae or 'crawlers' of a Coccid (*Antonica indica* Green) have also caused damage to greens, especially in Natal. Control in all cases can be affected by the use of insecticides mentioned earlier in this chapter.

As in many other instances in other countries, the value of sulphate of ammonia and sulphate of iron when considered as turf fertilisers, is very high. In the summer rainfall areas, dressings of phosphate and occasionally of lime, are necessary, but for the winter rainfall areas, the minimum of phosphate is desirable, and must be associated with the regular use of sulphate of ammonia and sulphate of iron.

Some of the many problems in South Africa are the maintenance of the optimum phosphate supply in the soil, the augmentation of the organic matter content, and the selection of strains of *Cynodon*, capable of remaining green in winter and more resistant to cold weather. Another problem is that of nap. Thus Florida grass is apt to form a nap, but the improved varieties are less given to this habit of growth.

East Africa

Varieties of *Cynodon*, Kikuyu, and Swazi grass (*Digitaria*) all have a place according to altitude, temperature and purpose of the turf.

Europe

There is an absence of published information about the upkeep of turf in the various parts of Europe. In the western countries conditions for growing turf are very similar to those in Great Britain, though they are subject to greater extremes of temperature and in summer water is more essential. As a result of examination of many samples from, or visits to, turf areas in Belgium, Czechoslovakia, Denmark, France, Germany, Holland, Italy, Luxemburg, Spain, Sweden, it appears that the bent and fescue grasses may be satisfactorily used, and that turf production in these countries is subject to much the same difficulties as those encountered in Great Britain. The establishment of new areas of turf by means of bent and fescue in these countries may therefore be carried out satisfactorily but there should be more emphasis on smooth-stalked meadow-grass and indigenous strains of red fescue and bent. Rye-grass is not winterhardy in northern latitudes.

In the central parts of Spain there are greater extremes of climate, though the establishment of turf with bents and fescues has been satisfactorily carried out. High temperatures may be experienced during the day, followed by bitterly cold nights, and the winter conditions are much harder. In the more southerly parts of Spain attempts are being made to produce turf from strains of *Cynodon* introduced from South Africa and Egypt, but here the difficulty is to obtain a sward capable of resisting the dry hot winds experienced in July and August from the Sahara.

The production of good grass in the Riviera also presents difficulties, partly owing to the climatic diversity and partly to the very much poorer depth of soil to be found. During the summer months continuous surface watering is necessary to save the turf from complete destruction through lack of rain and fierce sun, but it is possible, in spite of the difficulties, to establish turf from the usual grasses employed for turf formation in other European countries. In recent years attempts have been made to use the bulblets of *Poa bulbosa*, a grass found in abundance in the Mediterranean regions. This grass is at its best during the winter months, but dies away during summer. Another method is to establish rye-grass greens in the early autumn, these establishing quickly and providing a cover during the residential season. The study of strains of grasses for these parts and the improvement of the soil conditions for grass growing are amongst the most promising lines for future development.

In general the weeds found are almost entirely the same as in Great Britain so that the same methods of control can be carried out. Selective weed-killers are now being widely used.

Among turf diseases fusarium patch can be serious and much damage is done in winter by the snow mould form while species of *Typhula* are known to cause damage in winter in northern latitudes. Few records of brown patch disease of turf are available though the causative organism *Rhizoctonia solani* is widespread. *Sclerotinia homoecarpa* causing dollar spot is found and can be expected to cause disease on turf grasses whenever suitable conditions prevail. For methods of control reference should be made to the general chapter on fungal diseases and to the section dealing with turf diseases in the USA.

A serious problem in Norway and central Sweden is winter kill. This occurs mainly in spring as a result of alternate melting and freezing of snow. The chief grass affected is annual meadow-grass, so that greens mainly composed of this species can die right out. The solution seems to lie in the direction of diverting water from melting snow away from important areas like greens before it can re-freeze, in providing good surface drainage and thirdly in the greater use of indigenous smooth-stalked meadow-grass and indigenous strains of creeping red fescue and *Agrostis*.

In Holland and Belgium heavy infestations of leather jackets occur at times while periodically a species of cut worm (moth larva) can become a serious pest. Reports of it have been received from Belgium, France, and Switzerland. Lead arsenate powder and DDT dusts have proved completely effective, but probably other insecticides could also be used.

China and Japan

No literature dealing exclusively with lawn production in these countries has been found, though a number of references appear in some of the American publications.

In Japan the grass species most largely employed is Korean lawn grass (*Zoysia pungens Japonica*). Seed is produced in Japan and the turf formed is dense with a strong underground system of rhizomes. This species has also been used on the Gulf coast in the United States. Another species used is *Zoysia tenuifolia*, a fine-leaved species that forms a dense wiry turf.

From direct inquiry as to turf growing in the Shanghai area of China it would appear that the chief difficulty is the climate, since the district suffers from extremes of heat and cold. July and August are very hot, temperatures of 37°C in the shade being common, while the rainfall is fairly regular, and the growth of grass is good. Towards the end of November, however, a general browning of the turf takes place, and December and January are very cold months, often with biting winds.

Korean lawn grass imported from Japan has been tried out on the Hungjao Golf Course and reports indicate that it has a value for turf production in the Shanghai area. Trials with bent and fescue species on the Hungjao Golf Course failed completely.

The commonest species of grass used for lawns in China is centipede grass (*Eremochloa ophiuroides* (Munro) Hack.), a dwarf-growing and intensively stoloniferous plant. Perhaps the commonest turf weed in Shanghai is crab grass (*Digitaria ischaemum*), an annual summer species that invades turf rapidly, causing a great deal of labour to effect its removal.

United States of America

In such a wide area there are naturally big climatic differences, but rainfall and evaporation are the principal ones, and these largely determine the species of use in the different parts. It may be of interest to refer briefly to some of the diverse climatic conditions encountered in this vast country. Broadly speaking, and especially in regard to golf courses, the turf maintenance is on a much higher plane than in this country. More labour is used, more fertilisers, and the general equipment is on a more liberal footing. Furthermore much more investigational work has been done on all turf matters.

In most parts evaporation is relatively high and artificial watering is generally necessary—indeed, in some parts grass cannot be grown without it. Along the Pacific coast the total rainfall is low, most of it coming in the winter months. For example, at Los Angeles, the rainfall is 14·9 in (380 mm) and about 60 per cent of it comes in the three winter months; there is less than 1 in (25 mm) for the three summer months. Normally there is no rainfall from May to September, and evaporation is high, so that liberal sprinkling is essential.

At Denver, on the eastern slope of the mountains, the annual rainfall is similar, 14·1 in (355 mm), but the distribution is the opposite, most of the rain coming in the growing season while the winters are cold and dry. Near the cities of Oklahoma and Kansas, the yearly rainfall amounts to over 30 in (762 mm), and most of it is in the growing season, so assisting upkeep, but as evaporation is high, irrigation becomes essential. Throughout the middle-western territory the average rainfall may be as much as 48 in (1218 mm), fairly uniformly distributed throughout the year, but temperatures are high and dry winds absorb the moisture. In the eastern states the water requirements for turf are less than in the western, though provision for watering is now generally considered essential.

From the point of view of the suitability of the grasses an important line of demarcation is approximately 35° to 38°N; north of this line, bent, fescue, and Kentucky blue-grass will thrive, whilst south of it is the Bermuda grass country. The position may best be understood if the United States is divided into three regions, as shown in the diagram. In the first region Kentucky blue-grass (*Poa pratensis*) has no superior for general use as a lawn grass, and it may in suitable soil be sown alone with good results. Where the soil is acid, however, the bent grasses should be used, since the Kentucky blue-grass would not

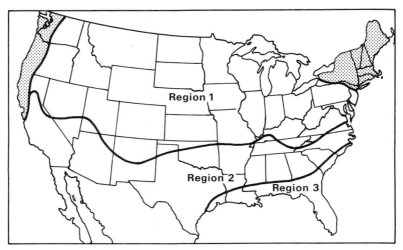

Map showing regions of the United States where various lawn grasses succeed best. (From US Dept. of Agric., Bull. 1677.)

survive. Soils suited to bent are usual in parts of New York, in the New England states, along the Pacific coast of Oregon, in Washington, and Northern California (shaded portion of diagram). In these areas the bent grasses, browntop, creeping bent, and velvet bent are dominantly used, and the creeping species are produced vegetatively from stolons. Whilst the fescues may be used in conjunction with the bents on the acid soils they do not survive well under the influence of close mowing. In Region 2 Bermuda grass is most suitable, though at higher altitudes Kentucky blue-grass does well. The Bermuda turf may be obtained from seed or prepared vegetatively; the chief objection to this species is that it dies down in winter and develops a poor colour.

In Region 3 most of the lawns are produced from single species. Bermuda grass and St Lucie grass (*Cynodon dactylon* var. *St Lucie*) are used for the dry areas where the soil is heavy, while carpet grass (*Axonopus compressus*) is especially desirable on moist soils. One of the most outstanding grasses is centipede grass (*Eremochloa ophiuroides*) produced vegetatively. It was originally introduced from China. St Augustine grass (*Stenotaphrum secondatum*) has no equal in Florida and in the southern states as a shade grass. It grows equally well in the sun, and if well watered and supplied with nitrogen forms a good turf but is too coarse for good golfing turf. In Region 3 (Florida) experiments have been done with Australian blue couch and species of *Zoysia*. *Z. tenuifolia*, Mascarene grass, sometimes called Korean velvet grass or Japanese velvet grass, produces a very fine textured turf and has been grown for a number of years in Florida and California. *Z. japonica* or Korean lawn grass is coarser than the above but hardier, while the third species *Z. matrella*, Manila grass, is intermediate in texture.

In areas where prolonged high temperatures are experienced in summer, the usual practice is to select a suitable warm season grass such as Bermuda grass and over-seed with a cool season grass or grasses. Winter turf quality in such areas is dependent on the cool season grass used, the rate of over-seeding, thatch build up, seed bed preparation, time of seeding and winter feeding.

The high winter over-seeding rates used tend to delay the development of the Bermuda grass in the spring, and therefore it is important that the cool season grasses do not deteriorate rapidly before the Bermuda grass has developed.

The timing of over-seeding is of paramount importance, and it is preferable to allow soil temperature to drop before over-seeding. Early over-seeding tends to encourage the growth of Bermuda grass, while late over-seeding will often inhibit the germination of the cool season grasses. Local conditions will govern the time of over-seeding.

The preparation of the seed bed has a very marked effect on winter cover. It is essential, to reduce competition of Bermuda grass, that close vertical mowing be carried out, immediately prior to seeding. It is also necessary to make certain that the seed comes into contact with the soil, and to help ensure this, top-dressing should be carried out immediately after over-seeding.

Lolium multiflorum, when used for over-seeding tends to deteriorate very quickly in the spring, and is not suitable for putting greens. A high seeding rate is essential to provide the density needed for good putting surfaces.

Pennlawn Festuca rubra however, provides a good density, has an excellent spring transition period, and is an eminently suitable variety.

Agrostis species are generally slow in establishment, providing poor surfaces in the winter, but are excellent in the spring transitional period.

In Florida, results have shown no difference in appearance of pure strands of over-seed *Penncross Agrostis palustris*, *Pennlawn Festuca rubra*, *Poa pratensis* or *P. trivialis*, but in Virginia and Texas, it was found that *P. trivialis* deteriorated very rapidly in the spring, and is therefore not considered suitable.

The rate of over-seeding will depend on the number of seedlings a particular variety will develop during the winter months. Because of the continual play on the golf course, and the fact that the grasses seldom develop beyond the seedling stage, over-seeding rates are of necessity very high to compensate for the high mortality rate.

Fertility must be maintained throughout the winter months, and nitrogen at the rate of 100 lb per 2·5 acres (50 kg per ha) from a quickly available source is necessary to produce suitable development. Poor turf cover often results where heavy thatch exists, but where thatch is removed from Bermuda grass during the summer months, an excellent cover was attained.

In the year-round semi-tropical climate of Florida, over-seeding is essential to retain the colour and quality of the surface. On golf courses, where colour is very important, bents, fescues and *poas* tend to emphasise the colour of *Poa annua*, so *Poa trivialis* and *Lolium* are more compatible. The selection of grass for over-seeding is dependent on the texture of the warm season grass to be over-seeded, as for instance, rye-grass would be used to overseed *Paspalum nodatum* and *Erimochloa ophiuroides* and *Stenotaphrum secundatum*.

Generally speaking, bents, fescues and *poas* provide better surfaces, but the cost of seed and maintenance is higher. The rate of establishment of bents, fescues and *poas* are slower than rye-grass, the bents, fescues and *poas* needing 5/7, 5/7 and 17/21 days respectively, while the rye-grass under ideal conditions will germinate in 3/4 days. Rye-grass requires about 4 weeks for establishment, while the bents need 6, the fescues 4 and the *poas* 10 weeks.

In the United States much attention has been devoted to experiments with fertilisers for turf, and a usual complete fertiliser for application to turf is one containing 6 per cent nitrogen, 8 per cent phosphoric acid and 4 per cent potash. The use of compost is also advocated, especially on creeping bent greens. The experiments to which reference has already been made earlier in this book, show the value of fertilisers that leave an acid residue in the soil for maintaining turf in a weed-free condition, and in eradicating weeds should they establish. The vastness of the country implies great variability in conditions, and local or state literature should be consulted.

Many of the weed species encountered in the United Kingdom are also common in the United States, but the widespread use now made of selective herbicides makes for easy control of them.

A serious weed of fine turf is crab grass, there being two common species, namely hairy crab grass (*Digitaria sanguinalis*) and smooth (*D. ischæmum*). Both are summer annuals, the seed germinating in late spring and early summer. They are widely distributed in northern and southern humid regions of the US. Indirect methods of control involve surface operations like raking and brushing before mowing, avoidance of too-close mowing and fertiliser treatment to secure a vigorous turf. For small areas hand weeding should be done but for heavy infestations all-over spraying is usual, thus a $\frac{1}{2}$ per cent solution of sodium chlorate at 10 gal per 1,000 sq ft (48 l per 100 m²) has been found effective. Experiments have also shown the value of phenyl mercury acetate (PMAS), 1 per cent potassium cyanate and weak solutions of sodium arsenite, 2 to 5 lb per acre (2 to 5 kg per ha), the last being the cheapest.

A number of soil pests occur in lawns, and if not specially dealt with may do much damage. The commonest of these are the grubs of Japanese (*Popillia japonica*) and Asiatic (*Anomala orientalis*) beetles and other 'white grubs,' which feed on the roots of grasses and may cause severe damage if many are present. Damage usually shows in early fall. It has been found that where grub injury is threatened, lead arsenate powder at 5 lb to 1,000 sq ft (2·5 kg to 100 m²) is effective. Protection against the grubs may be maintained by annual applications of the arsenate.

The sod webworm (*Crambus* spp.) is also a common pest of turf, and another common insect found, particularly in hot seasons, is the chinch bug (*Blissus leucopterus*) which caused damage by sucking out plant juices from the crowns of the grasses. The insecticides Chlordane, Aldrin and Dieldrin have all given good results.

As regards earthworm control, Chlordane, Carbaryl or arsenate of lead are quite effective, although the tropical earthworm (*Pheritima hupiensis*) has become a serious pest in the north-eastern states.

The value of aeration on small areas by hand or on large areas by machines designed for the purpose is now being more fully appreciated for the purpose of relieving compaction due to play and for breaking through surface mat formation.

Fungal diseases in the United States cause a great deal of damage and fine turf may be almost destroyed overnight by an attack of brown patch caused by *Pellicularia filamentosa* (Pat.) Rogers (*Rhizoctonia solani*). This disease is found where warm temperatures and high humidity prevail. It was first recognised in a turf garden near Philadelphia in 1914 and the causal fungus was isolated in 1915. The disease is carried over the winter by sclerotia which are found on the soil surface and on the dead grass. When suitable weather occurs the sclerotia germinate and eventually cause the patches. Many materials have been tried for the control of this disease but taken as a whole, mixtures of calomel and corrosive sublimate are those which are most commonly used. Phenyl mercury compounds (PMAS) and fungicides containing tetra-methyl thiuramdisulphide (TMTD) are also used to control the disease.

Dollar spot is also prevalent in the United States. The pathogen responsible is *Sclerotinia homœocarpa* F. T. Bennett, and it is recorded as well from Europe and Australia. It over-winters by means of very thin sclerotia and there are many different strains of the fungus varying in their optimum growth rate at various temperatures. Some have an optimum at 20°, others at 25°, and still others at 30°C. Taken as a whole this disease occurs in warmer climates than prevail in most parts of Great Britain. As regards control, large-scale trials in the United States indicate that cadmium-containing fungicides are very suitable for both prevention and cure while organic mercury compounds and inorganic mercury mixtures are effective preventatives, as is TMTD. Corticium disease may also occur in the United States. Good control has been obtained with PMAS.

In northern United States and in Canada *Fusarium nivale* is not the only fungus responsible for the dying out of turf (fusarium patch) which occurs following the melting of snow. Another fungus also found in northern Europe may in fact be responsible, i.e. *Typhula itoana* Imai, and *T. idahoensis* Remsberg. The mycelium is produced from sclerotia which lie dormant until late autumn. Growth may occur at as low temperature as −5°C. Control is normally carried out with mixtures of inorganic mercury salts. From time to time leaf spots occur on *Poa* species caused by the fungus *Helminthosporium vagans* Dreschsler. It is also found in Britain, being favoured by cool rainy weather. Several other species occur. The term 'melting out' is sometimes applied to diseases caused by *Helminthosporium* and sometimes to diseases caused by the fungus *Curvularia* spp. or a combination of both. These fungi are closely related and are becoming a problem in the United States. The antibiotic cycloheximide (Actidione) mixed with iron sulphate, a water-soluble cadmium compound and PMAS have given good control of these conditions.

Canada

The general principles for turf upkeep as described in the earlier chapters of this book may be followed fairly closely for conditions in Canada. A most important point in establishing lawns and greens is good surface drainage, and a free outlet for moisture must be assured, otherwise much grass will be lost through water-logging. A general principle advocated in Canada, as in this country, is modification of the soil to suit the grasses, and a common species used is Kentucky blue-grass. This species is able to tolerate a wide range of soil and climatic conditions, and is reasonably resistant to drought. It is therefore used for ordinary lawns and golf fairways, but cannot be used for greens since it fails to stand the close cutting. For second-class lawns, mixtures containing Kentucky blue-grass, redtop and browntop are utilised, whilst for the finest turf browntop and various strains of creeping bent are used. Turf formation is commonly carried out vegetatively. Canada blue-grass (*Poa compressa*) is sometimes advised, but it is only suited to the poorer soils, and it is best for fine turf to improve the soil and use better species. Canada blue-grass, however, is suitable for coarse grass such as is found in the rough on a golf course.

The general principles of fertiliser treatment as laid down in earlier chapters may be followed. Occasional seasonal dressings of sulphate of ammonia are advised.

Most of the common turf weeds of Great Britain are also found in Canada, and can be controlled by the use of selective herbicides.

A common turf disease of Canada is fusarium patch, the symptoms of which are dead areas of turf of various shapes and sizes as the snow melts in early spring. *Typhula* spp. are also a cause of winter damage, while 'melting out' has also been reported. General recommendations as for disease control in the United Kingdom will give satisfactory control.

Cyprus

Areas can be over-seeded for colour in a similar method to that used in the United States. Using a mixture of *Festuca rubra* (60 per cent), *Poa pratensis* (30 per cent) and *Lolium perenne* (10 per cent), the area is first scalped, brushed to remove clippings, then seeded and top-dressed. It is then irrigated lightly every day till germination is complete, and after germination, irrigated every second day depending on the weather, and eventually every third day till the sward is well established. Fertilisation is carried out at monthly intervals.

Persia (Iran)

Golf greens can be sown with a mixture of *Agrostis palustris, Poa pratensis* and *Festuca rubra,* fairways with *Festuca rubra* and *Poa pratensis.*

Further reading

Approved Products for Farmers and Growers—published annually by the Ministry of Agriculture, Fisheries and Food, London.

Drainage Problems on Playing Fields—National Playing Fields Association, London, 1972.

Fungal Diseases of Turf Grasses (2nd ed.)—J. Drew Smith—Sports Turf Research Institute, Bingley, Yorks, 1965.

Facilities for Athletics—National Playing Fields Association, London, 1971.

Grasses—C. E. Hubbard—Penguin, London, 1968.

The Groundsman—monthly publication to members of the Institute of Groundsmanship, London.

Insecticide and Fungicide Handbook (3rd ed. revised)—H. Martin (ed.)—Blackwell Scientific Publications, Oxford, 1969.

Journal of the Sports Turf Research Institute, Bingley, Yorks.

Principles of Turf Grass Culture—J. H. Madison—Van Nostrand Reinhold, Wokingham, Berkshire, 1971.

Sports Ground Construction—National Playing Fields Association, London, 1965.

Spon's Landscape Handbook—D. Lovejoy (ed.)—E. F. Spon, London, 1974.

Turfgrass Science—A. A. Hudson & F. V. Juska—American Society of Agronomy.

Weed Control Handbook—J. D. Fryer & R. J. Makepiece—Blackwell Scientific Publications, Oxford, 1973.

Composition of fertilisers and fertilising materials

	Total Nitrogen %	Total Phosphoric Acid %	Water-soluble Phosphoric Acid %	Total Potash %
Ammonium Phosphate:				
A	13·8	—	41·4	—
B	17·9	—	17·9	—
C	15·6	—	31·2	—
Basic Slag	—	8·0 to 18·5	—	—
Bone Charcoal	1·5 to 2·0	28·0 to 35·0	—	—
Bone Meal	3·0 to 5·0	20·0 to 22·0	—	—
Calcium Cyanamide	20·6	—	—	—
Castor Meal	4·0 to 6·0	1·5 to 2·0	—	1·5 to 2·0
Cocoa Husk	3·8	1·8	—	3·0
Distillery Residue	4·9	5·0	—	3·0
Dried Blood	12·0 to 14·0	trace to 1·0	—	—
Dried Sewage	1·5 to 3·5	1·0 to 3·0	—	trace to 0·3
Finely Ground Peat	0·7 to 3·0	—	—	—
Fish Guano	6·0 to 10·0	4·0 to 7·0	—	0·5 to 0·8
Fish Meal, White	8·0 to 9·0	9·0 to 10·0	—	1·0
Flue Dust	—	—	—	trace to 6·0
Fresh Farmyard Manure (with straw)	0·4 to 0·8	0·2 to 0·4	—	0·4 to 0·7
Ground Mineral Phosphate	—	25·0 to 39·0	—	—
Hoof and Horn Meal	12·0 to 14·0	—	—	—
Kainit	—	—	—	14·0
Leather Waste	5·0 to 7·0	—	—	—
Malt Culms	3·0 to 5·0	1·0 to 2·0	—	2·0
Meat and Bone Meal	3·0 to 8·0	10·0 to 20·0	—	—
Meat Meal	10·0 to 11·0	0·4	—	0·6
Muriate of Potash	—	—	—	40 to 60
Nitrate of Lime	13·0	—	—	—
Nitrate of Potash (Chilean)	15·0	—	—	10·0 to 15·0
Nitrate of Potash (Synthetic)	12·0	—	—	40·0
Nitrate of Soda (Chilean)	15·5 to 16·0	—	—	—
Nitro-Chalk	15·5	—	—	—
Peruvian Guano	5·0 to 18·0	6·0 to 25·0	—	2·0 to 6·0

	Total Nitrogen %	Total Phosphoric Acid %	Water-soluble Phosphoric Acid %	Total Potash %
Potassic Mineral Phosphate	—	20·0	—	10·0
Potash Salts (20% Low Grade)	—	—	—	20·0
Potash Salts (30% High Grade)	—	—	—	30·0
Poultry Manure (Dried)	1·0 to 4·0	1·0 to 4·0	—	0·5 to 2·5
Rape Meal	5·0 to 6·0	1·5 to 3·0	—	1·0 to 1·8
Seaweed	0·2 to 0·4	0·1	—	0·8 to 1·8
Seaweed Ash (Kelp)	—	—	—	15·0 to 20·0
Shoddy	5·0 to 14·0	—	—	—
Soot	2·0 to 11·0	—	—	—
Spent Hops	3·0 to 4·0	1·0 to 1·5	—	trace to 1·0
Steamed Bone Meal	0·75 to 1·0	27·5 to 29·0	—	—
Sulphate of Ammonia	20·6 to 21·0	—	—	—
Sulphate of Potash	—	—	—	48·0
Superphosphate	—	—	14·0 to 20·0	—
Supers, 'triple'	—	—	48·0	—
Urea	46·0	—	—	—

APPENDIX TWO

Equivalent measures

1 yard	= 0·9144 metre
1 metre	= 1·0936 yards

1 gallon	= 4·543 litres
1 litre	= 61·027 cubic inches
1 cubic metre	= 1·308 cubic yards

1 square inch	= 6·45 square centimetres
1 square foot	= 0·0929 square metre
1 square yard	= 0·9361 square metre
1 square metre	= 1·196 square yards
1 hectare	= 2·471 acres
1 cubic foot	= 6·2355 gallons

1 pound	= 453·6 grammes
1 ton	= 1,016·0 kilograms
1 kilogram	= 2·2046 pounds
1 hundredweight (112 lb)	= 50·8 kilograms

1 cwt (112 lb) per acre = 51 (approx.) kilos per acre = 125 kilos per hectare
   1 oz per sq yd   = 34 g per sq metre
   1 gal per sq yd   = 5·43 litres per sq metre
   1 oz in 50 gal   = 12·5 g in 100 litres
   1 oz in 50 gal per 100 sq yd = 33·75 g in 270 litres per 100 sq metres
   3 oz per 1,000 sq ft = 91·5 g per 100 sq metres

Fertiliser Mixing table

(Taken from Ministry of Agriculture and Fisheries bulletin no. 28.)

O May be mixed.

:: May be mixed if applied quickly.

X Should not be mixed.

Note.—Dry conditions of mixing are assumed in this table.

	Sulphate of Ammonia	Nitro-Chalk	Nitrate of Soda	Calcium Cyanamide	Sulphate and Muriate of Potash	Potash Salt and Kainitt	Superphosphate	Basic Slag	Bone and Rock Phosphates*	Ammonium Phosphate	Carbonate of Lime	Oxide of Lime
Sulphate of Ammonia	O	O	O	X	O	::	O	X	O	O	::	X
Nitro-Chalk	O	O	O	X	O	::	::	X	O	::	O	X
Nitrate of Soda	O	O	O	O	O	::	::	O	O	::	O	O
Calcium Cyanamide	X	X	O	O	O	::	X	O	O	X	O	O
Sulphate and Muriate of Potash	O	O	O	O	O	::	O	O	O	O	O	O
Potash Salt and Kainit	::	::	::	::	::	O	::	::	::	::	::	::
Superphosphate	O	::	::	X	O	::	O	X	::	O	::	X
Basic Slag	X	X	O	O	O	::	X	O	O	X	O	O
Bone and Rock Phosphates*	O	O	O	O	O	::	::	O	O	::	::	O
Ammonium Phosphate	O	::	::	X	O	::	O	X	::	O	::	X
Carbonate of Lime	::	O	O	O	O	::	::	O	O	::	O	O
Oxide of Lime	X	X	O	O	O	::	X	O	O	X	O	O

* Except dissolved bones should be treated as Superphosphate.

† The mixtures in this column can be kept for a time if they are dry.

APPENDIX FOUR

Conversion factors for fertilisers and lime

To convert:	Into terms of:	Multiply by
Ammonia (NH$_3$)	Nitrogen (N)	0·82
Nitrogen (N)	Ammonia (NH$_3$)	1·21
Tricalcium phosphate (Ca$_3$(PO$_4$)$_2$)	Phosphoric acid (P$_2$O$_5$)	0·46
Phosphoric acid (P$_2$O$_5$)	Tricalcium phosphate (Ca$_3$(PO$_4$)$_2$)	2·19
Sulphate of potash (K$_2$SO$_4$)	Potash (K$_2$O)	0·54
Potash (K$_2$O)	Sulphate of potash (K$_2$SO$_4$)	1·85
Muriate of potash (KCl)	Potash (K$_2$O)	0·63
Potash (K$_2$O)	Muriate of potash (KCl)	1·59
*Calcium oxide (CaO)	Calcium carbonate (CaCO$_3$)	1·79
Calcium carbonate (CaCO$_3$)	Calcium oxide (CaO)	0·56
Calcium oxide (CaO)	Calcium hydroxide (Ca(OH)$_2$)	1·32
Calcium hydroxide (Ca(OH)$_2$)	Calcium oxide (CaO)	0·76

* Approximately 20 cwt burnt lime = 26 cwt slaked lime = 35 cwt carbonate of lime.

APPENDIX FIVE

Dimensions of grounds

Association Football
Ground—Minimum, 100 yd × 50 yd (91·44 × 45·72 m).
        Maximum, 130 yd × 100 yd (118·87 × 91·44 m).

Athletics
Two parallel lines 84·39 m long and 73 m apart, joined by semi-circles with a radius of 36.50 m, will produce a track with a lap measurement of 400 m.

Where a track of different dimensions is required, the appropriate measurements can be calculated by using the formula:

$$L = 2S + 2\pi(R + 30 \text{ cm})$$

L = length of track in metres.
S = length of straights, and
R = radius to the track side of the inner line in metres.

It should be noted in the above calculations that π should be 3·1416.

Basket Ball
Court—85 ft (26 m) long and 46 ft (14 m) wide.

Bowls
44 yards square maximum, 33 yards square minimum (40·22 m max, 30·17 m min). Rinks; 19 ft (5·78 m) wide (for domestic play not less than 14 ft (4·25 m) wide).

Cricket pitch
Length of pitch 22 yd (20·10 m).

Croquet lawn
Full size 35 yd × 28 yd (32 × 25·60 m).

Hockey
Ground—100 yd × 55 to 60 yd (91·44 × 50·29 to 54·86 m).

Lawn Tennis
Court—78 ft × 36 ft (23·77 × 10·96 m) (single 27 ft (8·22 m)). Allowing for run back etc., the following measurements are given as a guide:

Grass: Maximum 110 ft × 55 ft (33·52 × 16·76 m).
Minimum 100 ft × 52 ft (30·48 × 15·84 m).
Hard: Maximum 120 ft × 60 ft (36·57 × 18·28 m).
Minimum 116 ft × 56 ft (35·35 × 17·06 m).

Polo
Ground—Length not to exceed 300 yd (274·32 m), breadth not to exceed 200 yd (182·88 m) if unboarded, 160 yd (146·30 m) if boarded.

Rugby Football
Ground—Not exceeding, and as near as practicable, 110 yd (100·58 m) long and 75 yd (68·58 m) broad, with a maximum of 25 yd (22·86 m) at each end for 'dead ball' line.

How to find a right angle
A piece of metal (or wood) 3 ft (0·91 m) in length, with cord attached at each end, one 4 ft (1·21 m) long, the other 5 ft (1·52 m).

The right angle is obtained by placing the metal (or wood) on the ground, and driving in a pin where the strings meet.

Diagrams of sports grounds

Ground marked out for Lawn Tennis

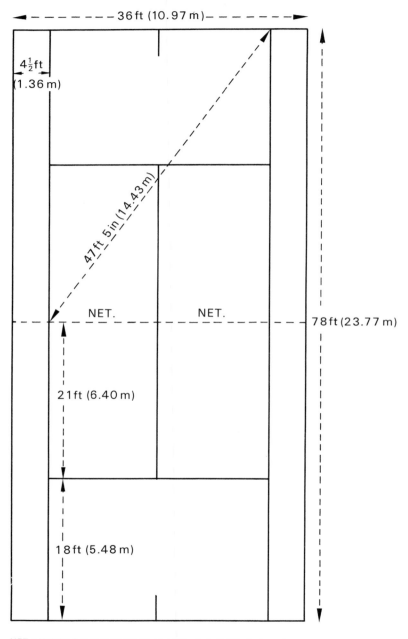

36 ft (10.97 m)

$4\frac{1}{2}$ ft (1.36 m)

47 ft 5 in (14.43 m)

NET. NET.

78 ft (23.77 m)

21 ft (6.40 m)

18 ft (5.48 m)

NET.– Height 3 ft 6 in (1.06 m) at posts, 3 ft (0.91m) at centre

Ground marked out for Rugby Union Football

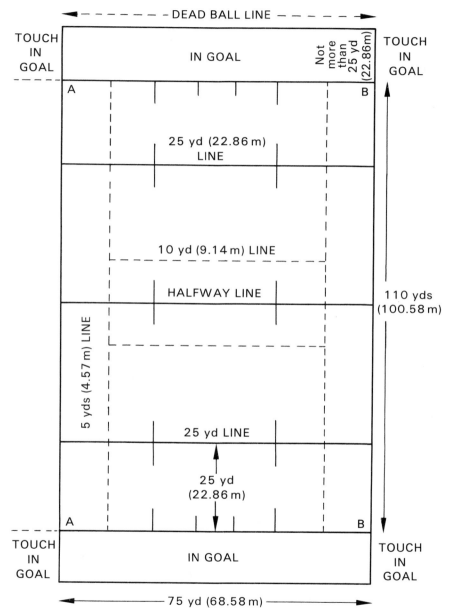

A to B, Goal line. A to A and B to B, Touch Line.
Goal Posts – Exceeding 11 ft (3.34 m) high. 18 ft 6 in (7.15 m) apart.
Cross bar 10 ft (3.04 m) from ground.
A 15 yd (13.17 m) mark is drawn parallel to the touch lines on the goal,
twenty five and centre lines.

Ground marked out for Polo

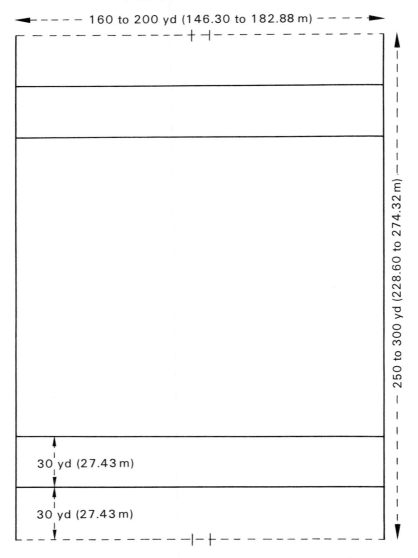

◀ ─ ─ ─ ─ 160 to 200 yd (146.30 to 182.88 m) ─ ─ ─ ─ ▶

250 to 300 yd (228.60 to 274.32 m)

30 yd (27.43 m)

30 yd (27.43 m)

A full sized ground should not exceed 300 yd (274.32 m) in length by 200 yd (182.88 m) in width, if unboarded; and 300 yd (274.32 m) in length and 160 yd (146.30 m) in width, if boarded. The goals to be not less than 250 yd (228.60 m) apart, and each goal to be 8 yd (7.31 m) wide. The goal posts to be at least 10 ft (3.04 m) high, and light enough to break if players collide with them. The board not to exceed 11 in (27.9 cm) in height.

Ground marked out for Croquet

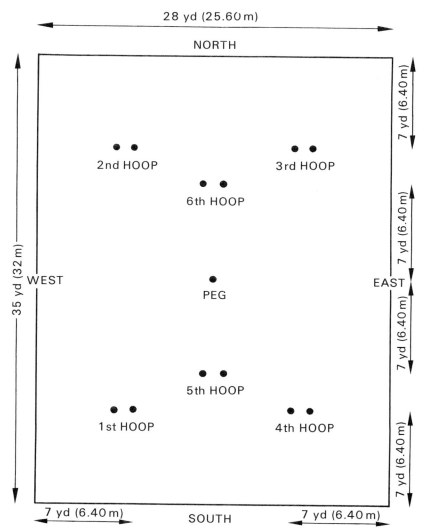

Ground marked out for Gents Hockey

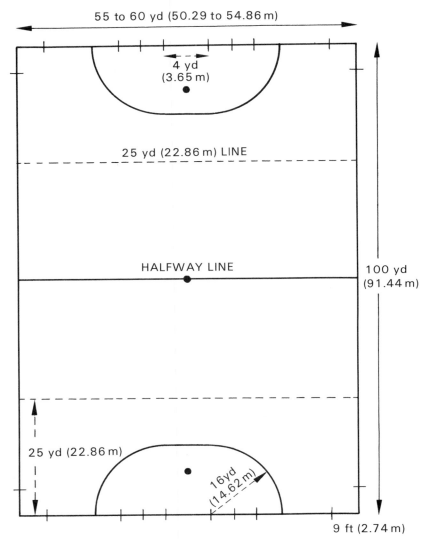

Ground–100 yd by 55 to 60 yd (91.44 m by 50.29 to 54.86 m)
Opening of Goal–7 ft by 12 ft (2.13 m by 3.64 m)
A penalty spot of not more than 6 in (15 cm) shall be marked 8 yd (7.31 m) in front of the centre of each goal.
12 in (30 cm) lines must be drawn at right angles to the goal lines and side lines as shown on the plan (i.e. at 5 and 10 yd (4.57 and 9.14 m)) from the goal posts and 3 yd (2.74 m) from the corners.

Portion of a Bowling Green

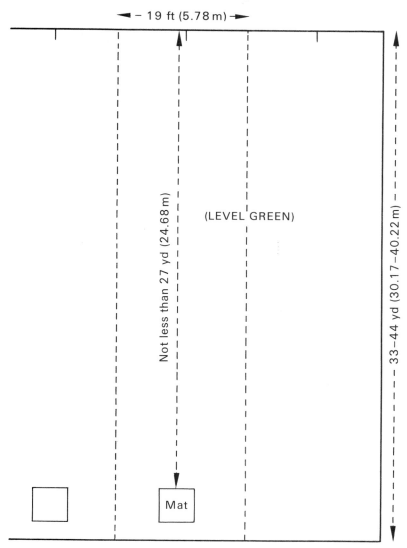

Ground marked out for Association Football

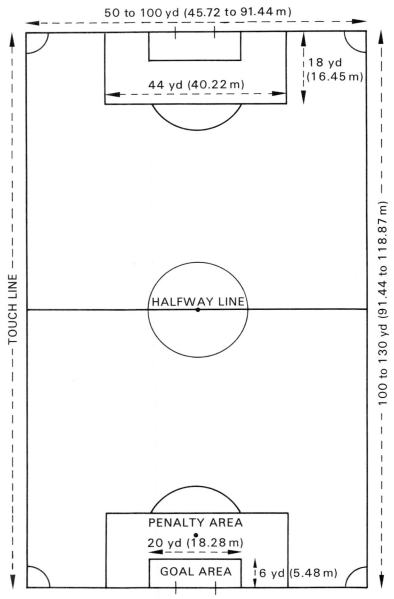

50 to 100 yd (45.72 to 91.44 m)

18 yd (16.45 m)

44 yd (40.22 m)

100 to 130 yd (91.44 to 118.87 m)

HALFWAY LINE

TOUCH LINE

PENALTY AREA

20 yd (18.28 m)

GOAL AREA

6 yd (5.48 m)

Goal posts–8 yd (7.31 m) apart. Cross bar 8 ft (2.43 m) from ground.
Penalty Kick Mark–Opposite centre of goal; 12 yd (10.96 m) from goal line . Arc of circle with radius of 10 yd (9.14 m) from penalty spot to be marked outside penalty area.
Corners–Flag with staff not less than 5 ft (1.52 m) high.
Kick Off Circle–Centre of ground, radius 10 yd (9.14 m).

Ground marked out for Cricket

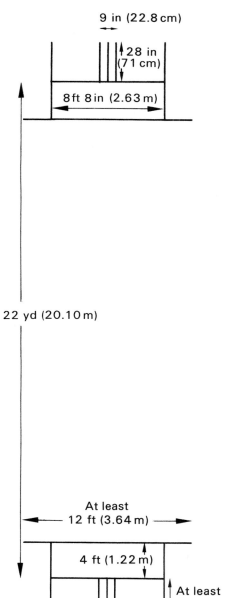

9 in (22.8 cm)

28 in (71 cm)

8 ft 8 in (2.63 m)

22 yd (20.10 m)

At least
12 ft (3.64 m)

4 ft (1.22 m)

At least
4 ft (1.22 m)

Adjustment and maintenance of mowers

The object of the following notes is to help the gardener or greenkeeper to deal with those minor faults that may ultimately lead to serious breakdown. In any case a faulty mowing machine cannot give the best results on the turf. Adjustment is largely a matter of common sense and most high-class machines rarely develop major faults; even cheaper machines have a long life and will withstand a surprising amount of ill-usage. With the better machines (both hand and motor) Instruction Books are issued by the makers and should be closely followed. These contain lubrication charts and lists of spares. Major repairs are best done by the experienced mechanics of the maker or his agents.

Care after use and storage
In dry weather brush down with a hard broom; in wet weather wash down using a hose. Immediately oil cutting edges using a paint brush, lubricate where required and put away under cover. Don't leave clippings in the box. When storing over the winter choose a dry shed and stand the mower on boards after thoroughly cleaning, oiling, and lubricating. Ease cutting cylinder off fixed blade and smear all cutting edges with grease. Clean and grease grass box. Remove driving chains from motor mowers and store in oil. Drain engine crank case with a view to refilling with clean oil at the beginning of the season.

Winter work on the mower
Thoroughly clean up hand mowers removing grass from gears and other parts, re-paint where necessary. On motors, dismantle and clean

carburettor and exhaust system, decarbonise engine and grind in valves. Check tension on chains. Paint frames and boxes. Examine all moving parts, including clutch and control cable, for wear and tear. If repairs are needed get mowers away to repair depot early in the winter.

Adjustment of hand mowers

Side-wheel mowers:

There are two types, those in which the cutting cylinder is driven by a set of gears and those in which the cutting cylinder is driven by cogs cast on the inside of the wheel acting on pawls and pinion on the cylinder spindle. Access is easily obtained by removing the split pin or unscrewing locking nut. Remove all grass clippings which tend to bind the gears. Regular lubrication of cogs and bearings as well as the pawls or free wheels is important. Adjustment of height of cutting is easily carried out by raising or lowering the back roller. Check height of cut on both sides of bottom blade with straight edge across roller and wheels. The fixed blade is adjusted by screws or hand wheel according to make. Only very gradual movement of screws is necessary. Test cutting by means of paper. If the blades are just touching the bottom blade, yet fail to cut, the cylinder has become dull and should be ground in. If the bottom blade is kinked or bent by accident, it may sometimes be cured on the grindstone but on the whole it is better to fit a new one. Occasionally the whole frame of the mower becomes strained and here return to the maker is essential.

Roller mowers:

There is much variation in the details of design in roller machines and there are varying degrees of precision. All the better machines are ball bearing, and transmission is usually by speeding-up gears, but sometimes there is a chain drive. Cutting speed is higher than on side-wheel mowers and free wheel is usually of the cycle type. Attend to lubrication carefully and see that the gear case is packed with grease. Height of cut is adjusted by one or two knobs, raising or lowering the front roller. Where there is only one knob, check both ends of the blade, using a straight edge, to see that there is strict parallelism. If out of line set the alignment of the front roller by the compensating screw. Setting of the bottom blade is by hand wheel or adjusting screws. In some machines the spring below the bearing housing closes up and there is danger of breaking the casting unless the spring is shortened. In cheaper machines the blade and concave may be in one piece with a central handle for adjusting. In setting the bottom blade it is important that it should be clear of the ground otherwise it may be knocked up against the cutting cylinder. Further, if too close to the ground the bottom blade tends to tear the turf on lumps and ridges. The height of set can easily be tested with a straight edge. Play on the front roller should be eliminated by the adjustment screws fitted, or by a new replacement. Careful attention to grinding-in and lubrication are important.

Grinding-in:

If the mower will not cut a piece of paper or a leaf cleanly at any point on the length of the cutting cylinder without undue pressure, then the blades are dull. In this condition they will only bruise the grass, leaving a ragged finish and at this stage grinding-in is necessary. The first step is to adjust the cylinder so that it only just touches the bottom blade. The blades should then be painted with oil and emery and the cylinder revolved in the opposite direction (i.e. anti-clockwise). A special stand may be bought for roller machines and a handle to screw into the main gear wheel. In the case of side-wheel machines this turning is done by inserting a stick between the spokes and revolving the wheels in the reverse direction, after turning over the pawl. Light pressure only is required and as the grinding proceeds the cutters are adjusted to the blades. They should be examined to see that they are touching throughout their length. Motor mowers are ground in the same way.

Adjustment of motor mowers

Transmission and cutters

The bottom blade in motor mowers is usually adjusted on the same system as hand mowers; the operation must be done very carefully and a little at a time until the cutting cylinder just brushes the bottom blade. Grinding-in is done as for hand machines though most owners of motor mowers will have this done by the service depot. Height of cut is adjusted by movement of front roller. Attention must at times be paid to the clutch; the lining of which beds down, unless of the metal to metal variety. The clearance between the collar and the operating mechanism is reduced, but there is a simple adjustment for correcting this. The conveyor or concave plate designed to throw the grass into the box occasionally requires adjusting. Driving chains are apt to work slack on motor mowers through constant use. In some machines this is taken up by sliding the whole engine forward and in others there are chain tensioners to take up the slack. Chains should not be made *too* tight but should be left with a slight slackness.

Lubrication

Some motor mowers used on lawns are of the 2-stroke variety. Lubrication of piston and bearings is done by the oil mixed with the petrol. When running in a new motor, more oil is needed than later in its life. With 4-stroke engines lubrication is by splash or by an oil circulating system. Oiling instructions are issued with new motor mowers and regular attention to all mowing parts is the best insurance against excessive wear and tear. All ball bearings need attention as well as the moving parts on the clutch and the starter and driving chain. Front rollers require careful attention. Being of small diameter they revolve at high speed and being in close contact with the ground are soiled frequently with earth.

Engine

The modern power unit is designed for reliability and trouble-free use. Often a few minor adjustments will keep the machine going but larger repairs are best left to the mechanic. When filling the tank always pour the petrol through a fine strainer. Regularly check over nuts and bolts as they are liable to shake loose and possibly lead to cutter damage.

Never stop a 2-stroke engine, when putting it away, by closing the throttle. Always turn off the petrol and allow engine to use up petrol in carburettor. This makes for much easier starting.

Starting of a motor mower is simple if the following procedure is adopted—turn on the petrol tap. If starting from cold, close the choke, partly open the throttle, depress kick starter or pull out the recoil starter. If difficulty is experienced, various throttle widths may be tried.

If there is still failure probably petrol and oil have accumulated in the crank case, this should be drained since this condition causes wetting of plugs and sooting up. If there is further difficulty in starting, the plugs should be removed, dismantled and electrode cleaned. Plug points should be checked leaving a gap of 0·02 in (0·5 mm), that is about the thickness of a visiting card. Petrol pipes should be checked for chokages and flexible joints examined as perisihing may have occurred.

Other failures to start may be due to the petrol jet or filter being choked. Popping in the carburettor is a sign of choked pipe, jets, or filter. Another cause of refusal is faulty ignition and, after cleaning, the dry plug may be tested by placing it on an unpainted part of the engine. On turning the starter sharply sparks should be seen. If sparks are not seen a new plug should be fitted and re-tested and if this fails probably the magneto is at fault.

The contact breaker should be examined periodically and any dirty deposit removed. Should the cam appear dry a single spot of thin oil should be applied to the surface on which the tappet runs as this will prevent rust and wear. Excessive oil causes mis-firing. The usual setting of contact points is 0·015 in (0·3 mm). Sometimes failure to start is due to a short circuit caused by insulation on the cable having perished.

At other times the machine will work satisfactorily for a time when after a few preliminary mis-fires it will stop; this may be due to lack of fuel, to faulty ignition, to hot bearing due to insufficient oil, to over-loading, or to dirt under the jets. There are times also when a machine may be giving a poor response to the work. This may be due to poor compression due to loose carbon under the valves, leaking or sticking valves, or possibly leaking piston rings. A knocking sound in the engine may be caused by over-loading, carbon deposit on piston top and cylinder head, or slack connecting bearing, or the mixture may be too hot. The above faults and failures are best put right by an experienced mechanic.

Index